D0977656

To:

From:

Date:

365 Devotions for Peace

Cheri Cowell

ZONDERVAN®

365 Devotions for Peace

Copyright © 2015 by Zondervan

Requests for information should be addressed to:
Zondervan, Grand Rapids, MI 49530

ISBN 978-0-3103-5956-2
ISBN 978-0-3106-3295-5 (custom)

Scripture quotations marked NIV are taken from the Holy Bible, New International Version®, NIV®. Copyright © 1973, 1978, 1984, 2011 by Biblica, Inc.™ Used by permission of Zondervan. All rights reserved worldwide. www.zondervan.com. The "NIV" and "New International Version" are trademarks registered in the United States Patent and Trademark Office by Biblica, Inc.™

Scripture quotations marked NCV are taken from the New Century Version®. © 2005 by Thomas Nelson. Used by permission. All rights reserved.

Scripture quotations marked NASB are taken from New American Standard Bible®. Copyright © 1960, 1962, 1963, 1968, 1971, 1972, 1973, 1975, 1977, 1995 by The Lockman Foundation. Used by permission. (www.Lockman.org)

Scripture quotations marked NKJV are taken from the New King James Version®. © 1982 by Thomas Nelson. Used by permission. All rights reserved.

Scripture quotations marked MSG are taken from *The Message*. Copyright © by Eugene H. Peterson 1993, 1994, 1995, 1996, 2000, 2001, 2002. Used by permission of Tyndale House Publishers, Inc.

Scripture quotations marked VOICE are taken from The Voice™. © 2012 by Ecclesia Bible Society. Used by permission. All rights reserved. Note: Italics in quotations from The Voice are used to "indicate words not directly tied to the dynamic translation of the original language" but that "bring out the nuance of the original, assist in completing ideas, and . . . provide readers with information that would have been obvious to the original audience" (The Voice, preface).

Any Internet addresses (websites, blogs, etc.) and telephone numbers in this book are offered as a resource. They are not intended in any way to be or imply an endorsement by Zondervan, nor does Zondervan vouch for the content of these sites and numbers for the life of this book.

All rights reserved. No part of this publication may be reproduced, stored in a retrieval system, or transmitted in any form or by any means—electronic, mechanical, photocopy, recording, or any other—except for brief quotations in printed reviews, without the prior permission of the publisher.

Cover design: Kathy Mitchell
Cover illustration: Kathy Mitchell
Interior design: Lori Lynch

Printed in the United States

19 20 21 22 23 /LSC/ 22 21 20 19 18 17 16 15 14 13 12 11 10 9 8 7 6 5 4 3 2 1

Contents

Strive to preserve your heart in peace; let no event of this world disturb it.

—Saint John of the Cross

PEACE FOR THE NEW YEAR

New Beginnings

In the beginning there was the Word. The Word was with God, and the Word was God.

—John 1:1 NCV

Happy New Year! Today marks a new beginning. No, we don't know what this year will hold. And, yes, we're still living with unresolved situations from last year—which, after all, was only yesterday! But still we can celebrate the fresh start that this blank calendar represents.

We are able to celebrate despite the unknowns of the next 365 days because of the truth of John 1:1. In the beginning of eternity (that sounds like a paradox!), God—Father, Son, Spirit—was there. Now, at the beginning of this year, God—Father, Son, Spirit—is here with us. And God will be with us every month, day, hour, and minute of this new year, which is ample reason for hope, anticipation, and peace.

God is all-powerful, all-knowing, all-loving; He is faithful and forgiving; He is gracious, good, and kind. And He is with us. He will be with us. That's why we can know peace.

God, I am grateful You're with me on January 1 and that You'll be with me through December 31. Teach me to be mindful of Your presence, which brings me peace. Amen.

Land for the Seasick

Jesus Christ is the same yesterday and today and forever.

—Hebrews 13:8 NIV

None of us completely avoided storms last year. The intensity of those storms may have varied, but they blew their way into each of our lives.

During those difficult times, you may have felt like a sailor standing on the bow of your battered ship, searching the horizon for calm seas and fair weather. With binoculars in hand, you scanned the waters looking for some solid land on which to toss your anchor until the storm passed. In the midst of the dark sky, pelting rain, and churning waters, you mostly found yourself looking at a lot of nothing—that is, until you saw the Rock that is Jesus Christ.

Jesus is the same yesterday, today, and for all your tomorrows. That promise offers hope: your gracious Redeemer brings good from storms. This year, when you find yourself tossed around by life's challenges, anchor yourself to Christ. He will hold you steady.

Jesus, help me to anchor myself to You in all I do this year. Only in You can I know safety, security, and peace. Amen.

Secure Foundations

"Have you not even read this Scripture: 'The stone which the builders rejected, This became the chief corner stone.'"

—Mark 12:10 NASB

Did you ever play with Lincoln Logs, those small, wooden, log-shaped pieces you could use to make any number of structures? If you played with more than one set, you could build an entire town. Of course, a favorite challenge was seeing how high you could construct your building before it toppled. You learned quickly that if you set the first level of blocks securely, your building had a better chance of standing tall.

Knowing the importance of a solid foundation, Jesus counseled His followers to make Him the cornerstone of their lives. The cornerstone of a building is the foundation upon which all other stones are set. Much like that first Lincoln Log, when we allow Jesus to be our foundation and build our lives on Him, we will stand tall for Jesus.

So live each new day wisely: place it on the cornerstone of Christ, and your building will rise secure.

Jesus, help me remember that only when I build my life on the sure foundation of who You are—God's Son, my Savior and Lord—can I know true peace. Amen.

Aiming High

Jesus looked at [His disciples] and said, "With men it is impossible, but not with God; for with God all things are possible."

—Mark 10:27 NKJV

Are you a planner, or do you prefer to make decisions in the spur of the moment? If you're a planner—or if you want to become a better one—the beginning of a new year is a great time to strategize and set some goals.

Most experts suggest making your initial goal achievable to build confidence and momentum. But these experts also advise having a significant goal that stretches you. Maybe you've heard it said that if you shoot for the moon and miss, you will still land among the stars. That saying may be encouraging, but another point of view is even more empowering.

Look again at Mark 10 and the truth Jesus proclaimed: God is in the impossible business. He makes what looks impossible *possible*. Keep that in mind as you dream, plan, and set goals for the new year.

Commit your plans to God, align them with His will, and rely on His guidance each step of the way. As you do these things, you'll experience the peace that comes with knowing that the God of the impossible is on your side.

God of the impossible, as I consider this new year, help me to aim high yet follow Your guidance each step of the way. Amen.

The Peaceful Garden

He has made everything beautiful in its time. He has also set eternity in the human heart; yet no one can fathom what God has done from beginning to end.

—Ecclesiastes 3:11 NIV

In 1904, cement industry pioneer Robert Butchart dug a limestone quarry in Victoria, British Columbia. After excavating the quarry, all that remained was a large, deep pit. Hardly a tourist attraction!

Robert's wife, Jennie, decided to turn the gigantic, ugly pit into something beautiful. She had many tons of topsoil carted in by horse and began planting flowers and trees. This labor of love took twenty-three years, and her son continued the project for another fifty years. Now every year Butchart Gardens welcomes almost a million visitors who delight in the fifty-five acres of the former quarry, now home to peaceful gardens.

Maybe you have an ugly scar in the landscape of your past. When you yield that scar, its cause, and the resulting pain to God, the master Gardener can turn it into something beautiful. Read His Word, allowing Him to plant its life-giving truth deep within your heart. As He waters it with His love, bursts of color will in time replace the ugliness.

God, I praise You for being able to turn the ugly scars on the landscape of my past into something beautiful. Amen.

Food for Life

Jesus answered, "It is written: 'Man shall not live on bread alone, but on every word that comes from the mouth of God.'"

—Matthew 4:4 NIV

Do you have a *life verse*, a verse or passage from Scripture that you've chosen to order your life around? Some people prefer having a verse to focus on for each new calendar year. Others choose a word, such as *joy* or *hope*, to be their theme for the year. The idea is to focus the heart and mind on some aspect of the Lord, His truth, or His calling on our life. After all, we need God's Word for our soul, heart, and mind just as we need daily bread for our body.

Imagine how life might be different if *peace* were our word one year. This world doesn't offer solid, lasting peace, and the pace of life reflects that. God offers peace unlike what the world gives, peace for the day-to-day despite all the peace-robbers in life.

Lord, thank You for Your Word, for its unfading beauty and richness as well as for the way You use it to teach me, guide me, and nourish my soul. Amen.

Win-Win

We know that God causes all things to work together for good to those who love God, to those who are called according to His purpose.

—Romans 8:28 NASB

Have you ever played a two-person game by yourself? The best part of playing by yourself is that no matter how bad things look, no matter which side is winning, *you* will win!

Maybe you wish life were more like the person who plays a game solo. You could control both sides of the playing field. Switching to the other side, you could make a move that would ensure your safety. Better yet, you could know what moves the other side was considering so you could plan your own.

The good news is that you have Someone who created the playing field and who always makes moves for your safety, your growth, your good. What peace this truth offers! You can be absolutely sure that, no matter how bad things look, no matter which side is winning now, God intends good and not harm for you in the end.

So the next time things aren't going your way, remember that the all-powerful, all-loving God is working all sides for your good.

God, when things look bad from my perspective, help me to remember that You will work all things for my good and Your glory. Amen.

Free Indeed

We have freedom now, because Christ made us free. So stand strong. Do not change and go back into the slavery of the law.

—Galatians 5:1 NCV

What does *freedom* mean to you? Some may see freedom as the opportunity to do whatever they want. Others may say freedom is limited because people are responsible for how their words and actions infringe upon those of others. Teenagers may equate freedom with a driver's license. Still others may associate freedom with the Declaration of Independence or the Bill of Rights. Then there's the gospel—the freedom to enter into a relationship with God.

Can you imagine going backward, though? No sixteen-year-old would readily surrender a driver's license. The United States would not return to British rule. Yet many of us still labor under the shackles of sin even though we have already received the Lord's forgiveness.

Decide this year to truly accept the freedom from sin's power, which Jesus offered when He died on the cross. Don't go back to the slavery of trying to earn God's acceptance or be the perfect follower of Jesus. With God's help, you can know the freedom of His grace. May this be the year you fully embrace freedom in Christ and all that it means.

Thank You, God, for the freedom of forgiveness, acceptance, and adoption that You extend to me through Jesus. What an incredible source of peace! Amen.

Do What's Important

Turn my eyes away from worthless things; preserve my life according to your word.

—Psalm 119:37 NIV

I dubbed it "constructive procrastination," and I first noticed it in college, specifically during finals week. When I should have been studying, I'd have the compelling realization that the car needed to be washed, my closet needed to be organized, and the mini-fridge needed to be cleaned out. I became a woman with a cause! I wasn't doing the most pressing activity—preparing for exams—but at least I was accomplishing something.

As a new year begins, many of us are thinking about goals to pursue, habits to change, healthy practices to begin. But have we taken any real steps in those directions? Maybe we have accomplished something (we *have* put away the Christmas decorations), but we haven't yet spent early-morning time with the Lord, encouraged a friend, or even made our health a priority.

We can easily find ways to keep ourselves busy with inconsequential tasks, neglecting our true priorities. But when we focus our energies on doing what's most important, we will experience peace.

Help me to recognize and move past those things that fuel my procrastination. I want the peace that comes with doing what I most need to do. Amen.

A Fitness Plan

Exercise daily in God—no spiritual flabbiness, please! Workouts in the gymnasium are useful, but a disciplined life in God is far more so, making you fit both today and forever.

—1 Timothy 4:6–10 MSG

Do you have a health goal for the new year? Right now TV commercials are offering a lot of suggestions. Lose weight! Stop smoking! Get in shape! Join a gym! Eat healthy!

If you do have a health goal, what is motivating you to try to make those lifestyle changes? Maybe you want to live longer, have more energy, or simply be a good steward of your body. Now think about a spiritual goal. What will help motivate you to make the right decisions and commitments to ensure your spiritual fitness?

Maybe determining how exactly you can labor for the kingdom of God will get you moving. Maybe you will feel convicted to strengthen a weakness, to surrender an aspect of your life to God, or to seek more of God's face.

When you spend time each day training on God's workout equipment—reading His Word, praying, meditating, fasting, serving—you will develop the muscles of a spiritually disciplined life, find yourself in better spiritual shape, and be blessed by a richer experience of God's peace.

God, help me to exercise more consistently on Your workout equipment so I may be all You want me to be for the body of Christ. Amen.

Much to Do

People may make plans in their minds, but the LORD decides what they will do.

—Proverbs 16:9 NCV

We've all had them: those days when we are off and running the moment our feet hit the floor. With one task after another to complete—errands to run, meetings to attend, emails to answer, and calls to return—we don't have time to take a breath. And as busy and productive as we've been, we reach the end of the day without even getting close to the end of our to-do list. Then, when our head finally hits the pillow, thoughts about what still needs to be accomplished fill our minds.

Sometimes what fuels this hamster-wheel pace is the sense that we are responsible for everything getting done, and done well. Yes, we are to do our best in order to honor God in all we do, but maybe an overinflated sense of responsibility has us stepping outside our jurisdiction. The good news is that we are not God. When we remember that, we can find peace, however long our to-do list may be.

Dear God, help me keep my eyes on You so that when my head hits the pillow each night, I can sleep in peace. After all, You are God; I'm not. Amen.

JANUARY 12

Laser-Like Focus

Let us run with endurance the race that is set before us, looking unto Jesus, the author and finisher of our faith.

—Hebrews 12:1–2 NKJV

What do you want to be when you grow up?" How many times were you asked that question when you were young? And what was your response?

Maybe you never had a specific answer—and maybe you still don't! Perhaps you've dabbled in various fields: you've tried several types of jobs and enjoyed some success, but you never landed on anything that was completely fulfilling.

Or maybe you've been able to answer that question since kindergarten. Some people know what they want to be when they're five—and they grow up to do exactly that! These people focus with laser-like vision on that one goal. They overcome obstacles because they clearly know what they want.

If you are still trying to discover what you want to be when you grow up, that's okay. But there is one thing we should all be single-minded about: our love for God and our commitment to knowing and obeying His Word. A laser-like focus on Him will give us peace—and God's peace is a great context for discovering what He is calling you to do.

God, help me this year to focus on You so that I will be able to hear Your guiding words and obey Your call and commands. Amen.

Going the Distance

Brethren, I do not regard myself as having laid hold of it yet; but one thing I do: forgetting what lies behind and reaching forward to what lies ahead, I press on toward the goal for the prize of the upward call of God in Christ Jesus.

—Philippians 3:13–14 NASB

Metaphorically speaking, when it comes to how you live, are you a sprinter or a long-distance runner? Sprinters are fast out of the blocks, they reach top speed quickly, and they hold back nothing as they compete for that short period of time. Long-distance runners, however, pace their stride based on milestones along the way. They know how to push beyond the pain, and they recognize when they are hitting their stride. An image of the finish line is engraved in their mind, propelling them to press on.

The Christian life is composed of sprints and long-distance runs. Some circumstances call for us to speed fast for a period of time, holding nothing back. But in the grand scheme of things, life is a long-distance race. Keeping our eyes on the finish line propels us forward.

Regardless of whether you are in a stretch of sprinting or just hitting your stride, keep your eye on the finish line, where God waits with your prize.

Almighty God, help me to run this race of life so that I honor You by finishing well. Amen.

A New Day

Because of the LORD's great love we are not consumed, for his compassions never fail. They are new every morning; great is your faithfulness. I say to myself, "The LORD is my portion; therefore I will wait for him."

—Lamentations 3:22–24 NIV

I cut the pizza into eight slices, put a couple on the paper plate, handed it to my daughter—and watched, in what seemed like slow motion, as the plate drooped and the pieces fell to the floor, cheese-side down.

Some days can't end soon enough. Everything you touched fell apart; everything you tried, failed. Or perhaps your day was on another level of bad altogether. When those days happen, you may find yourself longing for tomorrow's fresh start—and that, by God's grace, is exactly what you'll have.

Whatever your day holds, God won't use up His love, compassion, mercy, or faithfulness. He will have a fresh supply for you tomorrow and each new day after that.

So the next time you come to the end of your day more than ready for it to end, look to God, whose mercies are new each day. He is with you when you wake up, when you go to sleep, and every moment in between.

Lord, I am grateful You never run out of the love, compassion, mercy, and grace I need. Thank You that I can begin each new day with You. Amen.

PEACE AND LOVE

Peace-Filled Love

Brothers and sisters, keep rejoicing and repair whatever is broken. Encourage each other, think as one, and live at peace; and God, the Author of love and peace, will remain with you.

—2 Corinthians 13:11 VOICE

Think for a minute about how love is portrayed in today's media, and you'll realize that it is anything but peaceful. In movies, books, and television, love is too often supercharged, fueled by volatile emotions. Love can change in an instant, from heartwarming to heart-breaking, from soul-satisfying to soul-shattering. And it's depicted as self-centered and self-serving, rooted in narcissism and a desire for power or prestige.

The Author of true love, however, loves differently. God's love brings harmony and unity, not discord and dissension. God's love is not fickle or erratic but rather true, selfless, and steady. God's love is "patient . . . kind. It does not envy, it does not boast, it is not proud. It does not dishonor others, it is not self-seeking, it is not easily angered, it keeps no record of wrongs. [God's] love does not delight in evil but rejoices with the truth. It always protects, always trusts, always hopes, always perseveres" (1 Corinthians 13:4–7 NIV). God's love brings peace.

God, teach me how to love as You do because this world needs to see a more peace-filled kind of love. Amen.

The Color of Love

There is no room in love for fear. Well-formed love banishes fear. Since fear is crippling, a fearful life—fear of death, fear of judgment—is one not yet fully formed in love.

—1 John 4:18 MSG

There's a reason why the walls of some prison cells are painted pink: that color truly does calm people—and calm inmates are a good thing!

Colors not only impact emotions; they also reflect emotions. You probably wouldn't, for instance, choose pink to reflect fear. The choice would be a more ominous and foreboding color. Perhaps the top two choices would be black or red.

You might, however, choose pink to communicate love. Light pink is something of an opposite of inky black just as fear and love are opposites. The dark of night and the light of noon can't coexist just as dark fear and the light of God's love can't.

So when fear casts a shadow on your heart, turn to its opposite: remind yourself of the powerful, unchanging truth that God loves you and that nothing can separate you from His love (Romans 8:38–39). When you choose to focus on the love of your almighty God, fear fades.

God, I thank You that when my day is shaded by fear, I can stand in the light of Your love. Amen.

Truth and Love

Speaking the truth with love, we will grow up in every way into Christ, who is the head.

—Ephesians 4:15 NCV

It's never easy to be the bearer of bad news. The saying "Don't shoot the messenger" speaks not only to the challenge of sharing the news, but also to the difficulty of receiving it. We can, however, choose an approach to delivering unwelcome messages that will minimize the risk of—figuratively speaking—bullets coming our way.

Carefully and prayerfully choose an appropriate time and place to deliver the news. Given the situation, talking one-on-one may be essential; taking a third person may be biblical (Matthew 18:15–16). We must also consider the current mood or immediate circumstances of the person we approach. Timing is crucial if we want the person to hear the message as we intend.

As we deliver the bad news, the two key ingredients are truth and love. When the message is hard to receive, the speaker's truthful and loving manner make it easier to hear and respond. Speaking the truth in love brings a measure of peace to the conversation even when that truth is difficult to receive.

Lord, when I need to share difficult news, help me to choose the time and place wisely and wrap my words in truth and love. Amen.

Love Deeply

Now that your obedience to the truth has purified your souls, you can have true love for your Christian brothers and sisters. So love each other deeply with all your heart.

—1 Peter 1:22 NCV

It's a good truth to review from time to time: *love is a choice, not an emotion.* Yes, there is the heartwarming emotion of love, but that emotion comes and goes. The love God calls us to extend to one another is a choice, and sometimes it may seem like a superhuman choice. The apostle Peter explained why we are able to make that choice: "You have been born again" (v. 23 NCV).

When we acknowledge our sin, ask God for His forgiveness, recognize Jesus' death for our sin, and confess Him as our Savior, we are born again. Our new God-given nature enables us to choose to love. This love is intentional: we choose to love the hard-to-love; we choose to love in tough circumstances; we choose to love when it costs us. This also means that we choose to love the person behind the hurt that makes her harder to love.

Our new nature and our being filled with God's Spirit enable us to love with Christlike love, to "love each other deeply."

Lord, use me to love others with Your love and thereby be a channel of peace and hope. Amen.

Lessons About Love

Now about your love for one another we do not need to write to you, for you yourselves have been taught by God to love each other.

—1 Thessalonians 4:9 NIV

What did you learn about love when you were growing up? Who showed you genuine love, a selfless love that gave you a glimpse of God's love? Maybe it was Mom, Dad, or a grandparent; maybe it was a neighbor, mentor, or friend. In what ways did that person exemplify God's love?

From the opening pages of the Bible, God shows us how to love, how much real love costs, and how to love when the other person is unlovely. In His Word we also see pure love's power to transform. God's love lessons have been changing lives for thousands of years, and they continue to do so today.

Who is learning how to love from you? Are the lessons they are learning from your life ones worth repeating?

God, thank You for being the God of love. Make me a good reflection of Your love for those learning about You by watching me. Amen.

Creaking Gates

If I speak with human eloquence and angelic ecstasy but don't love, I'm nothing but the creaking of a rusty gate.

—1 Corinthians 13:1 MSG

According to most studies, the number-one fear in America is public speaking. (Death is a distant number five.) Sociologists have determined that most people don't fear the act of public speaking itself, but fear being judged, making a mistake, or simply not measuring up. Speaking requires an element of courage, speaking eloquently requires a lot of practice, and making eloquent public speaking look easy requires even more practice. Without practice, we can sound like a rusty gate.

The Bible tells us that our everyday-life speech can also sound like a rusty gate. If we aren't speaking with love, we will be as annoying and hard to listen to as a creaking gate. So whether you are opening your mouth to speak in front of hundreds or speaking one-on-one with a friend, speak your words with love. The result will be peace—and no creaking!

God, I desire my life to speak volumes of love. May the words that I speak always be filled with love and offering peace. Amen.

Abiding in God

We have come to know and have believed the love which God has for us. God is love, and the one who abides in love abides in God, and God abides in him.

—1 John 4:16 NASB

As a teenager, maybe you were told, "Tell me who your friends are, and I'll tell you who you are." This warning, usually reserved for less-than-desirable friends, reiterates the apostle Paul's warning in 1 Corinthians 15:33: "Bad company corrupts good character." The opposite is also true. If you hang out with inspiring and motivated people, some of that inspiration and motivation will rub off on you.

The word the Bible uses to describe this concept is *abide*. Today's verse explains that when we abide, or hang out, with God, we will become more like Him.

When we spend time with our loving Father, we will become more loving. When we spend time with our joyful, patient, and peaceful God, we ourselves will become more joy-filled, patient, and peace-filled. Are you spending enough time with the Lord to become more like Him?

God, help me guard my time with You so that I become more like You: more loving, joy-filled, patient, and peace-filled. Amen.

A Family Resemblance

Whoever does not love does not know God, because God is love.

—1 John 4:8 NCV

What characteristic distinguishes almost every family-member-by-blood in your family? Some families are known for the shape of their faces, their clear blue eyes, their barrel chests, or their charcoal-black head of curls. Members of other families may be identifiable by their laugh, their gait, or the way they use their hands when they speak.

God's family also has its telltale characteristics, and the primary one is this: a member of God's family is known by his or her love (John 13:35). If someone claims to be a member of the family of God yet doesn't demonstrate love toward others, that person clearly does not know the family Patriarch, the God of love. Because God is love, each member of His family exhibits such telltale signs as love, compassion, joy, and peace.

Do people see in your life the telltale Christian characteristics of peace and love?

Lord God, help me show others that I belong to Your family by the way I love them. Amen.

Clean and Pure

Now the purpose of the commandment is love from a pure heart, from a good conscience, and from sincere faith.

—1 Timothy 1:5 NKJV

Would you consider yourself a germaphobe? If you're not sure, see if any of the following statements describe you.

You keep hand sanitizers in your purse, car, diaper bag, and briefcase. You could eat off the sanitized counters and floors in your homes—although just the thought of that makes you shudder. And despite the results of scientific studies, you *know* that the "five-second rule"—picking up food dropped on the floor within five seconds and eating it without fear of germs—is just a myth. So are you a germaphobe to one degree or another?

All of us need to be as vigilant about our spiritual cleanliness. Many pollutants in this world threaten our hearts, minds, and spirits. Only the vigilant who rely on God's power can love from a heart that is clean and pure; with a clean conscience; and with a peace-filled and sincere faith. Spiritual cleanliness really *is* next to godliness.

God, please enable my love to be from a pure heart, from a good conscience, and from sincere faith. Amen.

Sticks and Stones

What you say can mean life or death. Those who speak with care will be rewarded.

—Proverbs 18:21 NCV

If you've ever been hurt by verbal stones, you know that the sing-song assertion "Sticks and stones may break my bones, but words will never hurt me" is simply not true. Words *do* wound, and sometimes those wounds run deep and sting—if not debilitate—for a long time.

Words carelessly thrown at someone can break spirits and hearts just as sticks and stones can break bones. On the other hand, words can also heal and spread joy. Uplifting words have prompted a turning point in people's lives.

The words we speak can give life to others as well as fill our own souls with joy as we speak them. But our words can also take life away if we speak them with evil intent or from a deceitful heart. Such words are poison; such words are death.

Verbal sticks and stones may not break bones, but they can destroy lives, even the lives of the people who speak the harsh words. So the next time you are tempted to throw verbal stones, replace those words with some that give life and make peace.

May I never use words as a weapon to wound, Lord. Help my words always to be full of life and love. Amen.

Given to Be Used

For the Spirit God gave us does not make us timid, but gives us power, love and self-discipline.

—2 Timothy 1:7 NIV

Imagine if merely receiving the gift of an exercise bike meant automatically experiencing its health and fitness benefits. Gifts don't work that way, though. We need to use the exercise bike: we need to rely on discipline, hard work, and sweat to experience any beneficial results from that gift.

The gift of flowers placed in a closet is not a gift we enjoy. A blender placed on the counter but never used is a gift of little worth. Good gifts are the gifts we use.

God gives the best and most appropriate gifts. For instance, He knew that as a young preacher, Timothy needed gifts that would counter his natural timidity and fear. So God gave him power, love, and self-discipline.

What gifts do you need? If you ask for and receive them, will you use them as Timothy did? God knows what you need, so ask Him for those gifts, and then be ready to use them to serve Him and others.

God, please give me the gifts of power, love, and self-discipline. Help me to use the gifts you've given me wisely and well. Amen.

Open Doors

Offer hospitality to one another without grumbling.

—1 Peter 4:9 NIV

It was one of my grandmother's most generous and most endearing habits. Once or twice a week, when she was making the family dinner, she also prepared an extra meal for someone in need; she liked to have one ready for whenever a need arose. Besides being generous and kind, this practice also helped broaden my understanding of hospitality.

Sometimes hospitality means opening your home, but it can also mean taking a meal to someone or visiting a homebound person for the day. Christian hospitality means living with open doors—literally and metaphorically—to welcome people who are searching, hurting, or hungry.

May we also live with open hearts, open calendars, and open checkbooks. May we be ready to offer the shoulder to lean on, the day at the soup kitchen, and the check to help the widowed mom. Showing hospitality is putting God's love into action.

God, give me boldness to live with open doors, welcoming people with Your love. Amen.

Puffed Up

Knowledge puffs you up with pride, but love builds up.

—1 Corinthians 8:1 NCV

Knowledge is power," the professor explained to the class of aspiring teachers. "And that's why at some schools even the teachers in your own department won't share lesson plans, worksheets, or any other classroom tips and tools."

Knowledge does indeed give one a sense of power, so how will we exercise the power that comes with knowledge? Will we humbly serve people or pridefully lord our knowledge over them? You know what the latter looks like: puffed-up chest, nose in the air, an attitude of superiority. The apostle Paul recognized the potential for such dangerous pride—and that includes pride in Bible knowledge.

The passionate new Christians in Corinth had been learning a lot about their life-transforming faith, so Paul felt it wise to warn them about the dangers of pride. He instructed them never to use their knowledge to discourage people but instead to use that knowledge—and their time and resources—to love. This focus on others rather than self deflates a puffed-up chest and honors God.

God, forgive me for my overly generous self-evaluation that puffs me up. Rather than focusing on myself—my abilities, accomplishments, or knowledge—may I focus on loving others. Amen.

JANUARY 28

A Kiss That Reassures

Greet one another with a kiss of love. Peace to all of you who are in Christ.

—1 Peter 5:14 NIV

Some kisses are tender; some are just a peck on the cheek. Kisses can be passionate, while others are friendly greetings. We kiss the boo-boos of children, and we kiss away tears when a heart is broken. Kisses can be blown across a room, and letters can be sealed with a kiss. And then there is the kiss that the apostle Peter speaks of: the kiss of love or, in some translations, the kiss of peace.

As a common greeting among Jewish people in Bible times, a kiss of love given in the name of the Lord spoke volumes to the recipient. This token of brotherly love communicated familial affection and sincerity of heart.

Though it's more common for us to greet one another with a handshake or a hug, we can do so with warmth and sincerity—the agape love that is God's very nature. When we offer an embrace in the name of the Lord and on His behalf, we remind the recipient of God's love, forgiveness, and acceptance. And the gift of peace often accompanies that reminder.

By Your grace, Lord, help me to embrace others with warmth and sincerity because You love them beyond measure. Amen.

A Big Assignment

Beyond all these things put on love, which is the perfect bond of unity.

—Colossians 3:14 NASB

Though we may be reluctant to admit it, some people are just plain annoying—but the people who get under my skin probably aren't the same people who irritate you. And we can only imagine the list of people who find us annoying!

Whether or not He was ever annoyed (by slow-to-understand disciples, maybe?), Jesus knew the rest of us would be. So He told us what to do when that happened (John 13:34–35). And the apostle John told us what to do (1 John 4:7–12). So did Paul (Romans 12:10; 13:8). And they're all pretty much quoting God Himself: love your neighbor as yourself (Leviticus 19:18). That's a big assignment, but—by God's grace—not impossible.

By the power of His Spirit, God is in the business of making us more like His Son—more compassionate, kind, humble, gentle, patient, forgiving, and, yes, more loving. Let's yield to the work of the Spirit, looking beyond the annoying behavior to the heart of the person.

God, let me see the people You put in my path today as fearfully and wonderfully made and deeply loved by You so that I might love them as You do. Amen.

The Greatest Mystery

My goal is that they may be encouraged in heart and united in love, so that they may have the full riches of complete understanding, in order that they may know the mystery of God, namely, Christ.

—Colossians 2:2 NIV

Do you like a good mystery? You know, the stories that offer clues along the way about whodunit but don't let you put the pieces together until the very end. Really good mystery writers toss in some twists and turns to throw you off. Maybe the best mysteries are those with not-too-obvious clues, which we better understand in retrospect.

One of the compelling elements of God's story is the mystery of His love. People in Jesus' day and for millennia before that thought they knew what love meant. Then Jesus came.

Jesus' love was sacrificial: He was beaten, He bled, and He died. Jesus' love was powerful: He brought hope, peace, and joy to people who had none. He left the purity and glory of heaven to walk this dusty earth and gave us a more complete understanding of what love really is.

God, help me each day to more fully understand the mystery of Your gracious, life-changing, life-giving love. Amen.

The Lord's Delight

The Lord God is a sun and shield; the Lord bestows favor and honor; no good thing does he withhold from those whose walk is blameless.

—Psalm 84:11 NIV

It's a great Mark Twain quote that can prompt a profoundly theological discussion: "Heaven goes by favor. If it went by merit, you would stay out and your dog would go in."

How true! And praise God that He doesn't open heaven's doors to us based on our merit. Imagine trying to earn our way in. How many of us would have made any progress at all today? Though we may not have done anything particularly bad, we definitely weren't perfect. And then there are those sins of omission we need to account for!

With Twain's observation in mind, let's consider the psalmist's words. The Hebrew word for *favor* is *ratson*, meaning "delight, grace, kindness, and willfulness." The word *bestows* means "to give as a gift." Then paraphrase today's verse in connotation: *The Lord delights in you, not for anything you have done, but as a gift He gives simply because He loves you.* What a wonderful and peace-giving truth!

Lord, I'm not worthy of Your grace, but You give it as a gift of Your love. I am grateful. Amen.

Knowing vs. Doing

"'Love the Lord your God with all your heart, all your soul, all your mind, and all your strength.' The second command is this: 'Love your neighbor as you love yourself.'"

—Mark 12:30–31 NCV

Maybe this observation is just a commentary on the limitations of the English language, but we can love golden retrievers, pizza, sunsets, sleeping in, rainy days, our child, our spouse, and the Lord. And we know that love "is patient and kind . . . not jealous . . . not proud . . . not rude . . . not selfish . . . does not count up wrongs . . . patiently accepts all things . . . always trusts, always hopes, and always endures" (1 Corinthians 13:4–5, 7 NCV). And we know that God's two greatest commands are to love Him and to love others.

We know those are the greatest commands because a Pharisee asked Jesus (Matthew 22:34–37). But knowing God's commandments to love and knowing how His Word describes love are meaningless unless we're acting on that knowledge. Let's ask Jesus to help us live out what we know about love. Talking about love is not the same as loving!

God, I don't want to just know about Your love; teach me to live out Your love. Amen.

Consistent Love

Let love prevail in your life, words, and actions.

—1 Corinthians 16:14 VOICE

We all have many roles. We are mothers or fathers, daughters or sons. We are friends, neighbors, and coworkers. We are coaches, homeroom parents, Sunday school teachers, and club members. We belong to a church family as well as our own family.

Imagine if I talked to a person who knows me in each of these capacities. If a friend, a neighbor, a coworker, a team parent, a schoolteacher, the club president, my pastor, my spouse, and one of my kids compared notes, would their sense of who I am, their understanding of what I value, their reports on how I act, and the way they describe my character be consistent?

I want to share God's love and mirror His character wherever I am and whatever I'm doing, even when I'm hungry, hurried, tired, or overwhelmed. Clearly, I need the Lord's help!

Lord, please help love to prevail in my words and actions throughout my waking hours, no matter the role I'm in or however weak I'm feeling. Amen.

Stuffed with Love

Long before he laid down earth's foundations, he had us in mind, had settled on us as the focus of his love, to be made whole and holy by his love. Long, long ago he decided to adopt us into his family through Jesus Christ. (What pleasure he took in planning this!)

—Ephesians 1:4–5 MSG

Have you ever visited a workshop where you can stuff your own teddy bear? When you enter, you've undoubtedly done some planning and anticipating. So you choose a boy or girl bear of the size and color you want. Next, you fill your bear with stuffing. Then you choose a heart to insert inside, after which the seam is stitched closed. At some stores you can even add clothes and accessories to your bear. Once complete, you can name your bear and create a birth certificate.

A child's excited anticipation of this new furry friend is nothing compared to the joy God found in planning both His creation and His adoption of us. Long before He made the earth, He anticipated creating us, loving us, and adopting us into His family. As today's verse says, "what pleasure he took in planning this!"

And what pleasure we can have in being chosen and loved like that!

I pray, Lord, that You would make this head-knowledge of Your pleasure in creating me, adopting me, and loving me become heart knowledge as well. Amen.

Loving the Unlovable

Pursue peace with all people, and holiness, without which no one will see the Lord.

—Hebrews 12:14 NKJV

Some people are just easier to love than others. Some are prickly and difficult to get close to. Some shoot words that wound. Other people destroy any good that comes their way. And I'm sure you can add other difficult-to-love people to this list.

But the most difficult people to love are probably the people who most need our love. At first they may not know how to respond to, receive, or trust our love. The past hurts that make them hard to love have undoubtedly caused protective walls, defensive behaviors, and even hurtful ways.

Yes, loving the unlovable is difficult, but doing so—choosing to love in obedience to God's command and as a step of faith—is absolutely life-changing . . . for you *and* for them.

Lord, You know the people I'm thinking about right now. The next time I'm with them, help me to pursue peace by loving them with Your love. Amen.

First Love

But I have this against you, that you have left your first love.

—Revelation 2:4 NASB

Who was your first love? The classmate who made your heart race? The singer whose posters adorned your room? Do you remember the sweetness of puppy love? I'm sure you can't forget the heartache of the first breakup. You may have experienced falling in love, you may be choosing to stay committed to your vow to love, or you may be blessed to experience a love that has grown richer through the years.

Now think about your first love for Jesus. Think about your hunger to be with Him and learn more about Him . . . your passion for Scripture, His love letter to you . . . your sensitivity to His presence with you. Has that love been tempered by time or disappointment? Has it been derailed by busyness or distractions? Or have you consciously walked away because of hurt or anger?

Whatever has distanced you from Him, know God can change your heart. Ask Him to rekindle your first love for Him. Being in a close relationship with Him brings peace, and so much more.

God, rekindle my first love for You, and teach me what You would have me do to fuel that flame. Amen.

The Real Thing

Let love be without hypocrisy. Abhor what is evil; cling to what is good. Be devoted to one another in brotherly love; give preference to one another in honor.

—Romans 12:9–10 NASB

It's a casualty of our busy world: cooking from scratch. Why would we want to spend time melting chocolate in a double-boiler when we could just add eggs and oil to a premade brownie mix? When the list of ingredients is three items long and we only have to clean a bowl and spoon, why would we cook from scratch?

Because the from-scratch version is so much better! The real thing can't be compared to the silver-medal imposter. The mix is satisfying enough only if you don't know what you're missing.

But I hope you notice a difference when it comes to love. If you've experienced God's love, then you've experienced the real thing. If you do know God's love, be ready to share His real love with those in your life who only know imposter love.

God, let me love with authentic, selfless, and steadfast love because I've experienced the real thing from You. Amen.

Better Together

In the same way that one body has so many different parts, each with different functions; we, too—the many—are different parts that form one body in the Anointed One. Each one of us is joined with one another, and we become together what we could not be alone.

—Romans 12:4–5 VOICE

The apostle Paul spoke of believers as the body of Christ. This analogy effectively communicates the way different parts contribute to the whole, the way different functions contribute to the overall well-being of the organization.

Paul also wrote about some of the ways an individual can contribute to the well-being of the body of believers. Some will prophesy, and others will serve, teach, exhort, and lead (Romans 12). Some will be blessed with wisdom, while others will be blessed with knowledge, faith, or healing (1 Corinthians 12).

No individual can always do or be all things all at one time. When we see ourselves for what we are—imperfect and incomplete—we will come to appreciate fellow believers, be grateful for who they are and what they can do, and therefore at peace with them. And we can be at peace with ourselves: God has made each of us unique.

God, thank You that we are indeed better together as Your hands and feet, as salt and light, in this world. Amen.

Wedding Joy

Let us rejoice and be happy and give God glory, because the wedding of the Lamb has come, and the Lamb's bride has made herself ready. Fine linen, bright and clean, was given to her to wear.

—Revelation 19:7–8 NCV

Have you been to a wedding lately? Some traditions have changed: not every bride is given away by her father; she doesn't always wear a white dress or a veil; and she is showered with birdseed rather than rice (a greener solution!).

But a few things remain the same. Mothers cry, and cake is still served. Vows are exchanged, and the couple is introduced as "Mr. and Mrs." for the first time.

In Revelation, the Bible describes the wedding that will take place at the end of all time, the wedding between the Lamb of God, who is Jesus Christ, and His bride, who is the church of all believers. In its glory and splendor, this wedding will be unlike any we've ever witnessed. In some ways the wedding will seem familiar: the bride will positively glow, the joy will be palpable, and the love, immeasurable.

As a member of Your church, Lord, I am that future bride. Help me to ready myself for the big day when I will say, "I do" for eternity. Amen.

Sacrificial Love

"Take your son, your only son Isaac whom I know you love deeply, and go to the land of Moriah. When you get there, I want you to offer Isaac to Me as a burnt offering on one of the mountains. I will show you which one."

—Genesis 22:2 VOICE

Some children break their parents' hearts. The parents have prayed, cried, yelled at God. They were loving and consistent; they let natural consequences teach and enforced logical consequences when necessary. Their children had every advantage, and they still chose the wrong path. It's not always predictable which way a child will go.

At some point in our parenting, though, we realize we have to let go. We who are Christian parents, though, have a distinct advantage. We know we aren't releasing our children into the unknown of a random universe of happenstance and fate. Instead, we let go and place our children in God's capable hands. We surrender our children to the One who loaned them to us in the first place, to the God who loves our children more than we ever could.

Peace comes with that transition. May our children grow from dependence on us to dependence on the Lord.

God, I place my children in Your good and perfect care and ask You for the blessings of comfort and peace. Amen.

Superman's Cape

As God's chosen people, holy and dearly loved, clothe yourselves with compassion, kindness, humility, gentleness and patience.

—Colossians 3:12 NIV

Do you remember watching Clark Kent turn into Superman? He was a quiet, normal, everyday newspaper reporter until he put on that cape. When he put on his costume, he became a new man—bold, fearless, take-charge, and able to leap tall buildings in a single bound!

The clothes Clark changed into had quite an impact on him. To be more specific, those clothes gave him cover to become someone he could not be otherwise. He stood strong and confident when clothed in garments that gave him a new persona.

We, too, can be strong and confident when, like Clark Kent, we put on new clothes—the clothes of Christ. God's Word gives the details, instructing us to clothe ourselves in "compassion, kindness, humility, gentleness and patience." When we put on these clothes, we can become bold and fearless, empowered by God's Spirit to do His work in this world.

Lord, help me be mindful not only every morning but throughout the day to put on compassion, kindness, humility, gentleness, and patience. Amen.

The Cupboard Is Bare

Better a dry crust with peace and quiet than a house full of feasting, with strife.

—Proverbs 17:1 NIV

Isn't it amazing how we can have a cupboard full of food, yet our families will still complain, "There's nothing to eat!" We know there is plenty of food in the house. They're not really saying they can't find *anything* to eat; they're just looking for something that will satisfy.

Our souls are like that. We long for something that will satisfy our inner hunger. We look at all the world has to offer—exhilarating relationships, custom-built houses, fancy cars, corner offices, impressive vacations—yet we see nothing that will truly satisfy.

When we look at our life at home, is there peace? If our home is filled with strife, it's like having a refrigerator full of food with nothing to eat. When our home is calm and we're all getting along, the cupboard may be bare, but our souls are satisfied.

The next time someone in your house claims there's nothing to eat, take a quick inventory of your family: whose soul needs some extra attention and love?

God, thank You for the food in my cupboard and especially for the peace and quiet in my home that satisfies my soul. Amen.

The Power of a Love Song

"I in them and You in Me, that they may be perfected in unity, so that the world may know that You sent Me, and loved them, even as You have loved Me."

—John 17:23 NASB

Love songs have a way of taking us back. If you hear a love song from your early years of marriage, aren't you immediately transported back to that time?

As you listen, memories of the simpler, more carefree love you shared may come to mind. You may remember the funny things you did to financially survive as newlyweds. Or perhaps you think of the tough times and tender moments of those early years.

True love is rarely, if ever, easy, but when we choose to unite our love with God's love, to ground our love for each other in His love for us, then our love will have staying power. When we as a Christian community love one another with a love rooted in God's love, we experience a unity that serves as a beacon of light and hope that draws others to the One who is love. And, like our favorite love songs, our loves—for spouse, family, and brothers and sisters in Christ—point us back to the One who first loved us.

Thank You, God, for Your love. As I love those You have given me to love, may my love for them be grounded in Your love so I might point others to You. Amen.

He Gave

God expressed His love for the world in this way: He gave His only Son so that whoever believes in Him will not face everlasting destruction, but will have everlasting life.

—John 3:16 VOICE

If you live on this planet, you've probably been betrayed at least once. And if you tried to count all the lies, disloyalties, and times you were treated unfairly, you'd probably run out of fingers and toes to tally them on.

A common reaction after being betrayed is, "I'll never let anyone do that to me again!" We wall ourselves off, believing that if we never again let anyone get close to us, we can protect our hearts from pain.

Our Savior understands the excruciating pain of being betrayed. Jesus knew it awaited Him before He left heaven's throne. God the Father knew, too, but God so loved us that He gave anyway. He gave His Son to us knowing we would reject Him and kill Him. He gave His Son to us in spite of our sin. And Jesus gave Himself knowing one of His own would betray Him and another would deny knowing Him. He gave until He bled and died so that we might truly understand the selfless, sacrificial nature of divine—of genuine—love.

Every time a little annoyance occurs or someone deeply wounds me, help me to remember all that You gave, Lord Jesus and Father God. Amen.

Love You More

May [you] be able to . . . know the love of Christ which passes knowledge; that you may be filled with all the fullness of God.

—Ephesians 3:18–19 NKJV

"I love you more than vanilla ice cream with hot fudge," a smiling dad said to his daughter. With a sparkle in her eye and an even bigger smile than her dad's, she replied, "I love you more than kisses from a puppy!"

It's hard to find the words to express our love for someone dear to us. Consider the ways God has chosen to express His love for us. God has given us the words of Scripture, but He didn't stop there. In fact, through His creation, God seems to play the dad's and daughter's game with us!

God gives us a breathtaking sunrise as if to whisper in our ear, *See this? I love you more than I love that.* He sends rain for flowers and sunshine to brighten the day and whispers again, *I love you more than that.* God's ultimate expression of His immeasurable love for us is the gift of His Son, whom He sent to die on the cross, taking on Himself the punishment we deserve for our sin.

So the next time you see a gorgeous sunrise or a delicately crafted rose, imagine God saying, *I love you more than I love this, so I sent Jesus.*

God, thank You for being a loving Father. Please give me eyes to notice the evidence of Your love. Amen.

Know-It-Alls

If I have the gift of prophecy, and know all mysteries and all knowledge; and if I have all faith, so as to remove mountains, but do not have love, I am nothing.

—1 Corinthians 13:2 NASB

No one likes a know-it-all. In the workplace, know-it-alls have an answer for every question, a solution for every problem, a plan for every obstacle. At the PTA meeting, they know the way it has always been done. In the neighborhood association, they know the way it is supposed to be. Know-it-alls have a better way and a bigger voice—and an ego to match. Every group, association, and organization seems to have its resident know-it-all.

However, if we could scratch beneath the surface of the know-it-all, we would find someone who knows a lot but is lacking the knowledge of one very important thing. As the Bible puts it, this person has many gifts, knows many facts, and does wonderful things but lacks a deep and genuine love of people. Know-it-alls don't know it *all*. Knowing it *all* means knowing the love of God and the peace that comes with it.

If you don't want to be a know-it-all, focus on knowing all you can of God's rich and amazing love.

God, I want to experience all that Your amazing love has for me—hope, purpose, joy, direction, and, yes, peace. Amen.

Serving with Love

If I give all I possess to the poor and give over my body to hardship that I may boast, but do not have love, I gain nothing.

—1 Corinthians 13:3 NIV

The phrase *social activism* refers to volunteerism paired with social justice. Social activists feel passionately about working with the underserved and unnoticed in society. They volunteer in soup kitchens, homeless shelters, and low-income housing communities. Social activists want to both change an unjust system and help those who have suffered because of that injustice.

However, the Bible says we can give away all we own, volunteer every hour of every day, and work our body to the bone on behalf of unjust causes, yet if we do so without loving people with God's love, we might as well stay home. Oh, we might feel better about ourselves and we may even do some good, but as God sees it, serving others without loving them is worthless.

Love changes everything, including the act of service. When we act out of love, no longer is our service all about us. So the next time we volunteer, let's not just check something off our list but truly love those we serve.

God, purify my heart motive. Fuel my love for You so that it overflows into the lives of others, especially those You call me to serve. Amen.

Seeing with His Eyes

Love never gives up. Love cares more for others than for self. Love doesn't want what it doesn't have. Love doesn't strut, doesn't have a swelled head.

—1 Corinthians 13:4 MSG

If you have a sibling, you may remember scenes like this. One of you shouted, "I hate you!" The other yelled, "I hate you back!" Mom entered the room and explained—again—"Now, you may not like what your sibling did, but you don't hate your brother/sister." Mom made a good point. Separating the person from the behavior is one of the first lessons in learning to love. The next step is harder.

With human eyes, we only see the trouble or pain this person caused. When—by God's grace—we see others with Christ's eyes, we see the person God created, one of His children, a person wounded in this life, a person covered with the filth of sin, yet a person whom Jesus loves.

When we see people with God's eyes of love and compassion, we find it easier to extend love and compassion. If this sounds like a difficult task, God will gladly help. Because He is love, He can enable us not only to see with the love of Christ, but also to love with the love of Christ.

God, thank You for seeing me with eyes of compassion and love. Give me Your eyes to see others the way You see them and to love them as You do. Amen.

Fighting Fairly

Love is not rude, is not selfish, and does not get upset with others. Love does not count up wrongs that have been done. Love takes no pleasure in evil but rejoices over the truth.

—1 Corinthians 13:5–6 NCV

If you've ever witnessed a heated argument between two people who love each other, you may have learned a great lesson in fighting fair. No name-calling, no blaming, no piling on past offenses, and no finger-pointing are good guidelines for conflicts with friends as well as spouses.

Love doesn't mean you never disagree. But it does mean you fight differently than the world fights. Love requires you to put the other person's needs before your own, no matter how hurt you are. Because of love, you choose not to be rude even in the heat of an argument, and you choose not to bring up past wounds that have nothing to do with the matter at hand. When when handled well, those conflicts are actually an opportunity for your love to grow.

The next time a heated discussion arises, consider every word you say: "Is it loving?" You just may learn how quickly a fight can end.

Lord, when I disagree, enable me to love enough to fight fairly so resolution can come and peace can reign. Amen.

A Tall Order

"You shall love the LORD your God with all your heart, with all your soul, and with all your strength."

—Deuteronomy 6:5 NKJV

Does Deuteronomy 6:5 seem like a tall order? It is! This verse is the commandment to love God with all that we are—with all our heart and all our soul and all our strength. "All our mind" is added in other places, but it is certainly implied in this trio.

So we are to love God with all that we are. Sounds simple enough—but how are we doing?

- What does your calendar reveal about how much you love God?
- What does your bank statement suggest about how completely you love God?
- What would a coworker say about your love for God?
- What would someone who lives with you say about your love for God?

Loving God with all we are is a tall order—but an appropriate one for our big God, who deserves nothing less from us.

God, You keep planets in their orbits, the law of gravity functioning, and my heart beating. You alone are worthy of my loving You with all that I am. Amen.

Costly Love

[Love] bears all things, believes all things, hopes all things, endures all things.

—1 Corinthians 13:7 NKJV

When couples say the words "for better, for worse; for richer, for poorer; in sickness and in health; to love and to cherish; from this day forward until death do us part," they mean them. But time will tell. When the worst happens, when richer becomes poorer, when health fades, the loving and cherishing won't be easy, but it will be precious. In fact, the most beautiful love is seen in the person who stays even when loving is difficult and costly. True love is most lovely when life is ugly.

Wedding vows are beautiful, but vows whispered in a hospital room, a bankruptcy hearing, or a prison's visitor lounge are powerful pictures of true love, of costly love. And this steadfast love blesses the recipient with a deep sense of peace.

It is one thing to say the words "I love you" on your wedding day, but it is quite another to live them. So if you are in a place where the cost of loving is on the rise, God understands. His love for you was very costly. He will give you what you need so you can love when it's hard.

God, when life tests the wedding vows I once made, give me a depth of love—of Christlike love—that bears, believes, hopes, and endures all things. Amen.

Character of Love

Faith, hope, and love remain; these three virtues must characterize our lives. The greatest of these is love.

—1 Corinthians 13:13 VOICE

Formation skydivers are a lot of fun—and a little nerve-racking—to watch. For many people the freefall isn't as frightening as the potential of hitting the ground. The only visible thing keeping these brave men and women from catastrophe is the parachute each one wears. They must trust that their harnesses, ripcords, and parachutes have been thoroughly tested and properly packed. Having that faith is easy when you're safely on the ground, but having that complete trust when you're freefalling at 120 miles per hour is a different matter.

Similarly, trusting God is easy when we have health, enough money, and kids making good decisions. Deliberately holding on to faith in God when circumstances head south—when the diagnosis is terminal, when the checking account is empty and no job can be found, when a child has chosen unwisely—is real faith. Our gracious God helps us hold on to our faith in Him, our hope in Him, and our love for Him whenever the circumstances of life make it tough.

God, when my faith is tested, when hope fades, and when love hurts, help me to hold on to faith, hope, and love. Amen.

PEACE WITH JUSTICE

A Grace-Filled Life

Grace and peace be given to you more and more, because you truly know God and Jesus our Lord.

—2 Peter 1:2 NCV

Do you have two left feet, or are you considered graceful? I would love to be graceful even for a single day. Walking across a crowded room involves hazards that the graceful don't see and can't even imagine! And forget playing sports. Instead of being a gazelle, I am more a duck-billed, beaver-tailed, otter-footed platypus. I'd love to be the reason for the winning goal on the soccer field, but most likely I'll be the reason the other team scores.

While gracefulness can help us on a soccer field, God's grace makes a far more significant difference in our lives. God gives us the grace of forgiveness of sins and salvation. He also gives us grace to accept other people despite their clumsy human limitations, idiosyncrasies, and even flat-out sins.

A grace-filled life means accepting people's mistakes and sins because we know what it's like to need and receive grace.

God, I need Your grace, and I thank You for Your grace. Help me to live a grace-filled life that blesses others with peace and love. Amen.

Three Requirements

He has shown you, O mortal, what is good. And what does the L*ORD require of you? To act justly and to love mercy and to walk humbly with your God.*

—Micah 6:8 NIV

Mention the word *justice,* and many people will picture the blindfolded Lady Justice holding her scales as she stands in front of a courthouse. Or perhaps they think of a big trial where justice prevailed—or didn't.

The book of Micah depicts a courtroom scene: the Lord is the plaintiff; Micah, His envoy; the mountains, the witnesses; and God's people, the accused. The charge against Israel was injustice, and their guilt was undeniable. Willing to do whatever it took, God's chosen people asked Him what they might do to again be at peace with Him.

Acting with mercy, God offered a simple, straightforward answer. He told His people that they could make restitution by acting justly, loving mercy, and walking humbly with Him as their Lord and King.

Those requirements for Israel offer each of us a mirror to consider our own actions. How are you doing on those three counts?

God, I know I haven't always acted justly, offered mercy, or lived humbly. I ask for Your forgiveness as well as for Your transforming work in my heart. Amen.

Justice Prevails

I am the Eternal One who acts faithfully and exercises justice and righteousness on earth. These are the things that delight Me.

—Jeremiah 9:24 VOICE

From time to time a high-profile court case will grip the nation. It's the lead story on every news app, a topic of conversation during coffee breaks, and a teachable moment in classrooms. Outside the courtroom, opposing sides set up camp. It's difficult to imagine a peaceful resolution with so much at stake.

Looking at our world, we might feel the same thing. What kind of resolution can God bring to the mess we have made? God is the ultimate Judge who presides over this earth, but where is justice now? And how will justice prevail and the guilty be punished? We don't understand because of our limited human perspective.

Let's remember that from the supreme bench of justice, God hammers the gavel with authority and strength. He will faithfully perform His duties: He will exercise justice, punish the guilty, and reward the righteous. He is the Judge of all judges; we can completely trust Him to do right. That truth gives us peace.

God, it is sometimes difficult to see how justice will prevail, but I put my trust in You. I know that, in the end, Your judgments will make all things right. Amen.

Our Merciful God

[God] says to Moses, "I WILL HAVE MERCY ON WHOM I HAVE MERCY, AND I WILL HAVE COMPASSION ON WHOM I HAVE COMPASSION." So then it does not depend on the man who wills or the man who runs, but on God who has mercy.

—Romans 9:15–16 NASB

Random isn't quite the right word. Definitely not *arbitrary*. *Wise* works. *Sovereign* may be the best word.

Sometimes we don't understand why God does what He does. That question may involve a personal issue, but it may also involve His actions in ancient history. Why, for instance, did God prefer the second-born twin Jacob to the firstborn son Esau? That was countercultural! Furthermore, Jacob was a liar and a deceiver.

Whenever we don't understand what God does—on however big or small a scale—we do well to remind ourselves that God isn't random or arbitrary. He is wise and good—and sovereign. Our sovereign God is the Creator of all and the Author of all history: He has every right to "have mercy on whom I have mercy, and . . . compassion on whom I have compassion."

Thank God for the peace we can know as we trust in His mercy.

I praise You, sovereign God, as You reign in justice and righteousness, as You reign with wisdom, compassion, power, and love. Amen.

Stranger Danger

Also you shall not oppress a stranger, for you know the heart of a stranger, because you were strangers in the land of Egypt.

—Exodus 23:9 NKJV

We teach our children about the danger of talking to strangers, and rightly so. We want to help our children stay safe, so we warn them about the lost-puppy ploy and the ice-cream lure. We teach them how to scream and even how to fight off an attack.

But that's not the only way—and it's not always the right way—to treat strangers. Our children need to learn how, in a safe context, to reach out to a stranger with God's love. After all, our God is the God of love, and He calls us to be people who love. As His representatives on this earth, we are to welcome people whose names we don't yet know, people who are different from us, and people who call another land "home." Such welcoming calls for wisdom and discernment, which God will provide.

Such love is golden-rule love: we are treating strangers not with oppression, but with the kind of welcoming love we would want if we were the stranger.

Lord, judging people I don't know, people who are different from me, can come more easily than reaching out to them in love. Forgive me and change me. Amen.

FEBRUARY 27

Pictures of Peace

The wolf will live with the lamb, the leopard will lie down with the goat, the calf and the lion and the yearling together; and a little child will lead them.

—Isaiah 11:6 NIV

A dog and an elephant playing in the water . . . The greyhound who adopted a baby owl . . . A parakeet and a kitten napping together . . . The Internet has captured in pictures and video some sweet and unusual animal friendships including a lamb lying down with a lion.

Although, as the verse above reveals, the lion/lamb image is a misquote of the prophet Isaiah, it represents the peace that will come to earth when Jesus returns. This profound peace is pictured as a wolf living with a lamb, a leopard with a goat, and a calf with a lion. Furthermore, the prophet Isaiah said, a child will lead. That child is Jesus, and the peace He brings will one day set aside all warring. One day His peace and justice will know no end. Even before that day, He blesses His followers with peace in the midst of struggle and pain, a peace that passes understanding.

I praise You, Jesus, for being the means of peace between God and me, for blessing me with a peace-filled heart, and for the promise of ultimate peace in this world. Amen.

For This Is Right

Children, obey your parents in the Lord, for this is right.

—Ephesians 6:1 NASB

There is something to be said for adults who required a respectful "Yes, sir" or "No, ma'am" from children. This fading practice offered a solid training ground for learning to ultimately obey God throughout a lifetime of faith. We need this kind of training because surrendering our will in obedience does not come naturally or easily to us.

Growing up, we didn't always understand why our parents did what they did, why they enforced such painful consequences for our disobedience, why they treated siblings differently than they treated us in seemingly similar situations, or why they didn't always explain themselves to us.

We may have those exact same issues with our heavenly Father. His ways—even His justice—can be hard for us to understand with our limited perspective and wisdom. Responding with a "Yes, Sir" and obedience will honor Him and serve us well.

Lord, thank You for the training ground for obedience I had growing up. Enable me to obey You, my heavenly Father, with a humble and willing heart, "for this is right." Amen.

On the Outside Looking In

As for the outsiders who now follow me, working for me, loving my name, and wanting to be my servants—all who keep Sabbath and don't defile it, holding fast to my covenant—I'll bring them to my holy mountain and give them joy in my house of prayer.

—Isaiah 56:6 MSG

There are insiders and outsiders. The insiders are the innately cool movers and shakers for whom life looks effortless and amazing. The outsiders can't fit in to that world. The divide is too great. But, as Old Testament insiders learned, the divide isn't too great for God.

God's people considered themselves insiders and pointed to the fact that God had specifically chosen them out of all the peoples on the earth. In Genesis 12:1–3, God chose Abram, promising to make his name great, his offspring beyond numbering, and his presence on this earth a blessing to others. But even in the Old Testament, the Bible makes it clear that many outsiders followed God and lived according to His commands. The Almighty never intended for people to be divided like that. He called His people to invite the outsiders in so that they, too, could experience peace with God and joy in relationship with Him.

Whom on the outside will you invite in?

God, help me recognize people who are on the outside looking in so that I may invite them to in to where Your peace and joy abound. Amen.

Our Liberator

"The Lord has put his Spirit in me, because he appointed me to tell the Good News to the poor. He has sent me to tell the captives they are free and to tell the blind that they can see again. God sent me to free those who have been treated unfairly."

—Luke 4:18 NCV

Try to imagine the day that troops opened the gates of the World War II prison camps. First think about being a soldier who saw those shriveled bodies but huge smiles. Then consider being a prisoner who had prayed for freedom. Imagine the overwhelming emotions of both those soldiers and those prisoners.

Like the soldiers who stormed Normandy so those gates could be opened and justice and peace could reign around the world, Christ stormed the gates of hell so that justice and peace could reign in the spiritual realm.

Christ is our Liberator. He came to set free the captives, those enslaved by sin—and that is all of us. If you have recognized your captivity to sin, confessed, and welcomed Christ's offer to open the gates and set you free, thank your Liberator. If you are still imprisoned, know your Liberator is ready to open the gates of your prison cell. He died and rose again: you have been set free!

Jesus, thank You for storming the gates of hell and opening the door to the prison of sin that held me captive. Amen.

When No One Sees

"Woe to you, teachers of the law and Pharisees, you hypocrites! You give a tenth of your spices—mint, dill and cumin. But you have neglected the more important matters of the law—justice, mercy and faithfulness. You should have practiced the latter, without neglecting the former."

—Matthew 23:23 NIV

Politics can be vicious, ruthless, and just plain dirty. Running for office, even staying in office, has become a cutthroat business. So it is nice when we see our politicians doing something for the less fortunate. Still, we may find ourselves questioning their motives. Only the Lord knows their hearts.

Doing good in order to appear good is exactly what the Pharisees did, and Jesus called them out on it. He knew, for instance, that they gave their tithe simply so everyone would see and praise them, and then they neglected the more important aspects of being God's people: the practice of justice, mercy, and faithfulness in their everyday lives, even when no one was looking. What hypocritical behavior! But . . .

What do you and I do or not do when no one is looking? Does the practice of justice and mercy contribute to the peace God wants us to know?

Lord, help me to not only do the right thing when all eyes are upon me but also when no one except You will see. Amen.

Telling the Truth

Truth shall spring out of the earth, and righteousness shall look down from heaven.

—Psalm 85:11 NKJV

In the 1950s, a game show aired that ran for six decades. Its format was simple enough: *To Tell the Truth* introduced three challengers, each claiming to be the same person. Two were lying and one was telling the truth. After the contestants asked the three a series of questions in an effort to discern who was lying and who wasn't, they voted for the person they thought was the truth teller. Anticipation grew until the game show host finally asked the big question: "Will the real [person's name] please stand up?"

It is important for people to stand up and tell the truth. Proclaiming truth—proclaiming *God's* truth—is intimately connected with justice and righteousness. Without honesty and truth, neither justice nor righteousness can be defined. The good news is that biblical truth is not dependent on human truthfulness. Biblical justice is predicated on Truth with a capital *T*, a reference not to a human attribute but instead to the Person of Jesus Christ. He doesn't simply represent truth; He *is* Truth. Whenever you speak truth, you honor your righteous God.

God, may the words I share and the actions I take always be truthful, representative of Your love, peace, and justice. Amen.

Right Angle

All have sinned and fall short of the glory of God, being justified as a gift by His grace through the redemption which is in Christ Jesus.

—Romans 3:23–24 NASB

For us not-so-handy types, the tools at the local home-improvement store can be scary. We know the job we want to get done, and we know there must be a tool to make that job easier, but we have no idea what that tool is called. Some tools have been named well: appropriately enough, names such as *level* and *screwdriver* describe what they actually do. Other tools have rather ambiguous names: what does a hacksaw or a droplight do anyway?

Consider the well-named right angle. The dictionary defines the word *right* as "conformity with standards or truth; just; set straight; vindicated; or assumes a vertical position." Jesus is our Right Angle: His life is a model of conformity to God's standards and truth, and He enables us to be in relationship with—to be set straight with—God.

The next time you pass the pegboard in your garage or enter the dreaded home-improvement store, thank God that Jesus is your Right Angle. He is the right tool for the job of living a life that glorifies the King of kings.

Jesus, thank You for setting an example of right and righteous living and for, by the power of Your Spirit, enabling me to follow You. Amen.

Wave the White Flag

Having been justified by faith, we have peace with God through our Lord Jesus Christ.

—Romans 5:1 NASB

Have you ever wondered what it must feel like to be an innocent person whom a jury finds guilty? An unjust verdict must prompt indescribable frustration and rage. In sharp contrast are the relief and peace that come when a just verdict is read.

According to Scripture, we are all guilty of sin: the just verdict is "Guilty!" We deserve the penalty of eternal separation from God, a separation we chose every time we sinned. Yet God's verdict for us is "Not guilty!" He has accepted Jesus' death on our behalf and deemed us justified. Our holy God has removed all charges from our records: it's as if they were never there. Legally, it is as if we had never even been accused. Spiritually, it's as if we have unfurled a white flag in our soul's war with God.

If your soul has not yet raised that white flag, now is a good time. Accept God's gift of grace and peace today.

God, help me to accept Your verdict of "Not guilty" and live in that freedom so that I may know Your peace. Amen.

Hand-Me-Down Wisdom

You who are younger, submit yourselves to your elders. All of you, clothe yourselves with humility toward one another, because, "God opposes the proud but shows favor to the humble."

—1 Peter 5:5 NIV

What comes to mind when you think of hand-me-downs? Maybe you've received some hand-me-downs that made you cringe, but maybe you've received hand-me-downs that were a money-saving answer to prayer. Maybe hand-me-downs were a painful commentary on your family's economic situation, but maybe hand-me-downs meant an unexpected "new" dress and other fun clothes. Or maybe your family refused, for whatever reasons, to receive hand-me-downs when they were offered.

Just as hand-me-downs can prompt a variety of reactions, so can the idea of receiving wisdom from others. Peter encouraged believers to submit themselves to elders, to those older chronologically but also to those older in the faith. Believers who have walked with the Lord longer than we have can offer hard-earned and pain-saving wisdom. However, it takes humility for us to receive it. Don't pridefully refuse those hand-me-downs. Choose to put on humility.

Lord, help me to graciously accept hand-me-down wisdom from my elders and each morning to first reach for the cloak of humility when I get dressed. Amen.

PEACE WITH GOD

Holy, Holy, Holy

Each creature was calling to the others: "Holy, holy, holy is the LORD All-Powerful. His glory fills the whole earth."

—Isaiah 6:3 NCV

Isaiah heard it sung in the vision through which God called him to be a prophet. The apostle John heard it sung in his vision of the throne room of heaven, part of God's revelation of the coming end of history. And we sing it in hymns and praise and worship songs today: "Holy, holy, holy is the Lord God Almighty."

The repetition of "Holy, holy, holy" was important to speakers of the Hebrew language: using a word three times was a way of emphasizing that point. The repetition indicated a state of completion, perfection, or absoluteness. In this case, the worshippers are proclaiming God's complete, perfect, and absolute holiness.

The next time you hear the refrain "Holy, holy, holy," allow your awareness of God's glorious majesty, absolute authority, and eternal kingship to fill your soul with peace.

God, I praise You for Your complete and absolute holiness. You alone are worthy! Amen.

Triggering God

Give freely and spontaneously. Don't have a stingy heart. The way you handle matters like this triggers GOD, your God's, blessing in everything you do, all your work and ventures.

—Deuteronomy 15:10 MSG

Psychology has helped us understand that even a subtle gesture or the tone of someone's voice can trigger a memory or a reaction. Some memories are good, such as times with a loved one, an especially fun vacation, or a time when God's presence was very real. Sometimes, though, painful memories or feelings of anger can be triggered. At times those triggers blindside us. Suddenly we're dealing with intense emotions we didn't anticipate.

Today's verse from *The Message* says that God has triggers and gives us a specific example. How we treat people—whether we lead generous, giving lives or cold, stingy lives—triggers God. When His children give spontaneously without regard for the cost, He is triggered to bless them. He will give peace to those of us who freely give to others in all we do.

Are you living in a way that triggers God's blessings?

God, enable me to me to live openly and give generously, not for Your blessing but to honor You with my life. Amen.

Thanks, Hubble!

For as high as the heavens are above the earth, so great is his love for those who fear him; as far as the east is from the west, so far has he removed our transgressions from us.

—Psalm 103:11–12 NIV

With much fanfare and high expectations, NASA launched the Hubble Space Telescope in 1990—and Hubble has not disappointed. It has relayed hundreds of thousands of images back to earth. Its powerful instruments have surveyed our planetary neighbors, revealing now-famous images of the Pillars of Creation and the Eagle Nebula. Hubble has documented thousands of galaxies, including the Hubble Ultra Deep Field, and shown us the most distant galaxies ever observed.

Thanks to Hubble, we believers understand in a new way what it means that "the heavens declare the glory of God" (Psalm 19:1 NKJV). God promised to remove our sins from us as far as the east is from the west, and Hubble photos give us a sense of just how amazingly far that really is.

The next time you see an image from space, thank God for removing your sin far from you—and imagine how mind-bogglingly far that must be to your Creator.

Heavenly Father, thank You for technology that gives us a glimpse of how far You've removed our sins from us and how big a God we serve. Amen.

Bubble Baths

Be diligent to be found by Him in peace, without spot and blameless.

—2 Peter 3:14 NKJV

It's one of life's simple pleasures: a bubble bath! Most of us don't make time to regularly relax in the tub, but when we do, we never regret it. There is something about washing away all the stress, pain, worry, busyness, and grime of the day. Light a few candles, enjoy some soothing aromatherapy, and find peace for your body and soul.

Peace is not something that comes naturally to us; neither are the spotlessness and blamelessness that Peter mentioned. Our daily lives often work against a sense of peace; our sinful nature works against our spotlessness. We would therefore be wise to take more bubble baths. In that quiet time, we can do important things like relaxing, regrouping, confessing our spots and guilt, and finding God's peace for our souls.

Lord, I want to know peace, and I know that's related to my making time to wash away the dirt of this world and the grime of my sin. Help me to do exactly that. Amen.

God's Face

"The LORD make His face shine upon you, and be gracious to you; the LORD lift up His countenance upon you, and give you peace."

—Numbers 6:25–26 NKJV

Have you been blessed to look into the face of someone who absolutely adores you? Maybe you saw unconditional love in the face of a parent, grandparent, teacher, or mentor. Such looks of absolute love can make a lasting impact on you. That kind of acceptance, from even one person, can stay with you throughout your life. Images of that person's face warm your heart, reminding you that you are loved, accepted, and approved, no matter what messages the world may tell you.

You may not have received this kind of look from a parent or other adult. If you haven't—but even if you have—know that Someone is looking at you today with an expression of absolute adoration and unconditional love. Gaze into God's face as He smiles on you with total love, and then bask in the peace that comes with knowing you are accepted by the Holy One.

God, I want to know Your approval and be assured of Your love today. Please enable me to see Your face. Amen.

Blank-Check Love

This is what real love is: It is not our love for God; it is God's love for us. He sent his Son to die in our place to take away our sins.

—1 John 4:10 NCV

God's love is beyond measuring and beyond description. I like the analogy that God's love is a blank check from the Not-of-This-World Bank that guarantees 24/7 access to its infinite resources. In the memo area of the check, God has written "For love—whatever amount you need, whenever you need it," and He signed it, "Your Loving Father." And God dated the check: "Good Friday."

We whom He created and dearly loved had chosen sin and were so far from God. Like the parent of a wayward child, God longed for us to know the peace that comes from a reestablished relationship with Him. Because of His love for us, He paid the debt we owed for our rebellion by giving His Son's life for ours. This truly is love: not that we loved God, but that He loved us.

Do you rely on your heavenly Father's blank-check love? And do you love others with the same blank-check love—love that is given whenever, wherever, and in whatever amount is needed, with no strings attached?

Thank You, God, for giving me the blank check of Your love so I can know the peace that comes with being in right relationship with You. Amen.

Spring Cleaning

Grace, mercy and peace will be with us, from God the Father and from Jesus Christ, the Son of the Father, in truth and love.

—2 John 1:3 NASB

What tasks come to mind with the simple phrase *spring cleaning*? And what is your least favorite task on that list?

I don't mind washing the windows (I'm ready to welcome the sun), and I don't mind cleaning baseboards, scrubbing walls, or even taking down curtains and rehanging them. But cleaning out closets? For me, that's the worst.

I've realized, too, that I'm not fond of cleaning out the closets of my heart and mind either. We've all stored away things we don't want to think about, we never want to talk about, and we aren't sure we've been forgiven for. Maybe we've shelved some apologies we should make, forgiveness we need to ask for, and reconciliation we could work on.

For a season we haven't thought about cleaning out those closets, but maybe God is nudging us to do so now. After all, He wants us to know a deep and abiding peace, not just an appearance of peace. Let's ask Jesus for His help as we clean out the closets of our hearts and minds. He longs to fill them with peace.

God, I've stored many dark things in the closets of my heart and mind. Enable me to address each one and make more room for Your peace. Amen.

Noisy Sheep

May the God of peace, who brought the great Shepherd of the sheep, our Lord Jesus, back from the dead through the blood of the new everlasting covenant, perfect you in every good work as you work God's will.

—Hebrews 13:20–21 VOICE

If you've ever stood in a field with sheep, you know it is anything but quiet and peaceful. Sheep are noisy: they bleat incessantly. So why do so many churches have, framed and hanging in the hallway, lovely pastoral scenes with sheep? Those pictures aren't based in the smelly, noisy reality of real-life sheep. Perhaps those idyllic, peaceful scenes speak more of the Shepherd and the impact He has on those in His flock.

The Bible likens us to sheep and often adds that we need a shepherd. We are very much like sheep: we are noisy—and if we ourselves are not noisy, we live in a very noisy world! Many voices clamor for our attention, shouting our name—deadlines, social media, family demands, bills, and chores.

Jesus, however, is our Good Shepherd, and His presence brings us peace as the noise rages all around us. So, when you feel like a lost sheep and the constant noise robs you of peace, turn to the Shepherd. You can know peace by simply being in His presence.

I am a sheep in need of You, Jesus, my Good Shepherd. Thank You for the privilege and blessing of sitting in Your presence and knowing Your peace. Amen.

The Ultimate Encourager

May our Lord Jesus Christ himself and God our Father, who loved us and by his grace gave us eternal encouragement and good hope, encourage your hearts and strengthen you in every good deed and word.

—2 Thessalonians 2:16–17 NIV

We all need encouragers in our lives. We need someone, even several someones, to cheer us and speak uplifting words. Encouragers may send cards, bring cookies, or pat you on the back and say, "You did your best, and your best is all that is expected." And I hope you have that special encourager whom you call when you need a friend: you'll know she will drop whatever she is doing and come hold your hand.

The encouragement Jesus offers us—and offers us through His people—is yet another form of God's grace. The encouragement of the cross—the grace of Jesus' death on our behalf—gives us solid hope of a future with our Lord. The presence of God's Spirit—another gift and grace—encourages us both *for* the day-to-day and *in* the day-to-day.

Whenever you need encouragement, know that the ultimate Encourager and Giver of peace is only a prayer away.

Lord Jesus, thank You for being the ultimate Encourager—and the Giver of peace, joy, hope, guidance, and love! Amen.

Someone Beyond Myself

May the Lord of peace give you peace at all times and in every way. The Lord be with all of you.

—2 Thessalonians 3:16 NCV

Is it really possible to have peace at all times? Let's face it: some situations are simply not peaceful. They produce anxiety and restlessness—exact opposites of peace. In addition, we may know people who are not the peaceful type: they are always on the move and antsy when they have to try to slow down.

Still, the apostle Paul prayed that we may have peace at all times and in every way. And Paul lived in prison for a while—not a peaceful situation. His personality would not be described as peaceful. *Driven* and *passionate* are better words; on occasion *angry* and *frustrated* work; not *peaceful*. But Paul was always *at* peace. He enjoyed a quiet confidence in something—in Someone—beyond himself. Paul lived at peace with who he was as a redeemed sinner, a mouthpiece for the Almighty, a child of the King. And Paul prayed that you would know this peace.

God, in You I have all I need to be at peace in any situation. Amen.

God of Order

God is the author of order, not confusion.

—1 Corinthians 14:33 VOICE

Some people like a neat and clean home. According to their well-established routine, they dust and vacuum three days a week. Some people, though, pull out a dust cloth only after the kids have written "Clean me" on the dust-covered coffee table. Wherever we fall on that spectrum, most of us will agree that a neat and clean house provides a deep sense of peace. Maybe that's because our God, "the author of order," created us in His image.

How pleased God was after finishing His creation! All He had made was clean and pure, balanced and orderly, perfect and peaceful. Then we let the dirt of sin enter, and it has left a layer of dust on everything.

Our God of order dealt with the disorder on the cross. He can help us deal with the disorder of life in this still-dusty world, and He can help us with any internal disorder caused by hurt, stress, indecision, worry, or fear. Turn to Him and know order as well as peace.

God, thank You for bringing order and peace to my internal world despite whatever is going on externally. Amen.

Believe!

"Let not your heart be troubled; you believe in God, believe also in Me."

—John 14:1 NKJV

We believe in a lot of things. We believe in love and in miracles. We believe in Santa Claus and the Easter Bunny—or at least the spirit of them. We believe in the innocence of children and the wisdom that comes with age. We believe in the value of working hard, serving others, and being people of integrity. We believe in sharing our toys and saying "please" and "thank you."

Those are good beliefs, but a few others are more fundamental and of greater eternal value. We believe the Bible is truth. We believe in God. We believe in His resurrected Son. We believe in God's goodness and power, His sovereignty and wisdom. Yet life's circumstances can shake our confidence in any or all of these facts. Then what?

Belief is a choice: we choose to believe whatever we're feeling and whatever we're seeing around us. Belief is a gift: we ask for it as the distraught father did—"Lord, I believe; help my unbelief" (Mark 9:24 NKJV). And belief is a source of peace: Jesus does not want your heart to be troubled.

Jesus, help me choose to believe. Help me receive the gift of faith. And help me know Your peace. Amen.

A Peaceful Place

"After I go and prepare a place for you, I will come back and take you to be with me so that you may be where I am."

—John 14:3 NCV

Turn on the television, read the paper, or listen to the news. The world seems to be crumbling right in front of us. Prior to the evil of September 11, 2001, some of us convinced ourselves that terrorist acts were not likely to occur in America. On that day, our eyes were opened. The bad stuff out there is here too. No wonder we find ourselves shaking our heads and asking, "How much worse can it get?"

We want hope and peace, and we find both in the promises of Scripture, like the one above. Jesus will return and take us to a peaceful place free of evil, sin, and war. So, when the news of this world overwhelms you, open God's Word. You'll find peace in the moment and the hope of peace—eternal peace—in the future.

The suffering, evil, and pain in this world are all too real and all too present—but they're not permanent. Thank You, Jesus, for the eternal peace You promise! Amen.

Listen Up!

Jesus overheard what they were talking about and said to the leader, "Don't listen to them; just trust me."

—Mark 5:36 MSG

Commercials tell us we should look a certain way, be treated a certain way, live a certain way—and that, with their product, we can. Bosses tell us we must measure up, or we're out the door. Society tells us that our disapproval of certain activities is evidence of our intolerance. There isn't much positive in these messages! Even the messages we speak to ourselves too often tear down rather than build up. Well, I have a good message for you.

Jesus knows all the negative messages that come at us like flaming arrows. He urged us to listen to a different message than our workplace and politics, than our culture's values and standards. Again, hear the urgency and passion: "Don't listen to them; just trust me." He knows you better than anyone else does, and He loves you more than anyone else can. His is a message of compassion that offers hope and peace, even a touch of joy. So sit still. Listen for Jesus' sweet and encouraging voice. And trust Him.

Lord Jesus, many messages are deafening and hard to ignore. Enable me to hear Your voice—and to listen to Your message of peace and hope—despite the din. Amen.

I'm So Proud of You!

Immediately coming up out of the water, He saw the heavens opening, and the Spirit like a dove descending upon Him; and a voice came out of the heavens: "You are My beloved Son, in You I am well-pleased."

—Mark 1:10–11 NASB

If you had a loving father who told you time and again how proud he was to be your father, how blessed he was that God entrusted you to his care, be thankful. Maybe your father didn't actually say the words, but you knew his heart. That, too, is a reason to be thankful. Other fathers didn't have such words coming from their mouth, and they gave no hint of having such feelings in their heart.

Consider this biblical picture of a Father and Son. The scene was John's baptism of Jesus, and God the Father opened the skies over His Son and sent a message through His Spirit, which descended like a dove. Hear the love and pride in the Father's words: "You are My beloved Son, in You I am well-pleased."

God was proud of Jesus because of who He is. In the same way, God is proud of you for who you are, His child. If your earthly father didn't or couldn't say such words, hear them spoken from your heavenly Father right now. May that truth be a touch of the Lord's healing and a gift of peace.

Heavenly Father, thank You for Your perfect love. Amen.

God's Protective Wings

"Jerusalem, Jerusalem, who kills the prophets and stones those who are sent to her! How often I wanted to gather your children together, the way a hen gathers her chicks under her wings, and you were unwilling."

—Matthew 23:37 NASB

Nature offers us many illustrations of truths about our God, His love, His character, and the principles of His kingdom. Consider a mother hen with her baby chicks. She's never comfortable having strangers near her babies. She noisily chirps and, with her wings, gathers her chicks. The little ones, unaware of any danger, have to be coaxed, and the mother doesn't settle down until all are safe and secure beneath her wings.

We are like those chicks. We don't always recognize that danger is near. We need coaxing to go to a safe place—sometimes even when we are aware of danger. Wanting us to be safe, Christ coaxes us—like that hen with her babies—to stop our dangerous and often sinful wanderings and to gather under His wings where we will find refuge and peace.

As defenseless as those chicks, you may be unaware of danger. Know that God is more powerful than any danger that threatens. Let Him gather you under His wings.

God, thank You for this picture of how You want me to slip beneath Your protective wings and know Your tender care, safety, and peace. Amen.

Happy Hearts

"Blessed are the peacemakers, for they will be called children of God."

—Matthew 5:9 NIV

You *bake* a cake. You wouldn't say you *build* a cake, but you do *build* a house. You *make* a movie. You don't *fashion* a movie, but you do *fashion* a question. But you never *make*—or *build* or *bake*—the question. You might make *up* the question, and you can make up your mind.

Words matter. So consider Jesus' choice of the word *peacemaker.* We aren't manufacturing it from raw ingredients. And we aren't building it as we build a tower by stacking blocks. So what does peacemaking mean?

Being a peacemaker means going where there isn't peace and interceding, brokering, and negotiating for peace. It's a dangerous assignment when the disputing parties are hostile. We risk getting hurt, but the possible payoff is bringing God's light to darkness. And when, by God's grace, peace replaces hostility, He is glorified, and we are blessed for serving Him.

One meaning of *blessed* is "happy." And happy are those who make or broker peace because that is what God calls His children to do.

Lord, give me the courage, wisdom, and strength I need in order to be a peacemaker who brings light to this world and glory to Your name. Amen.

God's Hands

Because of the Master, we have great confidence in you. We know you're doing everything we told you and will continue doing it. May the Master take you by the hand and lead you along the path of God's love and Christ's endurance.

—2 Thessalonians 3:4–5 MSG

Hands come in all sizes, ranging from the tiny hands of babies to the huge hands of athletes who can palm and dunk a basketball. Hands also range from soft to rough, from smooth to aging, from weathered to manicured. People's hands can often tell something of their story, but not always. Consider powerful and strong hands that can be tender.

Your heavenly Father's hands are powerful and strong. He did, after all, create everything that exists. But the power and strength of God's hands are limited by His love. That's why we can trust Him to gently lead us, through the toughest day and the darkest night, along the path of His love. When you place your hand in His, He will stay at your side and guide you to a place of peace.

Lord, thank You that I can reach for Your hand because it's dark, because I'm afraid, and just because! Amen.

Your Honor

"My agreement for priests was with the tribe of Levi. I promised them life and peace so they would honor me. And they did honor me and fear me."

—Malachi 2:5 NCV

Teachers will tell you that it is the biggest problem they face—and it's not truancy, failure to do homework, or even cheating. The biggest problem is at the root of these and others. That problem is the lack of respect and honor in American society today. Parents notice it in the home, yet the lack of respect and honor in society as a whole makes their attempts to instill these values even harder. And if we don't respect or honor teachers, parents, or one another, why would we honor God?

The Bible often uses the word *fear* to describe a special kind of honor or reverence for God. This is not the fear we experience when our lives are threatened. This kind of fear is better described as awe, and it rises from the deep and abiding sense of honor we have for the holy, all-powerful, and sovereign One inspiring that awe.

God blesses with peace those who fear, honor, and respect Him. May we learn to honor God with all we are and all that He has entrusted to us.

Lord, I want to live out my heartfelt awe and deep sense of honor for who You are. Amen.

MARCH 27

Innocent by Association

He was pierced for our transgressions, he was crushed for our iniquities; the punishment that brought us peace was on him, and by his wounds we are healed.

—Isaiah 53:5 NIV

No one likes to be reprimanded. Nor do we enjoy suffering the punishment that comes as a result of breaking the rules. Whether we're paying for a speeding ticket or being demoted at work, facing the consequences for our missteps isn't fun. When we've broken the rules and the punishment is justified, it's easier to take. But when we've been unjustly accused and are suffering consequences for something we didn't do, that is much, much harder.

Yet that is exactly what our Savior did. He had not broken a single law of God or of the Romans or the Jews. Still, the undeserving Jesus let Himself be crucified: His blood was spilled for the forgiveness of our sins. He took on Himself the punishment for our rebellion against God.

The pure and holy Jesus was pierced and crushed for our sins. As a result of that punishment He didn't deserve, we were healed, and our relationship with God was restored. Divine peace is now ours because our punishment became His. Receive the peace Christ wants to give you today.

Thank You, God, for Your gift of peace, which I can experience only because You took the punishment meant for me. Amen.

Sleep Aid

He enters into peace; they rest in their beds, each one who walked in his upright way.

—Isaiah 57:2 NASB

We are a nation of insomniacs. A survey revealed that nearly 9 million Americans take some form of sleep aid even though there are solutions that don't involve medicine. You could try forming a bedtime routine, removing the television from the bedroom, and lowering the temperature in your home. If you've tried these or other suggestions and are still tossing and turning, consider some wisdom from your heavenly Father.

God's sleep advice applies not when we are getting ready for bed, but when we are starting the day and as we go through it. We are to order our steps, God's Word says, so that we walk uprightly. We are to live in a way that honors Him, holding our head high as we walk in His light and on His path. When we do so, we can rest assured that as our heads hit the pillow at night and our minds review the steps of the day, we will be at peace.

If you want to fall into peaceful sleep each night, try God's sleep aid and practice walking in upright and godly manner from the first step of the day to the last.

God, please guide my steps throughout the day so I can sleep in peace when I lie down at night and rest in You. Amen.

Singing and Dancing

He will rejoice over you with gladness, He will quiet you with His love, He will rejoice over you with singing.

—Zephaniah 3:17 NKJV

You've probably seen one of those talent-based reality TV shows featuring amateur talent, professional judges, and dreams of fame and fortune. Auditions are held around the country where not-yet-famous individuals sing before the judges in hopes of being awarded a coveted spot on the program. Eventually, brave contestants who have weathered the earlier rounds try to impress a panel of judges and the nation with their singing. When we watch, we may marvel at the competitors' courage and hope that the American dream comes true for them. We want a nobody to become a somebody. After all, none of us is that different from the performers: we all want to be a somebody.

The good news today is that you don't have to audition or compete in order to be "somebody." And the reason is simple: God has already discovered you; you are somebody to Him. You don't have to perform to earn His love, but know that *He* performs: He sings and dances because of His joy in you. Be blessed by His joy and quieted by His love and peace.

Thinking of You as a God who sings and dances with joy over Your people—over me!—brings joy to my heart and peace to my soul. Amen.

Your Hand in God's

"I am the LORD your God, who holds your right hand, and I tell you, 'Don't be afraid. I will help you.'"

—Isaiah 41:13 NCV

When we take an oath, we raise our right hand. When we are sworn into the witness stand, we raise our right hand and place our left hand on the Bible. To sit at the right hand of a king was to hold his authority. And according to Isaiah 41:13, God holds our right hand.

Most of the human population is right-handed, which means most of us would be limited in what we could do if someone were to hold our right hand. Yet, if we are feeling fearful, nothing is more comforting than having our hand held, especially if it's being held by someone who is able to protect and defend us. Furthermore, our almighty God knows that we need His help whether we have only one hand or both hands available to do what we need and want to do.

What a blessing that God takes our hand when He knows we need Him—which is always!

God, as You hold my right hand, I take comfort in knowing that You are with me. Amen.

Keep Going

We know that all things work together for good to those who love God, to those who are the called according to His purpose.

—Romans 8:28 NKJV

Have you ever watched marathon runners battle the messages their bodies send them toward the end of a race? Every muscle is telling them—screaming at them—to stop. But they know that if they push through the pain, the reward of finishing will be theirs: a goal will be reached.

The pain and suffering that can come during the journey of the Christian life can also make us wonder if the race is worth the effort. But then we notice Jesus at our side, offering His strength and encouragement. He will not let this be wasted effort. As He runs along with us, it's as if we can hear Him say, *Keep going!* and *You've got this!* He reminds us, too, that He will use every experience along the way—the good and the bad—to make us more like Him, more trusting and more sensitive to God's presence.

When you hear Jesus' voice and remember He's at your side, peace floods every cell of your body, and you catch a second wind. You aren't racing alone, and because of that, you can keep going.

Lord Jesus, You know that running the race of faith is hard. Thank You for running it with me. Amen.

Confident Trust

Do not throw away your confidence; it will be richly rewarded.

—Hebrews 10:35 NIV

Doesn't the word *confidence* bring peace to your soul? Confident trust in the One who gave His life for you means life eternal and purpose in this life. Your trust in God will enable you to live with confidence.

This is what that confidence won't look like: it isn't an oversized ego or being puffed up about your own abilities. It isn't ignoring the facts, believing you can do something you don't have the gifts or talents to do. It isn't cockiness or arrogance, and it needn't be bold or brash.

Confidence has no need to brag. Truly confident people don't need glory; they know what they've achieved, and they know all glory belongs to God. Confidence doesn't need the validation of other people; genuine validation comes from God. Confidence also doesn't mind sharing the spotlight because God's "Well done" is reward enough.

Let's place our confident trust in God—in His goodness, in His plans for us, and in His presence with us. Then we can be humbly confident and at peace.

Thank You, almighty God, that You are so worthy of my confident trust! May You be glorified as You enable me to live out that trust. Amen.

Sparkling Clean

Now may the God of peace Himself sanctify you completely; and may your whole spirit, soul, and body be preserved blameless at the coming of our Lord Jesus Christ.

—1 Thessalonians 5:23 NKJV

There is something settling about a clean house. When the floors have been mopped and vacuumed, the cobwebs have been swept away, the dust is gone, the piles are put away, and the pillows are fluffed, it feels good. If there were a magic wand that could create and maintain this wonderful scene, stores wouldn't be able to keep them in stock. Unfortunately, this sparkling-clean home happens only when someone does the work.

The same is true for our hearts. There is something special and wonderful about a pure heart, a heart completely cleansed of sin. That happens not by some magic wand, but by Someone doing the work. *Sanctification* is the big word that describes the cleaning God does in our hearts when we submit our lives to Him. God desires to present us blameless when Jesus returns. Our part is to submit to His cleaning process. We need to open every room, every closet, and every cupboard of our lives to Him.

God, I want to be pure, holy, and blameless for Jesus, who died so that such a cleansing is possible. Amen.

Strong Gates

He has strengthened the bars of your gates; He has blessed your children within you. He makes peace in your borders, and fills you with the finest wheat.

—Psalm 147:13–14 NKJV

Gates come in all shapes and sizes. No matter how ornate or simple, a gate has two basic functions: to keep things out and to allow things in.

The people of Jerusalem had fortified gates in the walls that surrounded the city to protect the people inside from danger. They knew, however, that unless God strengthened the bars of those gates—unless He also served as their Protector—they were vulnerable to the enemy.

We need to be wise about protecting ourselves, but we also need to remember that if we don't turn to God—if we place our trust in our own ability to provide for our safety and security—our effort will prove insufficient. To use the psalmist's metaphor, we will find the bars on our gates to be weak. Only God can strengthen those bars. Peace inside the gates of our hearts and our lives comes only when we place our trust and security in God.

Where are you placing your trust? To whom are you looking for security and peace?

God, thank You for reminding me: only in You may I find my strength and security. Amen.

Love to Learn

Those who love your teachings will find true peace, and nothing will defeat them.

—Psalm 119:165 NCV

For some children and for a variety of reasons, school is a struggle, while at the same time some of their classmates absolutely love school and the learning, discovery, and acquisition of new skills. Wherever you were on that spectrum when you were in school, I pray that the school of God's Word will be richer and more rewarding than you can imagine.

Studying God's Word offers students joy, peace, and a chance to fall in love with learning. The love of learning God's Word happens because it fuels love for God's living Word—Jesus Christ. The love of God's written Word means learning solid truths about genuine peace. The love of God's living Word means experiencing that peace.

May our love for God's written Word fuel our love for the living Word—and may sparks ignite in people around us that same love for Jesus.

God, continue to increase my love for Scripture and my desire to know it better. Amen.

Redefining Wealth

The Lord *is the portion of my inheritance and my cup; you support my lot.*

—Psalm 16:5 NASB

Have you thought about what it would be like to inherit a couple million dollars? How do you think you'd react to the news—and how do you think it would impact your values, your lifestyle, your interactions with people, and your everyday routine? And what would you do to honor the deceased for his incredible generosity?

Most of us don't have that millionaire relative, but in Christ, we can anticipate receiving an even greater inheritance. God's Word says that the Lord Himself is our inheritance, and that inheritance—that saving knowledge of Jesus as Savior and Lord that means eternal life in heaven—makes us truly wealthy people. What we do with that inheritance tells God and others how much we value both the gift and the One who gave the gift.

What are you doing with your inheritance? May we live a life worthy of the gift and freely share that rich knowledge of Jesus with others.

God, because of the great inheritance of Your saving truth, I am wealthy beyond measure. May I live a life worthy of that gift. Amen.

Like an Eagle

When your soul is famished and withering, He fills you with good and beautiful things, satisfying you as long as you live. He makes you strong like an eagle, restoring your youth.

—Psalm 103:5 VOICE

The eagle is one of nature's most beautiful and majestic birds, admired throughout the world as a symbol of power and freedom. Every year, during molting time, eagles shed some feathers. New feathers grow, essentially giving eagles a renewed appearance of youth.

Above, the psalmist sang of God making us who are famished and withering "strong like an eagle, restoring [our] youth." Think about what happens when God saves us, His people, from our decaying ways: He fills us with new life. We become young again as He refreshes our souls, renews our spirits, and fills us "with good and beautiful things." God promises that, when we are tired and worn out, He will return to us the joy of our youth, making us soar like eagles.

If you are worn out and tired, ask God to renew you like the eagle. He will lift you up.

When I am tired and weak, Lord, please give me Your renewing strength. Amen.

Fuel for the Moment

The LORD will give strength to His people; the LORD will bless His people with peace.

—Psalm 29:11 NKJV

It takes every ounce of strength you have to make it through . . . How would you end that sentence? I can only imagine the variety of responses. It takes every ounce of strength you have to make it through a job loss, a long-term illness, a marital conflict, a wayward child, a car on life support. These and so many other situations can sap our physical, emotional, and spiritual strength.

As God's people, though, we don't need to stay low on energy. We are to turn to our God, who will give us the strength we need to get through our days with grace and peace. God's strength enables us to deal with the big obstacles and the little irritants, to simply put one foot in front of the other, to choose to believe despite our unbelief.

If you are weary, whisper, "Lord, give me strength," and He will.

Great is Your faithfulness and, when I need it, Your strength. Thank You for Your willingness to restore and renew me when I turn to you. Amen.

Sure-Footed

Who is a rock, except our God, the God who girds me with strength and makes my way blameless? He makes my feet like hinds' feet, and sets me upon my high places.

—Psalm 18:31–33 NASB

The mountain goats of the Rockies are some of the most sought-after subjects of photographers from around the world. The goats' long beards, short tails, and black horns make them especially photogenic. The quest for that great photo is so powerful that photographers are not deterred by the challenge of getting close to these intrepid goats. And it is challenging!

These mountain goats have cloven hooves that are well suited for climbing steep, rocky slopes, even slopes that are angled at more than sixty degrees. The tips of the goats' cloven feet have sharp claws that keep them from slipping. With only their hiking boots, the photographers find the topography a bit more difficult to traverse!

Like the mountain goats that God created for this terrain, those of us who choose to walk in God's ways are divinely enabled to navigate the narrow and rocky paths of this life. We can have complete confidence and total peace that God will make our feet sure.

God, when life gets rocky and I feel unsteady, I am grateful that You will strengthen me and enable me to walk on the path You have for me. Amen.

The Look

I will instruct you and teach you in the way which you should go; I will counsel you with My eye upon you.

—Psalm 32:8 NASB

All parents have it—and all children know it. You undoubtedly remember *the look* from your growing-up years. From across in the room, the front seat of the car, or a few feet away on the same pew, you knew the look. It says, "You'd better straighten up!" It tells you, "I know everything there is to know about what you are doing!" It clearly communicates, "I'm onto you!" and "You've been warned!" No spoken words are necessary.

God also has a parental look in that He can speak a thousand words with it. With His look, He instructs and teaches us "in the way which [we] should go." His look, like that of our earthly parents, can warn us that the way we're headed is not going to end well. His look, if heeded, can save us a lot of heartache and bless us with much peace.

Are you heeding God's look, or are you simply looking the other way?

Father, help me to notice and then to heed Your look of warning, correction, and instruction. Then I will know Your direction and Your peace. Amen.

PEACE IN THE WORKPLACE

Whom Are You Working For?

In all the work you are doing, work the best you can. Work as if you were doing it for the Lord, not for people.

—Colossians 3:23 NCV

There is something different about doing a disagreeable chore when you're doing it for someone else. Church workdays are a perfect example. Tons of people show up to sweep, scrub, trim, paint, and weed for people they don't even know. Interestingly, chances are good that some of these same tasks are on their own to-do list at home. The difference is, when they do that work for someone else, they work with smiles on their faces.

All of us have chores we dislike, and some of us have nine-to-five jobs we don't especially enjoy. But in many cases we don't have the choice *not* to do these chores and work these jobs. However, today's Scripture just might bring us peace by giving us a different perspective on these situations. Let's tackle the task at hand or do the nine-to-five that God has provided as if we are doing it for Him.

Lord, forgive my grumbling. Help me do that job and the to-do list chores as if I were doing them for You. Amen.

Pleasing the Boss

Then the LORD God took the man and put him in the garden of Eden to tend and keep it.

—Genesis 2:15 NKJV

What was your first job? Mowing lawns? Babysitting? Maybe in high school you had job in retail, working at a restaurant or a local store. Regardless of where you worked, you undoubtedly learned some of the same things: you are to put in a full day's work for the full day's pay you're receiving, and it is wise to do a quality job that pleases the boss and therefore makes the workplace peaceful.

God gave Adam a job to do right at the start: he was to tend and keep the garden. Adam learned what we learned about the value of putting in a good day's work. At the end of his workday, he could enjoy the cool evenings with God. Adam also learned that loving God and His creation as he worked greatly pleased the Boss. Working as a way of showing our love for God still pleases Him, who is ultimately our Boss.

Regardless of where you work today, determine to work hard, love God, and care for all of creation, so that in the evening you can sit with the Boss and enjoy the peace of His presence.

God, I look forward to being with You in the cool of the evening and enjoying Your peace after every hard day's work. Amen.

I Got the Job!

That each of them may eat and drink, and find satisfaction in all their toil—this is the gift of God.

—Ecclesiastes 3:13 NIV

If you or someone you know has ever lost a job and been unemployed for a long time, you know how stressful and discouraging that season can be. The job search can seem unending, and the loss of purpose may feel overwhelming. When that much-sought-after job finally does come, so does a silly grin. You find yourself excitedly repeating the words "I got the job!" over and over to anyone who will listen. The joy is not necessarily about the specific job, but more about simply having *a* job to do.

God created us to be productive. By His design, we want to use our gifts, talents, and abilities. All of us have complained about our jobs, and those complaints are often justified. However, we need to balance our complaints with our gratitude that we have work to do.

So the next time you're about to complain about work, don't. Instead, thank God for the gift of work to do—and know His peace.

Forgive me for complaining about my job, Lord. Help me to replace the complaining with gratitude. Amen.

Keeping a Balance

The best that people can do is eat, drink, and enjoy their work. I saw that even this comes from God, because no one can eat or enjoy life without him.

—Ecclesiastes 2:24–25 NCV

Some people are all about work. They aren't sure of the name of the person in the next cubicle, and they never ask a coworker about her weekend. Other people do nothing but have fun and therefore accomplish little actual work. Oh, they put in the hours, but those hours are filled with water-cooler gossip, trips to the office supply store, and plans for the next coworker's birthday party. There has to be a balance between work and fun.

God wants us to enjoy the work He has provided for us during this season of life. God also wants us to enjoy the people we work with, even if, by nature, we're not particularly social. We need to take breaks from our work to enjoy both our colleagues and the fruits of our labor. All work and no play makes for a stressful life. But all play and no work makes for a poor employee.

Look for a good balance: work hard *and* enjoy your fellow laborers and the fruits of your collective effort.

God, You know the drive I have to work hard and do a good job. Help me learn to keep a better balance between work and play. Amen.

Wealth Envy

As for every man to whom God has given riches and wealth, and given him power to eat of it, to receive his heritage and rejoice in his labor—this is the gift of God.

—Ecclesiastes 5:19 NKJV

Daddy, are we rich?" asked the young daughter of her wealthy businessman father.

He replied, "We are very rich in health, family, and good friends."

"No, Daddy. I mean, do I have a lot of money?"

The father answered, "Until you are eighteen you do, but then you will be poor like I was, and you'll work your way up."

Some of us fall prey to wealth envy: we feel that if someone has more than his or her fair share, there is less for us. The Bible teaches a different perspective. First, God provides the wealth. Second, God also gives us both the ability to use that wealth wisely and the freedom to enjoy its blessings.

Whether you have a storehouse of money or you count your riches in other ways, God is the Source of that wealth. So thank Him for the wealth you have. Then go a step further and praise God for what others have. By God's grace, you'll find that peace replaces envy.

God, help me to avoid wealth envy and instead enjoy the wealth You have generously blessed me with. I know that all good things come from You. Amen.

A Working and Wise God

[Jesus] answered [the Jewish leaders], "My Father is working until now, and I Myself am working."

—John 5:17 NASB

How do you see God? Is He distant and aloof—a sort of bystander as the world spins on its axis? Or is He active and always busy at work? Perhaps you cringe at the thought of a too-busy God: having a micromanaging boss who hovers over you makes you crazy. Sometimes you want a bystander God who doesn't get involved in your business. But there are also times when the idea of a distant and idle God is utterly frightening.

The good news is that we don't have either a bystander God or a micromanaging God. He is neither aloof, nor is He a busybody. But He is at work. He is always working on your behalf, and He always knows when you need Him working beside you and when you need a little space. Yet He is never far away.

To become more like God toward others at work, learn to discern when to come in close and when to step back.

God, thank You for always working on my behalf. Help me to learn from You how to be sensitive to the needs of others at my place of work. Amen.

Chain of Command

It is important that all of us submit to the authorities who have charge over us because God establishes all authority in heaven and on the earth.

—Romans 13:1 VOICE

There is little respect for authority today. Children don't respect their parents or their teachers. We as a culture don't respect police, rules, or laws the way we once did. We have less respect for the workplace and its deadlines, policies, and dress code. Civil discourse is anything but civil these days. So where did we go wrong?

One reason we are in this current situation is the ripple effect: when we lose respect for the ultimate Authority, we lose respect for lesser authorities. If we believe God has ultimate authority and establishes all other authority—even authority we disagree with—then we must be respectful of those whom He has given leadership positions. When we lose sight of that chain of command, when we don't live as if God is on the throne, we will be a disrespectful people. However, when we believe that all authority in heaven and on earth comes from God, we respond to everyone in that chain of command with respect.

Respect will breed respect, and respect means peace.

God, help me learn to respect those in authority out of respect for the chain of command, which begins with You. Amen.

National Prayer

I urge, then, first of all, that petitions, prayers, intercession and thanksgiving be made for all people—for kings and all those in authority, that we may live peaceful and quiet lives in all godliness and holiness.

—1 Timothy 2:1–2 NIV

America's leaders first called this nation to prayer in 1775. The Continental Congress asked the colonies to pray for wisdom as they worked to form a nation, and the call to prayer has continued throughout our nation's history. The National Day of Prayer was organized in 1952 to mobilize the Christian community to intercede for America's leaders. It continues to stand as a call for us to humbly come before God for our nation.

The idea of praying for people in government didn't originate with America. The apostle Paul called the Jews to pray for their Roman rulers and oppressors. He urged the Christian community to not only pray for the Roman leaders who were persecuting them, but to pray for blessings on them. Paul also called the believers to pray for the leaders with thanksgiving so that peace might reign.

Are you praying for blessings for America's leaders, local and national, even those you disagree with?

God, I don't always agree with our leaders, but I do desire peace in our land. So help me to do as Paul urged and pray faithfully. Amen.

Payday

Those who are stealing must stop stealing and start working. They should earn an honest living for themselves. Then they will have something to share with those who are poor.

—Ephesians 4:28 NCV

Perhaps the best day of the workweek is payday. When we hold that check or see the deposit that has been made to our bank account, the work we did seems worthwhile. We can forget the pain of the overtime hours we logged when we are rewarded with a paycheck. As workers, we feel we've earned every dime. We should also be at peace knowing that we earned an honest day's pay for an honest day's work. However, God views our paydays differently.

In God's world, everyone works for the same Boss. At times some of us are blessed so we have something to share. At other times we may find ourselves needing the blessings of other people's help.

You see, our paychecks aren't solely for our benefit. Rather, our paychecks are a means by which we can help and encourage others. So the next time you deposit your paycheck, thank God that payday gives you the opportunity to share with others from the bounty He provides—and ask Him to show you whom to share with this time.

Thank You, God, for the chance payday offers me to pay my blessings forward to those in need. Amen.

Holy Days

Six days you shall labor and do all your work, but the seventh day is the Sabbath of the LORD *your God. In it you shall do no work: you, nor your son, nor your daughter, nor your male servant, nor your female servant, nor your cattle, nor your stranger who is within your gates.*

—Exodus 20:9–10 NKJV

The British call their vacations "holidays." That word is derived from the phrase *holy days*, when a day of rest was built into each calendar week for the express purpose of celebrating the Lord's generous blessings. On these holy days, men and women gathered in the church to praise God and to thank Him for His faithfulness, goodness, and generosity.

Unfortunately, in the twenty-first century, our holidays are no longer holy days at all. But we can recapture something of that spirit by using our days off from work to refocus on the Giver of all that we have. Our vacations and any other days we have off from work should be holy days, with time set aside for us to enter God's presence and rest.

Whether your day off is Sunday or some other day of the week, be sure to set aside time to rest and refocus on God. You will know peace as you rest in Him.

Lord, help me be sure to set aside time to enter Your rest so my spirit will find peace. Amen.

How Light Works

"In the same way, let your light shine before others, that they may see your good deeds and glorify your Father in heaven."

—Matthew 5:16 NIV

It's a fact. Two subjects are lightning rods in the workplace: politics and religion. Some workplaces are zero-tolerance zones when it comes to religion. Even if you are blessed to work in a business run by believers according to Christian principles, the differences on religious views can still be tricky to navigate. So to keep peace at the workplace, do you simply leave your Christian values in the car from nine to five?

Today's Scripture suggests essentially the opposite approach. Jesus tells us to "let [our] light shine." Think about that. First, light doesn't use words. It doesn't argue its point. It doesn't lash out. It doesn't put people on the defensive. It doesn't offend or anger. Light simply brightens a room, and it does that by simply being present.

When we let our inner light of Jesus' love shine, we can brighten a room and warm the hearts of people nearby. If you work where it is unwise to discuss your faith, determine to let your light do all the talking.

God, help me remember that arguing my point is often much less effective than simply letting Your light shine through me. Amen.

Food Insecurity

The one who stays on the job has food on the table; the witless chase whims and fancies.

—Proverbs 12:11 MSG

It is difficult to fathom that in our prosperous nation, people go to bed hungry. Estimates are that 49 million Americans do not have access to enough affordable, nutritious food (called "food insecurity"), and this number includes almost 16 million children. Furthermore, food banks used to service mainly the homeless and unemployed, but they now serve a new group of people, namely, the working poor. Some of these individuals work several jobs yet still end up short at the end of the month.

So where *is* God when someone is hungry? We need to understand that the Bible doesn't connect a paycheck to having enough food. The Bible does connect working and having food, saying those who work will have food. Sometimes that food will come through other people.

Look for ways you can help provide for those who are in need in your community. Thank God for the opportunity your work gives you to help provide food for others—and then help.

Lord, forgive me for passing judgment on those who need help with food, and enable me to recognize my job as a means for helping those willing to work to provide food for their families. Amen.

God Provides

Let the favor of the Lord our God be upon us; and confirm for us the work of our hands; yes, confirm the work of our hands.

—Psalm 90:17 NASB

It used to be that the worth of someone's work was easily determined. Everyone worked with their hands, and what those hands produced—crops, woodwork, fabric—everyone could see. Through the years, new ways of earning income arose, and new ways of calculating the worth of the work had to be developed. No longer was it easy to see how much God had blessed one's work.

Recognizing God's blessing on work was important in Old Testament days. People built monuments to God to honor Him for blessing their work. These altars in the desert reminded passersby that God blessed the work of His people's hands. What encouragement, hope, and peace those monuments must have brought!

What are you doing to build a monument in honor of Jehovah-jireh, the God who provides by blessing your work? Maybe a plaque with a simple verse or phrase sitting on your desk, the tithe you give to your church, or the grace you say before eating will be seen by others and understood to mean that your God provides.

God, You have graciously blessed the work of my hands. Thank You for Your provision. Amen.

Not a Divine Santa

God will use your hard work to provide you food. You will prosper in your labor, and it will go well for you.

—Psalm 128:2 VOICE

You may have heard it preached that God wants to bless you, to prosper you, even to make you wealthy. Taken to an unbiblical extreme, this so-called prosperity gospel message can lead us to reduce God to a divine Santa. In this way of thinking, God simply doles out wads of money and lavish gifts to anyone who believes and trusts in Him.

But God is not Santa. He *does* want to bless you and prosper you, but not necessarily in the ways the world defines *blessing* and *prosperity*. God doesn't promise all of us mansions and million-dollar bank accounts. If He did, everyone would be a Christian!

What God actually promises is that we won't labor in vain. He also says we will prosper, just not as the world defines *prosper*. And He promises "it will go well for you." We can work hard, knowing that our labor won't be in vain. God will use our hard work to supply our needs.

God, You are my heavenly Father who rewards my hard work by providing what I truly need. Thank You. Amen.

Reach Down!

I showed you in all things that you should work as I did and help the weak. I taught you to remember the words Jesus said: "It is more blessed to give than to receive."

—Acts 20:35 NCV

Whether you work for a large corporation or a small business, climbing the corporate ladder is still the name of the game. To get a promotion, you must first know where you are on the ladder and then figure out what you need to do to get to the next rung. In many places, this effort becomes cutthroat. People standing on the rung someone wants may be targeted and destroyed. While you personally may not choose to play this game, that decision won't keep someone from targeting you.

The stress of the corporate ladder can wreak havoc on a person's health, family, friendships, and even spiritual life. If you want a way out, here's a suggestion based on today's Scripture: reach down to the rung below you to give someone a hand. Help someone look good in front of the boss. Or publicly recognize someone who rarely receives any acclaim. It is more blessed to give than it is to receive—even in the workplace. And giving rather than working to receive just might change the corporate ladder game.

Lord help me play the corporate ladder game by different rules! Show me whom You would have me reach down and help. Amen.

Staying Busy

If anyone will not work, neither shall he eat.

—2 Thessalonians 3:10 NKJV

Perhaps you work with someone like this: everyone else is busy with the computer, files, the phones, or the copier, but this person is busy just talking. Despite the amount of work to be done, she has a problem that the Bible calls idleness. The apostle Paul had already written to the church at Thessalonica about a problem with idleness, yet the problem had gotten worse: the idlers had become meddlers. The Greek word for *idler* is *periergos,* and it also means "meddler."

When we don't have enough work to keep our minds and hands busy—or when we choose not to do the work we have in front of us—we too easily move from being idle to meddling in other people's business. God wants us to stay focused on the work He has asked us to do. Nothing good comes to idlers or meddlers!

So when work gets slow, guard yourself against the tendency toward idleness. Find constructive things to do: help a coworker, take on an extra project, or clean and organize the breakroom. We can always find something constructive to do when we look—or ask.

Keep me busy, Lord, so I will not become an idler and a meddler in other people's business. Amen.

The Man at the Top

Commit to the LORD whatever you do, and he will establish your plans.

—Proverbs 16:3 NIV

When you are implementing big policy changes or sweeping shifts in the organizational structure, communication to everyone impacted is essential, and consensus is ideal. People at every level of the organization need to be informed. If someone feels threatened by the proposed changes and doesn't agree to set aside his own views, those plans can be sabotaged before they even begin.

Similarly, you and I might have great plans for our futures, but if we haven't cleared those plans with the Man at the top, we are sabotaging our own plans. If our plans are not aligned with His ways, we'll be heading in the wrong direction. That's why the wisdom of Proverbs calls us to commit our plans to God, to align them with His will, to be open to His guidance and revisions. Only plans that have been committed to God and, if necessary, tweaked or overhauled by Him will succeed and bring us peace.

Have you set out strictly according to your own thoughts and desires, or have you committed your plans to God?

Lord, help me to always commit my ways to You for my own good and for Your glory. Amen.

People Pleasers

[Be obedient . . .] not by way of eyeservice, as men-pleasers, but as slaves of Christ, doing the will of God from the heart.

—Ephesians 6:6 NASB

Pleasing the boss is good business practice, but some people carry it too far. These are the yes-men who will do anything to make the boss happy—with *anything* being the key word. Their efforts are fueled not by their hearts, but by sheer ambition. Most of us recognize these people and shy away from them because we don't trust their motives—and motives are what separate Christians from others in every aspect of life. When we align our wills with God's, our motives in the boardroom and in the backroom will be pure.

The Bible explains that, as slaves to Christ, we are to place our motives and wills under the God's authority. When we do, we will be more focused on pleasing God than pleasing man. We will no longer be people pleasers, but instead we'll be God pleasers—and *that* is the best business practice.

God, I want my motives as well as my thoughts, words, and actions in the workplace to always be aligned with Yours. Amen.

Laboring Together

We are gardeners and field workers laboring with God. You are the vineyard, the garden, the house where God dwells.

—1 Corinthians 3:9 VOICE

We get up each day and go to work. Some of us drive long distances, and others drop kids off at day care or school before heading to the office. The day ends, and we retrace our steps in the opposite direction, often adding an errand or two. We cook dinner, do homework and chores, and go to bed so we can do it all over again the next day.

If that routine sounds rather pointless, zoom out to get a more accurate picture of what is being accomplished. Do you see that millions of us Christians are actually laboring together in a giant vineyard? Perhaps from your vantage point it seems the little things you do for Jesus aren't having an impact. But God sees that we are all toiling together and making progress: the soil is being prepared, seeds are being sown, the field is being weeded, and the grapes are being readied for harvest, but only because each one of us has done what we could from wherever we are.

The little things you do, combined with the little things others do, make a big difference.

Lord, thank You for today's peace-giving reassurance that, by Your grace, my small efforts contribute to the big picture. Amen.

PEACE AT HOME

Real Security

My people will dwell in a peaceful habitation, in secure dwellings, and in quiet resting places.

—Isaiah 32:18 NKJV

Home security systems have become quite sophisticated. You can use a cell phone to view the interior of your home. Today's security systems can also alert you to dangerous carbon monoxide levels or leaks in your water heater. Whether it has lots of bells and whistles or is entry-level standard, the purpose of a security system is the same: to help ensure peace and security.

God is our ultimate and fail-safe Security System. In His protective presence—and only in His presence—can we know real security and genuine peace. But just like the security systems we place in our homes, God's system won't help us when we're out and about—it won't warn us of danger—unless we access it. We do that by studying His Word, aligning our wills with His, and putting on the armor He provides. Then we will live in peace, and our dwellings will be secure from Satan's attacks.

God, guide me as I study Your Word, align my will with Yours, and put on the armor You provide me. Amen.

Construction Dust

Unless the Lord *builds the house, they labor in vain who build it.*

—Psalm 127:1 NASB

Have you ever been involved in the construction of a home or a major remodel? Was it true for you that it came out double the estimated time and triple the financial cost?

So many issues—ranging from unforeseen foundation or mold problems to backordered appliances to delayed subcontractors or inspectors—can hold up project like this. That fact makes a good foreman or general contractor worth his weight in gold. A good foreman knows how to keep the work on track. He also knows when an obstacle is a critical matter or a normal bump in the road.

Construction of a God-focused home and family can also be more challenging than we anticipate. But our Lord is willing and able to help with any and all structural issues we may encounter, and He is an expert at setting a firm foundation. He knows how to get things moving and keep the work on track. He also can identify and address critical matters. When the construction dust becomes overwhelming and the structure doesn't seem to be matching the plans, we can always call on our Lord.

God, I am grateful You for Your expertise and 24/7 availability. What peace comes with knowing You are only a prayer away. Amen.

No Place Like Home

The LORD's curse is on the house of the wicked, but he blesses the home of the righteous.

—Proverbs 3:33 NIV

When we hear the word *wicked*, a lot of us picture the green-faced Wicked Witch from *The Wizard of Oz*. That movie frightened many children, and it may still frighten some of us as adults because that Wicked Witch is, well, wicked. When the house falls on the Wicked Witch of the East, we may cheer, but not nearly as much as we do when Dorothy melts the Wicked Witch of the West with a bucket of water. Wickedness was defeated in the end.

Scripture promises that same ending for all history. It may look like the wicked are winning and evil is darkening all the earth. But in the end the homes of the wicked will be cursed, and we will celebrate not their demise, but God's victory over evil. So however dark the stormy days and nights are, we can hold on to the Lord's promise to bless the homes of His people. For those of us who are righteous in Christ, there is no place like a blessed home.

God, thank You for the peace that comes from knowing that You bless my home. Amen.

A Godly Family

It takes wisdom to have a good family, and it takes understanding to make it strong. It takes knowledge to fill a home with rare and beautiful treasures.

—Proverbs 24:3–4 NCV

Once used to identify friend or foe, a coats of arms or family crest represented not only a family or clan but also the values that group held dear. The colors and symbols might tell the story of a family's ancestry, and the crests would indicate whether a family was known for its strength and valor or its generosity and compassion. Much was communicated in a family's coat of arms.

Maybe a rainy-day project would be to design a twenty-first-century family crest that reflects your faith in Jesus. A Christian family's crest would undoubtedly feature a cross, but what designs and symbols could you use to reflect important traits of a godly character, traits like wisdom, understanding, joy, patience, compassion, and integrity? What symbols would remind you of a time when God showed you His faithfulness and goodness in a remarkable way?

A family crest can tell a story. A Christian family's crest can tell part of God's story.

God, bind my family together around Your values. Keep us rooted in Your love. Amen.

One Person's Faith

From that moment on, God blessed the home of the Egyptian—all because of Joseph. The blessing of God spread over everything he owned, at home and in the fields, and all Potiphar had to concern himself with was eating three meals a day.

—Genesis 39:5 MSG

Being the only follower of Jesus in your home can make life lonely. Your parents, siblings, in-laws, even your spouse may not understand your choices, and they may be hostile toward your faith. Perhaps they feel threatened or judged even if you've been careful to do neither and you haven't tried to impose your views.

Joseph knew about being alone in his faith. He lived in the home of his Egyptian owners, a husband and wife who did not share his faith. Joseph held fast to his beliefs, though. God not only blessed faithful Joseph, but He also blessed the family Joseph lived with. Eventually, the Egyptian master realized that God was indeed with Joseph.

May Joseph's story encourage you and give you peace. Hold fast to your faith, and continue to pray that as God blesses your family through you, they will one day make your God theirs as well.

Lord, may my faith in You and the generous blessings You shower upon me bless my family and bring them to faith. Amen.

Make Yourself at Home

Jesus replied, "Anyone who loves me will obey my teaching. My Father will love them, and we will come to them and make our home with them."

—John 14:23 NIV

Make yourself at home," says your hostess. What a warm welcome—but what a shock to the gracious woman if you actually followed through on her invitation. She would be horrified if you took off your socks and shoes, made yourself a sandwich, grabbed the television remote, and, settling in to your favorite TV-watching position, put your feet on the coffee table. Your hostess wasn't really inviting you to act the same way in her home as you do at your own. Rather, she wants you to be as comfortable in her home as you are in your own.

When God said He desires us to make our hearts His home, however, He *was* speaking literally. He wants us to fully welcome Him into our hearts, to give Him complete control over our lives—even control over our remotes.

Are you willing to open your heart's door and then welcome God?

God, please come into my heart and make Yourself at home. Amen.

Good and Acceptable

If any widow has children or grandchildren, let them first learn to show piety at home and to repay their parents; for this is good and acceptable before God.

—1 Timothy 5:4 NKJV

Even for believers, the death of someone we love can be very difficult. Despite our confidence that he or she is pain-free and with the Lord, good-bye is hard. We still have to grieve, in our own way and according to our own timetable. At the same time that we are sorting out our internal thoughts and emotions, often we have to sort out family dynamics. And the numbness of loss and pain can make thinking clearly a tough assignment.

God's Word gives us a clear guideline for decisions that we'll need to make: children and grandchildren are to care for the widow and widower. Whatever our age, we are responsible for loving and respecting the remaining parent no matter how difficult the situation. When we do what is good and acceptable, God may heal and bring peace to family rifts. The Bible promises that as we show honor and respect for our parents and grandparents, God can heal the childhood wounds and bring peace to the adult soul.

God, please help me honor my parents and grandparents, which is good and acceptable in Your sight. Amen.

Missing

"Suppose one of you has a hundred sheep and loses one of them. Doesn't he leave the ninety-nine in the open country and go after the lost sheep until he finds it?"

—Luke 15:4 NIV

When you see a photograph of a missing child, does your heart skip a beat like mine does? I find myself praying, asking God to protect the child, to bless the family with hope and peace, and to guide the searchers to the young boy or girl. Unless we have experienced this situation, we can only imagine how terrified and worried the parents must be. But God doesn't have to merely imagine; He knows their pain.

From the beginning of time, God also knew that children today would get lost—literally and figuratively. So our heavenly Father lets us parents know that He understands. He placed today's verse, among others, in the Bible not only so we parents know that He cares about us, but also to let lost sheep know Someone is looking for them. May parents who pray constantly for their lost child find a measure of peace in knowing that God understands their pain.

God of mercy, bless the children who are missing as well as their parents with comfort and Your peace that passes understanding. Amen.

Go and Tell

[Jesus] said to [the man who had been possessed by demons], "Go home to your people and report to them what great things the Lord has done for you, and how He had mercy on you."

—Mark 5:19 NASB

Over the years some stories shared in families become legends. We love sitting around at family gatherings and hearing those stories repeated. Sometimes the stories make us laugh, and other times they are tender and poignant. Whatever the story, we find joy in hearing it told again and again.

Jesus knew the power of stories to communicate and to be remembered. Over and over, when Jesus did marvelous, and wondrous things, He commanded His people to go and tell everyone what they had experienced.

"Go home! Go back to your people," He told them. "Go and tell your family, your friends, your neighbors what the Lord has done for you."

Stories are powerful; accounts of what happened to us personally, even more so. In light of that truth and Jesus' command, think about all that the Lord has done for you. Who will you go and tell today?

God, give me the courage to go and tell people all about the great things You have done for me and about the great God I serve. Amen.

He's Got You Covered

God makes homes for the homeless.

—Psalm 68:6 MSG

Researchers tell us that most of us are only a few paychecks away from homelessness. That's a sobering thought! Have you ever thought about what homelessness would be like? Imagine having all your belongings reduced to what you can carry. Consider, too, that every single day you would be consumed by two concerns: where your next meal would come from and where you would lay your head that night. What a tough existence.

When God promised to make homes for the homeless, though, He wasn't addressing this tragic social issue. He was instead saying that He wants to free you from worrying about your things, your next meal, and where you will rest your head. He has all that covered: He knows what you need, and He will provide what you need.

Whether you are not at risk of losing your home or already in foreclosure, find peace in knowing God has you covered.

I confess, Lord: I worry too much about my house, about my things, and about not having enough. Knowing You have me covered, may I find peace. Amen.

Generations of Faithfulness

To [God] be glory in the church and in Christ Jesus throughout all generations, for ever and ever!

—Ephesians 3:21 NIV

What comes to mind when you hear the words *family reunion*? Matching T-shirts? Once again trying to figure out second-cousins as opposed to once-removed? Maybe an all-day picnic with sack races and egg tosses? Maybe musical families enjoying a jam session? Some families go more elaborate, with cruises or a visit to a national park. No matter how simple or extravagant the reunion, the focus is still the same: gathering the generations and the various branches of the family tree to celebrate God's blessings—and to share some stories.

If you are blessed to be part of a faith-filled family, some of those stories will be incredibly meaningful and encouraging as, together, you trace God's faithfulness through the generations to the present day. What a joy to be reminded that someone generations ago prayed for you before you were even born. Thank God for that person—and then be that person for someone in the family who is not yet born.

Thank You, God, for Your faithfulness to generation after generation of my family. Amen.

God's Wallet

In [Jesus Christ], you also, after listening to the message of truth, the gospel of your salvation—having also believed, you were sealed in Him with the Holy Spirit of promise, who is given as a pledge of our inheritance, with a view to the redemption of God's own possession, to the praise of His glory.

—Ephesians 1:13–14 NASB

Do you know someone who has done all she can to be a good parent, yet her child still struggles, disobeys, or even rebels? Perhaps it started with normal pushing-the-limit types of behavior, but it didn't stop there. She tried suspending privileges and monitoring friends. She sought counseling, as a family and individually. But the child's behavior and decisions have gotten worse. Maybe that parent is you.

If so, in the midst of this heartbreak and turmoil, may this news bring you peace: God has your child's picture in His wallet. Your child's wandering, questioning, doubting, disobedience, and rebellion will not change their heavenly Father's opinion of His child. Picture God looking at your child's picture and smiling warmly. His loving eyes clearly say, "I'm not letting go. Ever." May that image fill your heart with peace.

When I am afraid, Lord, help me to rest in the peace of knowing You love my child and always will. Amen.

Anger Management

Fathers, do not exasperate your children; instead, bring them up in the training and instruction of the Lord.

—Ephesians 6:4 NIV

There is a difference between *discipline* and *punishment*, but that may not have been your experience growing up. Maybe it was the silent treatment; maybe it was rage. Maybe it was a belt or a rubber flip-flop. And maybe anger was more the message than loving concern.

We figure out parenting as we go. A baby doesn't come with an instruction manual, and our own parents are the model we know best. No wonder the Lord included this verse in the Bible. Our Creator knows that the parent/child dance can be tricky, to say the least. We parents needn't make it any harder by exasperating our children. We aren't to provoke anger in them; we are to discipline them so they learn that their actions have consequences. Our discipline of our children might prompt their anger, but our intent should never be to make them angry.

May love, not anger, be the message of our discipline. May feeling convicted by a loving parent be our child's experience of that discipline.

Heavenly Father, thank You for the example of parenting that You give me. You are consistent and loving as You discipline. Enable me to be that kind of parent as well. Amen.

Dear Mom and Dad

"Honor your father and mother" is the first commandment that has a promise attached to it, namely, "so you will live well and have a long life."

—Ephesians 6:2–3 MSG

Moms and dads get a bad rap these days. Somehow all the problems a child grows up with are the parents' fault. While in some families that may be true to some degree, the mysterious balance between nature and nurture is not fully understood. But it's easier to blame someone or something for our weaknesses and bad decisions than to take responsibility for them.

That said, some adults need to take a look at some childhood experiences: trauma and pain should not be ignored. Even if we address some issues, the existence of those issues is not permission to be disrespectful. No matter what bad we experienced and what good we didn't experience because of (from our perspective) our parents, God's command to honor our mothers and fathers means what it says. This command doesn't have any disclaimers written in fine print; no loopholes or exceptions are identified. The honor we show our parents will mean, God promised, a long life well-lived.

Lord, help me to always respect and honor my parents with my words and my actions. Amen.

A Family of the '50s

[Older women] can teach the young women to love their husbands, to love their children, to be wise and pure, to be good workers at home, to be kind, and to yield to their husbands.

—Titus 2:4–5 NCV

Old television shows like *Father Knows Best* and *Leave It to Beaver* showed family life that some have deemed too idealistic, too perfect. That may be true, but let's first look at the values these sitcom families modeled for us.

Fathers led their family with wisdom and compassion. Fathers were present, not absent; they were respected, not the butt of a joke. Mothers raised their children with nurturing love without letting them think the world revolved around them. These moms also seemed content rather than discontent. Wives honored their husbands, husbands honored their wives, and children respected their elders. In these homes, when an issue arose, families worked together toward the goal of peace.

That description of a TV family of the 1950s reflects many of the values the Bible teaches. None of us needs to have a *Leave It to Beaver* family; all of us need to aim for the worthy goals of love, honor, and respect.

God, my home life isn't perfect, but please help it to be a place where love rules, respect guides speech, and we work through family matters with the goal of peace. Amen.

An Open-Door Policy

Don't forget to extend your hospitality to all—even to strangers—for as you know, some have unknowingly shown kindness to heavenly messengers in this way.

—Hebrews 13:2 VOICE

When was the last time you had people over for dinner? If it's been awhile, why? If you regularly host, what motivates you to do so?

Of course, some people are naturally more comfortable cooking, cleaning, hosting, and welcoming people into their homes than others of us are. We all have our gifts, our strengths, our loves. But this statement from Hebrews is an invitation—a command—to all believers. The author didn't say, "If you are a Martha Stewart or Julia Child type, this job is for you!" No, the call to extend hospitality is issued to all believers.

Rather than making the meal about you (your cooking, decorating, cleaning, charming personality, engaging conversation), make the meal about your guests. Love them with Jesus' love, listen with His compassion, encourage them with gospel hope, and bless them with peace. No one will notice the dust on the entryway table or care that you used paper napkins.

Thank You, Lord, for a home to open, a meal to share, and friends to invite. May visits to my home be blessings of love and peace for my guests. Amen.

Onions or No Onions?

[The Shunammite woman] said to her husband, "Look now, I know that this is a holy man of God, who passes by us regularly. Please, let us make a small upper room on the wall; and let us put a bed for [Elisha] there, and a table and a chair and a lampstand; so it will be, whenever he comes to us, he can turn in there."

—2 Kings 4:9–10 NKJV

Tacos may be the one meal everyone in the family likes. But the real favorite for some is pizza; others prefer pasta. You might have a family member who hates onions, while others love them.

Putting others first is a gracious form of hospitality. Like the Shunammite woman who provided Elisha a table, chair, and lampstand in addition to the bed, we put our guests first when we make sure there are hangers in the closet, a glass for water by the bedside, and an extra toothbrush available just in case.

But doing such thoughtful things for those we live with takes more effort. It's too easy to simply tend to the basics when it comes to caring for our families.

What would happen in our homes if we occasionally but regularly did little extras for our family members?

Lord, may I be creative with little extras for my family, not just our company. I want my actions to tell my family as well as my guests that I love them. Amen.

Noisy, Hungry Birds

"Look at the birds of the air, that they do not sow, nor reap nor gather into barns, and yet your heavenly Father feeds them."

—Matthew 6:26 NASB

It was not the rooster's quaint and charming cock-a-doodle-do. It was not the sweet song of a tiny wren. It was the cawing—the almost cackling—of big, black crows. And maybe you know pigeons. They can generate quite a racket—and they get even louder when you toss bread-crumbs their way. Birds can be noisy.

Children can be like noisy birds. If your house is the neighborhood hangout, you're not only doing something right, but you also get to decide how to feed them. No, it can't always be carrots, but it can't always be chips either.

Whatever you stock the shelves and fill the fridge with, think about always serving up a hearty portion of encouragement, love, and peace. This feast for the kids' souls will keep them coming back for more. You'll regularly be hosting a hungry, chattering flock—and the noise will be music to your heart.

Lord, please use my home to point people to You and the love, joy, and peace You have for them. Amen.

The Top of My Lungs

Let the word of Christ richly dwell within you, with all wisdom teaching and admonishing one another with psalms and hymns and spiritual songs, singing with thankfulness in your hearts to God.

—Colossians 3:16 NASB

Think about all the places we hear music these days. It is played at the mall and in our cars. We play it on our headphones when we run; we play it on our computers at the office. Think, too, about the power of music. A few notes can take us back to a moment in time. The right melody can make us cry—happy tears or sad. Another song gets sports teams fired up for the big game.

God's Word can also take us back to a moment of His faithfulness or tenderness, make us cry tears of conviction and tears of gratitude, and get us fired up for the circumstances we find ourselves in and the calling He has for us. And God's Word can put a song in our hearts. Hiding His truth in our hearts—memorizing passages of Scripture—can be music to our souls. And may we share that music with our family by praying Bible verses, using Scripture in notes of encouragement, letting God's Word offer comfort and hope, and singing praise songs as we go about our day.

God, may I fill my home with words of praise to You. Amen.

No "D" Word for You

God called us [husbands and wives] to live in peace.

—1 Corinthians 7:15 NCV

Whatever the statistics about the rate of divorce inside the church compared to outside—and reports widely—any divorce is tragic. And the divorce of a Christian husband and a Christian wife is even more tragic.

Two people committed to God who then commit to each other have a much stronger starting point than individuals who don't. That stronger commitment to the Lord may make a Christian couple more of a target for the Enemy, who hates marriage. And that's all the more reason we need to support one another's marriages. Marriage isn't easy: two broken people aren't made whole by getting married.

So may we turn to God and seek the peace that comes from knowing that He heals—knowing that He heals us in our brokenness, He heals our spouse's brokenness, and He heals broken marriages whether cracks are just now appearing or the relationship is on life support.

Pray for healing in your relationship with your spouse. God is in the business of healing.

Lord, teach us to pursue You and Your peace, individually and as a couple. Amen.

Disagreeing Kindly

"A family that's in a constant squabble disintegrates."

—Matthew 12:25 MSG

"If you don't have something nice to say, don't say anything at all" is a phrase I heard growing up. I used a shorter version when I was the mom: "Be nice . . . or be quiet."

But being quiet with our words doesn't mean being quiet in other ways. We can communicate volumes by rolling our eyes, for instance. Too often we ignore this parental wisdom and speak cruel words with a disrespectful tone. Parents who both find that behavior unacceptable and *make* it unacceptable in their family discussions have established some good guidelines for their disagreements.

A family who has learned how to argue and disagree without being unkind to one another is a family who lives at peace. The lack of unkindness doesn't mean we're not angry, and living at peace doesn't mean we put up false fronts or shove problems under the rug. Disagreeing kindly means holding our tongues when only unkind words come to mind. Choosing kind words—or choosing not to speak—when disagreements arise will keep a family from disintegrating.

Lord, help each member of my family choose to speak kind words or no words at all when we are trying to resolve a situation. Amen.

Blue-Ribbon Worthy

"If the household is worthy, let your peace come upon it. But if it is not worthy, let your peace return to you."

—Matthew 10:13 NKJV

These were some of Jesus' instructions to His disciples when He sent them out to serve. The homes that welcomed them, Jesus said, were worthy to receive the blessing of peace that the disciples would speak over them. Those homes that did not receive the disciples did not receive that blessing. Yes, peace is a blessing that God bestows.

We don't have a disciple to welcome or to turn away, so how will God determine whether our homes are worthy of His blessing of peace? Surely trying to live by the most important commandments would make us worthy of God's blessing. Hear Jesus' words: "'You shall love the Lord your God with all your heart, and with all your soul, and with all your mind.' This is the great and foremost commandment. The second is like it, 'You shall love your neighbor as yourself'" (Matthew 22:37–39 NASB).

So God is looking for families who put Him first and families who do the hard work of loving one another when loving is not easy. God is not looking for perfection—He's available to help, and He longs to bless you.

Lord, my family is far from perfect, but we try to put You first and to love one another even when loving is tough. Please bless us with Your peace. Amen.

Rest for Your Soul

My people will dwell in a peaceful habitation, in secure dwellings, and in quiet resting places.

—Isaiah 32:18 NKJV

Isn't it amazing how a vacation or even a quick getaway can change our outlook and improve our attitude? But as wonderful as the change of pace and change of scenery can be, after a while, many of us look forward to going home. One of those reasons is our bed. There really is nothing like our own bed and our own pillow.

Similarly, as wonderful as vacations are, there is nothing like our gracious God and the profound rest we find in Him. The world offers great spots for our bodies and minds to rest and relax, but nothing offers rest for our souls like time we make to be with God. And that rest for our souls doesn't require reservations, TSA clearance, or bags that weigh less than fifty pounds.

So enjoy the long weekends and long-awaited vacations, but don't let it be too long between the times you get away with God. Be quiet in His presence, and find refreshment for your spirit and rest for your soul.

Sometimes I think I need to get away when I really need time with You, Father. Help me recognize when what I actually need is the peace and rest found only at home in You. Amen.

First Things First

Complete your work outside, and get your fields ready for next season; after that's done, build your house.

—Proverbs 24:27 VOICE

We all understand how important it is for a building to have a solid foundation, and that doesn't happen without planning and preparation. Similarly, a strong, solid, carefully planned financial foundation is also important—even essential—for a peaceful home. Whether you're single and starting out in a career, engaged and preparing for life with a spouse, or nearing the retirement years, you won't regret investing time and energy in charting a course. You don't have time? Maybe you don't *not* have time!

Consider the verse above from the book of Proverbs, one of the Bible's wisdom books. Here's the even more straightforward statement from *The Message*: "First plant your fields; then build your barn." First things first!

God will help us identify what needs to come first. These two versions of Proverbs 24:27 suggest that providing for our future comes before pouring ourselves into the present. Careful financial planning for our future is a matter of good stewardship in the long-term, and it means more peace at home as that future unfolds.

Lord, help me plan and establish a stronger financial foundation for my family. I want to do that to honor You and give my family some financial peace. Amen.

Scrapbooking for God

Someday your children will ask you, "What do these stones mean?" And you will tell them, "Israel crossed the Jordan here on dry ground."

—Joshua 4:21–22 VOICE

Are you a scrapbooker? Many people I know are, and their books are truly amazing. They are beautiful ways to preserve family memories, celebrate milestones, document memorable vacation times, pass traditions from one generation to another, and remember those who've gone before us. Sharing a special scrapbook with the younger members of the family and telling the stories depicted on its pages can create additional memories that last a lifetime.

To memorialize an event in biblical times—especially an experience of God's great faithfulness—people built altars. When families passed by one of these stone structures, the children would ask, "What do these stones mean?" The adults would then share the story of those stones: a story of God's provision, guidance, protection, and love.

When you craft your scrapbook pages, be sure to include pages that tell of God's faithfulness to your family. Those are the best kinds of stories to pass along to your children and grandchildren.

God, I want to tell stories of what You have done in our lives so my children and grandchildren will have the peace that comes with knowing You are faithful to us. Amen.

PEACE WITHIN

Drawn by His Grace

Grace and peace be yours in abundance through the knowledge of God and of Jesus our Lord.

—2 Peter 1:2 NIV

While the roofing crew hammered away in the summer heat, neighbors watched from the shade in amazement. Even as they scurried around on top of the two-story home, not a single member of the crew seemed at all concerned about the possibility of falling. The crowd also noted how carefully the crew cleaned up. Their last task of the day was to walk around the house with a huge magnetic roller that would pick up any remaining roofing nails.

The neighbors watched as nails, attracted to the magnet, came tumbling out of the flowerbeds. One observer commented, "God's grace is like that giant roller, and we're the nails drawn to Him by His grace."

God is always in the process of drawing us to Himself. He moves around in our lives with His magnet of grace and peace. When we feel His tug, we simply need to let ourselves be pulled up. No matter how far away we may have fallen from the Lord or what weeds we may be tangled in, His powerful grace can pull us out.

God, thank You for always working to draw me to Yourself. May I not resist, and may I be used to draw others to Your grace as well. Amen.

Putting on Glasses

The word of God is living and active and sharper than any two-edged sword, and piercing as far as the division of soul and spirit, of both joints and marrow, and able to judge the thoughts and intentions of the heart.

—Hebrews 4:12 NASB

Is this how your hair appointment ends? When the hairdresser has finished cutting your hair, she hands you a mirror so you can see the back of your head. Some of us can't see a thing until we put on our glasses. The mirror that was handed to us doesn't do us any good without the proper lenses.

We may be a lot like that person sitting in the salon chair. God hands us a special mirror and says, *Look inside and see what great things I have done in you*. We strain to see what He is talking about, but we miss it.

God wants us to look at our hearts to see the ways He has been at work as well as what things still need to change. We try, but we don't see what He wants us to see. We pick up the Word of God, and through that lens we begin to see what we were unable to see on our own: the changes He is working in our hearts as well as opportunities for growth. God's Word is our prescription lens.

God, thank You for the reminder that You are working in my heart and that Your Word can help me see. Amen.

A Holy Remote

God did not give us a spirit that makes us afraid but a spirit of power and love and self-control.

—2 Timothy 1:7 NCV

Perhaps the most coveted device in the house—and therefore the most in-demand and argued-about device—is the remote control. Today's remote allows us to do a lot more than just choose which channel to watch. We can also pause the broadcast and rewind it, increase the volume, block certain channels, and record shows for future viewing.

Just as the remote control has power over the TV, the Holy Spirit is our power Source. When we call on the Holy Spirit, we will find that we have the ability to control our impulses, to limit our power for the sake of others, and to turn up the volume of our peace and love. We can even call on the Holy Spirit for strength to block the channels we ought not to view. When you start relying on the power of the Spirit, the unfolding plot of your life will please God, and you will know peace.

Thank You for Your Holy Spirit, God. I need His power to help me control my impulses, limit my power, and turn up the volume on peace and love. Amen.

Enough

I've learned by now to be quite content whatever my circumstances. I'm just as happy with little as with much, with much as with little.

—Philippians 4:11 MSG

How would you define *enough*? Is there an amount or a quantity that, when reached, you would be able to say, "I have enough"?

Our consumer society would say no! Commercials tell us many times an hour that we deserve more—but how much more? At what point would you be able to say you had accumulated enough possessions, enough money, enough status, or enough security?

Today's verse suggests that the apostle Paul had defined *enough* for himself, and he was very much at peace in his circumstances. Paul had experienced having it all, as society defined it, and he had also lost it all. Having lived in both extremes, he had gained some insight into what made for contentment and peace.

What *is* the secret? *Enough* is not found in the occurrence of perfect circumstances or the accumulation of a specific amount of stuff. *Enough* is found only in knowing that Jesus is all you need for now and for eternity. Jesus is enough—and that truth brings contentment and peace.

I long to be content regardless of my circumstances. Help me to focus on You, Jesus, and the fact that You are enough. Amen.

Dressed for Success

Stand firm then, with the belt of truth buckled around your waist, with the breastplate of righteousness in place, and with your feet fitted with the readiness that comes from the gospel of peace.

—Ephesians 6:14–15 NIV

Whatever the social setting—from weddings to parties to intimate gatherings—when we look good, we feel good. Yet looking good is not an easy mark to hit. What if we find ourselves overdressed or underdressed for the occasion? No matter how good we look, we don't feel good. What if the accessories—the jewelry or shoes—aren't quite right? Or aren't quite affordable? Again, the right look has proved unattainable.

Whatever our day holds, though, we can attain the right look—the look we need—for the battles we will encounter. The Bible describes the perfect outfit, and God provides it tailor-made for each of us. Every morning we can confidently put on the belt of truth, the breastplate of righteousness, and shoes that will enable us to go where we can share the gospel, the message of peace. Now you're dressed and ready for anything!

Lord, may I never start a day without putting on the armor You provide: truth, righteousness, the gospel of peace, faith, and salvation. Amen.

Beyond Our Understanding

The peace of God, which surpasses all comprehension, will guard your hearts and your minds in Christ Jesus.

—Philippians 4:7 NASB

It's difficult to describe the kind of peace God gives us. His own Word says that His peace "surpasses all comprehension"! But even though we can't adequately describe it, we know it when we see it; we especially know it when we experience it.

She had just buried her third child . . . He had just lost a position at his company that he'd held for thirty years . . . Their son was in trouble again, this time with a felony charge that would follow him throughout his life. Yet this devastated mother, this discouraged provider, and these heartbroken parents experienced God's peace. Maybe you've experienced it too.

In the midst of whatever darkness surrounds you or whatever chaos is swirling internally or externally, may the peace that passes understanding make you mindful of God's presence with you and His love for you.

When darkness comes, help me cling to You, confident in Your power and presence, strengthened by Your truth, and blessed with peace that surpasses all human understanding. Amen.

A Believer's Hope

I pray that the God who gives hope will fill you with much joy and peace while you trust in him. Then your hope will overflow by the power of the Holy Spirit.

—Romans 15:13 NCV

My grandmother had a hope chest at the foot of her bed. It was made of cedar and had a hinged top. Why did she call it a "hope chest"? Tradition!

In the past, in anticipation of a marriage, a young girl would put household linens, some of which she had stitched and embroidered, into such a chest. Maybe Mom would add some family heirlooms, a quilt she had made, a blanket she had crocheted. In a variation on that theme, some hope chests—filled with items a new married couple would need to start a home—were presented to the bride and groom as a gift. Either way, that chest was tangible evidence of the bride's hopes for the future.

Because of Jesus, we have solid hope for our eternal future. It is kept in heaven rather than a cedar chest. It can never be taken away from us: the author of Hebrews called it "both sure and steadfast" (6:19 NASB). God is worthy of our trust. When we place our confident hope in Him, we will overflow with joy and peace.

Thank You, God, that my hope for eternity *with* You and *without* pain and tears is certain. Amen.

Faithful Friend

We were saved in this hope, but hope that is seen is not hope; for why does one still hope for what he sees? But if we hope for what we do not see, we eagerly wait for it with perseverance.

—Romans 8:24–25 NKJV

One of the most viewed YouTube videos shows a German shepherd welcoming his master home from deployment. The dog can hardly stand or sit. He is so excited that he doesn't know what to do with himself. The friend who took care of the dog while his master was deployed said that each day the dog waited for the front door to open and his master to come home. That dog never lost hope: he always knew his master would return.

We are to be like that dog, never losing hope that God's promises are true, that He will act as He has said He will act, and that our Master—Jesus Christ, Victor over sin and death—will return. When Jesus comes for us in all His glory, we will not know whether to sit or stand, to jump into His lap or bow at His feet. Our steadfast hope in Jesus' return will give way to an incomparable joy like we have never experienced this side of heaven. What a glorious time that will be!

Jesus, may I be just as patient and confident as I wait in hope of Your glorious return. Amen.

Your Choice

The mind set on the flesh is death, but the mind set on the Spirit is life and peace.

—Romans 8:6 NASB

From an early age we're taught the concept of opposites: night and day, black and white, beginning and end, right and wrong. The Bible often uses contrasts to make important points to help us learn a lesson more effectively.

Today's verse contains two other pairs of opposites—flesh and Spirit, death and life—as it communicates an important truth. When we set our mind on the flesh, we surrender ourselves to our feelings and appetites rather than to the guidance and strength of the Spirit. And where will our feelings and appetites lead? The apostle Paul was clear: to death. Our being led by the Spirit takes us in the opposite direction, toward life.

Put differently, if we want life as God intends us to live and peace despite the circumstances and situations of this fallen world, then we must choose to set our mind on God's Spirit. When He guides our decisions, steps, thoughts, and actions, we will know peace. Let's set our mind on life and peace, and the Spirit of God will be with us.

Lord, the choice between the Spirit and life or the flesh and death is easy. Living out that choice isn't easy: teach me and empower me to choose with my actions the Spirit and life. Amen.

God's Peace

"Peace I leave with you; my peace I give you. I do not give to you as the world gives. Do not let your hearts be troubled and do not be afraid."

—John 14:27 NIV

Some people are naturally peaceful. Nothing seems to rattle them; they move calmly through life at a pace that calms others. Others find peace elusive at best. They are happier doing, going, getting things done. The good news is that the kind of peace a Christian knows has nothing to do with personality or other external factors. Whether we are naturally peaceful or we struggle to find peace, we can have the kind of peace God gives.

God-given peace is the inner sense that all *will be* well even though all *is* not well now. In fact, inner peace is not based on circumstances or personality. God's peace either pushes fear aside or wrestles it to the ground. God's peace is a balm that quiets a troubled heart in the midst of real-life crises. The question isn't "Are you a peaceful person?" but rather "Are you filled with God's peace?"

God's peace is a gift anyone can receive. All we need to do is ask.

Thank You, God, for the peace that pushes fear aside, quiets a troubled heart, and fuels confidence that all will be well. Amen.

I Owe It All to . . .

God, order a peaceful and whole life for us because everything we've done, you've done for us.

—Isaiah 26:12 MSG

We've all heard acceptance speeches from an individual receiving an award. Instead of receiving all the praise for herself, the honoree names a mentor or a coach, her parents, or her teammates as the reason for her success. Sometimes an individual gives God the glory by thanking Him for His role in her accomplishment.

Those speeches are good reminders that even though we work hard to reach our goals, we never succeed on our own. We always can identify someone who has walked alongside us or who sacrificed for us. These speeches also remind us that our skills and talents, although developed and sharpened by us, are gifts from God. When we know God, we begin to understand that everything good that we've ever done was because of Him.

In the end when we stand before God to receive life's rewards, may we humbly acknowledge the basic truth that we owe it all to Him.

God, thank You for skills and talents, for providing opportunities for me to develop them, people to support me, and Your grace and empowerment. Amen.

We Just Know!

"God even knows how many hairs you have on your head. Don't be afraid. You are worth much more than many sparrows."

—Luke 12:7 NCV

They just *know* what to do! Mama birds know to get worms to feed their babies. Mama kangaroos know to keep their babies in their pouches. Mama monkeys know to let their babies cling to them as they swing from branch to branch. And we human mamas just know—as we count toes and fingers, marvel at the tiny nose, and stroke the soft hair—that we are to love the precious child whom God has entrusted to our care.

When we have our first child, we quickly learn just how powerful this mother love is. We would do anything for our little one, even get up all hours of the night for months on end!

Our powerful love for our children is but a taste of God's love for our children and for us. Our God knows us by name (Isaiah 43:1; John 10:14), He collects our tears in a bottle (Psalm 56:8), He knows to give us good gifts (Matthew 7:11), and He even numbers the hairs on our head. What a blessing to know God loves us!

Father, thank You for Your intimate and powerful love. Knowing of Your love gives me much peace. Amen.

Listening with Your Heart

"He who enters by the door is a shepherd of the sheep. To him the doorkeeper opens, and the sheep hear his voice, and he calls his own sheep by name and leads them out."

—John 10:2–3 NASB

It is an interesting phenomenon: we can walk past the church nursery as crying kids are getting settled and recognize the cry of our temporarily unhappy child. Or we can find ourselves at the neighborhood playground and know that our child is the one of the fifty calling, "Mommmm!" In reverse, when we are called from the worship service to the nursery, our baby settles down when she hears our voice. And, like that child, as God's children we settle down and know His peace when we hear His voice.

Too often, though, we don't realize that God is calling us. He calls each one of us to different things at different times in our lives. Right now He is calling some people to accept Him as Savior. He is calling others to a deeper relationship and still others to take a bold step of faith. His call to you might be a specific task, an answer to a prayer for guidance, or even a request to get together with Him for a little while.

God is calling. Ask Him to help you hear Him.

Despite the world's noise and the noise of my life, I want to hear Your voice, Lord. Teach me to be in tune to it and to listen with my heart. Amen.

Worry Habit

"Do not consume yourselves with questions: What will we eat? What will we drink? What will we wear? Outsiders make themselves frantic over such questions; they don't realize that your heavenly Father knows exactly what you need."

—Matthew 6:31–32 VOICE

Some people have no trouble admitting it: "I'm a worrier." They worry about what others think, what would happen if they lost their job, where to live, what direction their kids are headed, what to say in a given situation, and even what to wear. But Jesus said, "Don't!"

"Do not consume yourself with questions" is not as straightforward as the "Do not worry" that appears in many translations. But "Do not consume yourself with questions" points to an important fact about worry: we can find ourselves consumed by it. Anxiety can impact our health, home, relationships, and so much more. Worry can make us entirely me-focused, which doesn't allow God into the situation.

Stop worrying and instead focus on God. Learn and recite Scripture that gives you peace. Ask God to forgive you for the doubt in Him that your worry implies and to help you break the worry habit. He will gladly do both.

God, please forgive me for choosing worrying over trusting You. Please help me break that habit and learn to be God-centered, not me-centered. Amen.

Heavy Lifting

"Do not worry about tomorrow, for tomorrow will worry about its own things. Sufficient for the day is its own trouble."

—Matthew 6:34 NKJV

My back went out, and I wasn't even doing anything out of the ordinary." "It was that sharp twist I took when I bent down to try to pick something up." "I forgot I'm not nineteen anymore. I shouldn't have picked that up." There definitely are some things in life we just shouldn't pick up: objects that are too heavy—and, according to Jesus, our worries.

We can usually avoid lifting heavy objects. But it's hard for many of us to not pick up our worries—and then carry them for long distances.

But Jesus said, "Don't!" Yesterday we read that we are not to worry about what we need today. Now we read the command to "not worry about tomorrow." The Source of all wisdom and peace tells us not to focus on things that have not yet happened. Tomorrow may not even come. And if tomorrow does come, it may not bring the things we're worried about. Furthermore, those worries may both distract us from what we need to do today and rob us of joy.

My back is bent over with the burden of worry, a burden that You tell me I don't need to carry, that You in fact command me *not* to carry. Help me obey. Amen.

The Tree of Life

[Wisdom's] ways are ways of pleasantness, and all her paths are peace. She is a tree of life to those who take hold of her, and happy are all who retain her.

—Proverbs 3:17–18 NKJV

Who are the wise people in your life? Do you go to a parent or mentor for wisdom? Do you trust a friend or coworker when you need wise counsel? Most likely these aren't people who have only book knowledge about the area of your concern; they are examples of success. When you need financial wisdom, you go to someone who knows financial success. If you need wisdom about your marriage, you go to someone who has a great marriage. What you see in their lives shows you that they have lived wisely and have wisdom to share.

And they will undoubtedly share that wisdom humbly because wisdom is not haughty. After all, a wise person knows what he doesn't know: he knows there is still much to learn about God and about the virtually infinite subjects His world offers. Being with this humble and godly person will be like finding refreshment in the shade of a tree on a hot and muggy summer day. Today's verse describes wisdom as a tree of life. Sitting in its shade will mean refreshing strength and godly advice.

When I need advice, guide me to people with true wisdom, with wisdom from You, God. Amen.

Peace Like a River

"If you had obeyed me, you would have had peace like a full-flowing river. Good things would have flowed to you like the waves of the sea."

—Isaiah 48:18 NCV

When was the last time you heard a sermon about obedience—or even heard the word *obey* mentioned from the pulpit? It may have been quite a while. We no longer talk much about obedience in our churches and our families, perhaps because we who would be doing that talking struggle with our own obedience. And obedience may be a struggle because it requires humility: we are to yield, to surrender, our wills to another.

When that Other is God Himself, however, the step of surrendering results in a flood of blessings, among them peace that fills your heart to overflowing. To make that step easier, think about the fact that God is your heavenly Father. Like most earthly fathers, God does not and will not require you to do anything that would be bad for you. Neither is God arbitrary or vindictive. His command to surrender, then, will mean good for you. Obedience to God—surrendering to Him—will bring peace and, as today's verse adds, "good things."

Lord, I struggle to obey, and my lack of humility is undoubtedly a factor. Help me surrender my will to Yours. Amen.

Righteousness and Redemption

The work of righteousness will be peace, and the service of righteousness, quietness and confidence forever.

—Isaiah 32:17 NASB

In the movie *Liar, Liar,* the five-year-old son of a high-powered and not-so-honest attorney makes a wish as he blows out the candles on his birthday cake: that his dad would stop lying for twenty-four hours. We laugh at the dilemmas that arise when the attorney has to always tell the truth. But there is another reason we enjoy this movie.

Liar, Liar is the story of redemption. The attorney's son wishes—or prays—for his dad to become the better person that he believes his dad actually is. The haughty attorney doesn't immediately see the error of his ways, and he fights it before finally accepting the new life offered him.

God also offers us a plan of redemption. We may fight against it and struggle. When we finally come to accept the righteousness of Jesus that God offers us sinners, He blesses us with peace. Have you accepted the redemption and new life offered to you?

God, help me to receive rather than resist Your gift of righteousness so that I may know Your redemption, Your powerful transformation, and Your peace. Amen.

A Good Friend

You're blessed when you meet Lady Wisdom, when you make friends with Madame Insight. She's worth far more than money in the bank; her friendship is better than a big salary.

—Proverbs 3:13–14 MSG

Has God blessed you with a good friend? You may not see her often, but God keeps your heart connection strong. This good friend loves you when you are unlovely, she knows exactly when you need her even before you say anything, and she offers wisdom and encouragement whatever the situation. Her friendship truly is a gift.

Today's Scripture translation personifies wisdom as that kind of priceless friend. Lady Wisdom is "worth far more than money in the bank," the writer stated, implicitly inviting us to befriend her. We gain this priceless wisdom by reading God's Word and spending time with His Son, Jesus. When we spend time with Jesus, we learn to value His wisdom just as we value the input of a good friend.

How much time will you set aside for this good Friend?

Thank You for the gift of earthly friendship—and for the opportunity to befriend my wise Savior. Amen.

Better Than a GPS

Trust in the LORD with all your heart, and lean not on your own understanding; in all your ways acknowledge Him, and He shall direct your paths.

—Proverbs 3:5–6 NKJV

Do you use a GPS? If so, that tells me that you trust someone you don't even know to have correctly drawn the maps. In other words, when you enter your destination, you are trusting that the GPS will direct you to that location—and not off a cliff or into a lake.

Trust is difficult for many of us, and the call to "trust in the LORD with all your heart" can seem utterly impossible. Yet when God follows up that command with the promise that He will direct our paths, we can be encouraged to trust Him. God has good paths for us. The paths won't always be easy, and we won't always understand what God is doing as He proves His trustworthiness and keeps His promises. God wants us to know that He is better than any GPS.

So take a step of faith today. Exercise your trust muscle, allowing God to show you how good He is at directing you to your destination.

Lord, I want You to direct my paths. Help me to be able to fully trust You to get me where You want me to be. Amen.

Surprise!

On the evening of that first day of the week, when the disciples were together, with the doors locked for fear of the Jewish leaders, Jesus came and stood among them and said, "Peace be with you!"

—John 20:19 NIV

Have you ever been scared silly? Some people love to watch scary movies with the anticipation of being frightened out of their wits. Others enjoy going through a fright house. But we don't have to look for ways to be afraid. The unfolding of our lives can provide the scariest moments of all. What will the test results be? Will the tornado touch down? Scary, right?

The disciples experienced a scare shortly after Jesus' resurrection when He entered the room where they were gathered. Jesus entered when the door was locked! Imagine the shock, disbelief, and fear that must have filled the room. Jesus recognized these emotions and said, "Peace be with you." Undoubtedly His very presence—showing the disciples His hands and side—further drove out the men's fear and blessed them with His peace.

When fear overwhelms you, Jesus has those same words for you. Whenever you find yourself filled with fear, ask Jesus to surround you with His presence and fill your heart with His peace.

When I am afraid, God, allow me to hear Your voice and feel You near me. Amen.

The Prescription

Stop doing evil and do good. Look for peace and work for it.

—Psalm 34:14 NCV

When asked why she had come to the doctor's office, the patient kicked her heel hard against the floor and explained, "Doctor, whenever I do this, my foot really hurts." The doctor rubbed his chin and nodded. "Hmm . . . I see." Grateful that he was taking her problem seriously, the concerned patient asked, "What do you recommend?" With a slight smile, the doctor answered, "Stop hitting your foot on the floor like that."

Just as that solution may have seemed too simple for the patient, God's suggested approach to the world's rampant evil and to our own tendency to do the wrong thing may seem too simple. God's Word basically says this: "Stop doing that! Instead, do good." When we are busy doing good, we have less time to be tempted by evil, much less time to look for it. Furthermore, when we look for peace and work for it, we will find that evil flees. When we simply stop doing evil, our foot—figuratively speaking—won't hurt anymore.

The Doctor has written you the prescription. Are you willing to follow the Doctor's orders?

God, it sounds simple—stop doing evil, do good, and work for peace—but I know it won't be easy. I need Your help to follow through. Amen.

Thirsting for Peace

The Lord will continually guide you, and satisfy your desire in scorched places, and give strength to your bones; and you will be like a watered garden, and like a spring of water whose waters do not fail.

—Isaiah 58:11 NASB

Have you walked through a garden after a rain? You can almost hear the sighs of contentment coming from the plants. Oh, these plants appreciate what the watering cans and sprinklers provide, but there is nothing as wonderful as the rain from heaven. In response to the rain, the plants show their joy and contentment by growing bigger and stronger and turning more lush.

We are like that. We can go for quite a while with a little watering, but after some time, we begin to show how sun-scorched and parched—how needy—we are. We may become irritable, easily frustrated, angered, and overwhelmed. When we see these warning signs, we need to call upon the Lord to send rain.

The full context of Isaiah 58 promises His faithful response. When we cry out to God, forsake our sin, and—as a result of His forgiveness and transforming love—serve those in need, the Lord will in turn provide for us. We can know His soul-satisfying peace only if we ask for it.

Lord, thank You for You promise of such tender and faithful care. Amen.

Listen Carefully

I will hear what God the Lord will speak, for He will speak peace to His people and to His saints; but let them not turn back to folly.

—Psalm 85:8 NKJV

It's been said that God gave us two ears and one mouth to show us that we ought to listen twice as much as we talk. Some people do a better job of this than others. We have no trouble meeting our quota for talking, but when it comes to listening—to truly listening and to listening twice as much as we talk—we struggle.

We would do well not only to apply this 2:1 ratio to our conversations, but also to our prayer conversation with God. When we think of prayer, we think about what we want to say. When we seek instruction for how to pray, we focus on what we say to God. Far less frequently are we reminded that we need to listen. Knowing His written Word will help us recognize His voice; choosing to ask for the Spirit's guidance will help us listen and obey.

Key to all of this is making time to shut out the world. When we are still, we will have an easier time hearing God's voice and, at the same time, experiencing the peace of His presence with us.

God, help me to work toward that 2:1 ratio and make a concerted effort to hear Your voice, listen, and obey. Amen.

Count What?

In peace I will lie down and sleep, for you alone, LORD, make me dwell in safety.

—Psalm 4:8 NIV

There are all kinds of tips and tricks for helping us shut off our minds and fall asleep. Counting sheep is perhaps the oldest trick in the book. Writing down your to-do list rather than repeating it in your mind sometimes helps. You might picture yourself doing whatever helps you relax: lying on a beach, floating down a river, walking through a garden. Other people stretch and relax or imagine drowsiness flowing into each muscle, nerve, and fiber of their body.

Perhaps the best advice comes from Scripture, though: "Oh give thanks to the Lord, for he is good; for his steadfast love endures forever!" (1 Chronicles 16:34 ESV). Thanking Him for every good thing He has given us—counting our blessings—is a great way to fall asleep. We come before our Prince of Peace with a thankful heart, each blessing a reminder of His love and care. No wonder peaceful rest can soon follow.

Try it tonight. Don't count sheep; count your blessings instead.

You are good, and Your love endures forever. What comforting and peace-giving truth to meditate on at day's end! Amen.

JUNE 18

Splashes of Love

May God our Father himself and our Master Jesus clear the road to you! And may the Master pour on the love so it fills your lives and splashes over on everyone around you, just as it does from us to you.

—1 Thessalonians 3:11–12 MSG

On hot, humid days, there is nothing better than a spring or fountain. Children and adults alike can be found splashing around in a city fountain or jumping into clear, cool springs in a local park. Water slides and sprinklers are wonderful respites from the sweltering heat. Even if you are in a high-rise with no access to a spring or fountain, a splash of cool water from the faucet is welcomed relief.

Even more refreshing than ice-cold lemonade on a hot afternoon, God splashes us daily with His peace and love. He encourages us with the beauty of the world He created, with random acts of kindness from strangers, and with the sacrificial service of family and church members. When we learn to recognize these splashes of love, we will come to look to the One who sent them.

The next time you're splashed, be ready to praise God and soak in the peace of His presence.

Lord, I don't want to miss any splashes of Your love and peace today or any day. May these blessings point others to You. Amen.

Stop and Smell the Roses

One hand full of rest is better than two fists full of labor and striving after wind.

—Ecclesiastes 4:6 NASB

Be honest. Are you the kind of person who takes two things off your to-do list and immediately adds six more? You like a full schedule; you thrive on being busy. Yet, there are times when your own pace wears you out, when there aren't enough hours in the day, when you think you might get caught up if only you could clone yourself for an hour or two.

But maybe more is going on than our simply liking the busyness. Maybe we wouldn't know what to do with ourselves if we got to the end of our to-do lists. We know people who are able to relax despite the mounting laundry piles and the paperwork to be shredded or filed, and we don't understand. How can they relax when there is so much to do?

Perhaps they realize that not one of us is promised another day or even minute of life. So they wisely slow down, stop, and smell the roses; they rest and relax once in a while, however long their to-do list may be. Take some time today to smell the roses—both literally and figuratively—and thank God for another minute of life.

Lord, help me to resist the urge to keep going and going and going so that I might savor the beauty and blessings of this world and of the gift of life itself. Amen.

Beaten Up

If you diligently obey the Lord *your God, being careful to do all His commandments which I command you today, the* Lord *your God will set you high above all the nations of the earth.*

—Deuteronomy 28:1 NASB

We all have those days when we feel like the stuffing has been beaten out of us. Without even realizing we'd entered a boxing ring, we've been punched in the gut and our nose has been bloodied.

How can so many things be going sideways all at once when we have been diligently trying to obey God and follow His commandments? Rather than trying to formulate an answer, we remember that He who committed no sin had it even worse: He was betrayed, flogged, mocked, and crucified.

When we are feeling bruised and beaten, we need to remind ourselves that the Lord has been in the boxing ring with us. He knows the blows we've taken, some because of our obedience to His commands. He has taken His own blows, as His hands and side attest. Yet even now He—who defeated sin and death—is lifting us up and will set us high above all nations.

Lord, when I'm feeling bruised and beaten, help me to remember that You are in the boxing ring with me, which gives me peace. Amen.

The Puzzle

By entering through faith into what God has always wanted to do for us—set us right with him, make us fit for him—we have it all together with God because of our Master Jesus.

—Romans 5:1 MSG

What kind of jigsaw puzzle do you like? The classic landscape? Interlocking pieces?

Fitting together the most complicated of jigsaw puzzles is nothing next to the challenge of figuring out the pieces of life. Why are we here? What is our purpose on this earth? Why is life painful? What happens after we die? Since the beginning of time, people have struggled to answer these questions and fit them together. Through the ages, though, we have discovered the secret to putting together this human puzzle: if we begin with the center piece rather than the edges, the rest of the pieces fall into place.

That Center Piece for a Christian is Jesus. Getting to know Jesus—through His Word and by His Spirit—helps us understand why we are here, our purpose on earth, and what happens after we die. When we get to know Jesus, the puzzle pieces of life come together.

Lord Jesus, thank You that the puzzle pieces of life come together when I first put You at the center. Amen.

PEACE OF MIND AND HEART

Angel Armies

He will redeem my soul in peace from the battle which is against me, for they are many who strive with me.

—Psalm 55:18 NASB

One of Satan's most effective ploys is to convince us that we are alone. He often whispers in our ear that it's us against the whole world. He tells us that no one understands us, no one is on our side, the battle is rigged, and there is no way we are going to win. Satan points to fake evidence to support his evil words.

What the Enemy chooses to ignore—and what we don't always remember—is that God's angel armies are on our side. Thousands upon thousands of warriors stand with us, angels who are described in Scripture as large and fearsome. Their very presence ensures that this battle—the battle against Satan and his lies—is already won.

So stand against the lie; stand confident that you are never alone. Knowing God and His angel armies are with you every step of the way means also knowing peace.

Lord, help me to recognize Satan's lies for what they are and not believe them! Amen.

Safe in Jesus

To all who have been called by God. God the Father loves you, and you have been kept safe in Jesus Christ: Mercy, peace, and love be yours richly.

—Jude vv. 1–2 NCV

Safety is big business. Cars are built with safety features and safety belts and then rated for safety. Buildings have safety exits, cabinet doors have safety locks, and medicine bottles have safety caps. We have safety glasses, safety nets, safety harnesses, safety gates, safe zones, and safe havens.

Clearly, we long to be safe and secure, and we're willing to spend a lot of money to feel that way. We wouldn't crave safety if we weren't aware of the dangers—physical, relational, emotional, mental, and spiritual—in this fallen world.

This desire for safety can be fully satisfied in only one Person, and that is our Father God. His mercy, peace, and love provide genuine security. Only in God, only in His love, will you find the safety your heart longs for.

The next time you turn to something or even to someone in hopes of finding security, remember that only temporary feelings of security can result. Solid, lasting, genuine safety—physical, relational, emotional, mental, and spiritual—comes only from God.

God, I surround myself with all sorts of safety gear, but You are the only Source of genuine safety. Help me find peace in this truth. Amen.

The Perfect Gift

"Peace I leave with you; my peace I give you. I do not give to you as the world gives. Do not let your hearts be troubled and do not be afraid."

—John 14:27 NIV

Some people seem to be really gifted at giving the right gifts! If you are blessed to have someone like this in your life, then you understand. These gift givers not only have great ideas, but they also know how to execute them. They search until they find what they're after. They are just as particular about the presentation: they know the perfect wrapping. They consider every detail about the gift and then put it in their closet until the perfect time for giving it arises.

Jesus is also gifted at giving gifts—the gift of forgiveness of sins, of life eternal, of hope and purpose. He also offers us the amazing gift of His peace. His gifts always fit us perfectly; they are always an ideal match for our circumstances. His timing is always right: He gives us His peace whenever we ask, sometimes even before we cry out to Him.

His gift of peace is always exactly what you need when you need it. Jesus is the perfect gift Giver at the same time that He, our Lord and Savior, is the perfect Gift.

Jesus, thank You for giving Yourself as my Savior and Lord on the cross. Thank You for the gift of Your perfect peace when I ask. Amen.

It's All in the Focus

You will keep him in perfect peace, whose mind is stayed on You, because he trusts in You.

—Isaiah 26:3 NKJV

It's an urban legend that we use only ten percent of our brains. In an interview with *Scientific American*, behavioral neurologist and cognitive neuroscientist Dr. Barry Gordon explained: "We use virtually every part of the brain, and [most of] the brain is active almost all the time. Let's put it this way: the brain represents three percent of the body's weight and uses 20 percent of the body's energy." And most of that energy fuels the millions of rapid-firing neurons that are doing their job. It sounds dizzying in there!

Life can be dizzying, too, and we can struggle to focus on what we need to focus on. Jesus offers this solution: focus on Him. Imagine training our amazing brain to do exactly that! From the moment our eyes flutter open, we focus our thoughts on Jesus as the Giver of a new day. When we get dressed, we think of the One who provides for our needs. As we handle all that the day holds, we focus on the One who gives us those tasks and the ability to do them. Such a focus on Jesus would mean peace in our hearts.

Jesus, help me learn to focus on You every waking moment so I may know peace as well as be sensitive to Your presence, strength, and love. Amen.

I'll Do It Myself!

Those who think they can do it on their own end up obsessed with measuring their own moral muscle but never get around to exercising it in real life.

—Romans 8:5 MSG

"I'll do it myself," the strong-willed toddler insists, sometimes with hands on hips or a foot stomp for emphasis. The child struggles, but eventually the jacket does get put on, the shoes are tied, and some juice finds its way into the cup.

You may have a child like this, or perhaps you were this child. Perhaps you and I are like this child even today! After all, when we grow up, we don't outgrow this drive for independence. We simply become more sophisticated in expressing it, or we hide it. Whatever our strategy, though, we stand before God with our hands on our hips declaring we will do it ourselves. Like the toddler, we think we are exercising our strength, determination, and muscle.

The truth is that we can't do life well on our own. To live in a way that truly honors God, we must admit—daily—that we need God's help.

Heavenly Father, You know I like to do things myself. Forgive me! I want to honor You with my life by walking the path You have for me. Amen.

The End of a Hard Day

Blessed is the man who trusts me, God, the woman who sticks with God. They're like trees replanted in Eden, putting down roots near the rivers—never a worry through the hottest of summers, never dropping a leaf, serene and calm through droughts, bearing fresh fruit every season.

—Jeremiah 17:7–8 MSG

An old farmstead on the Blue Ridge Parkway in Virginia offers a chance for modern-day folk to experience life the way it used to be. Down a dirt path sits a two-room cabin where a woman irons linens on the porch.

In sharp contrast are the twenty-first-century teens and their parents, grumbling about the heat. As the family walks away from the cabin, their mood lifts because the temperature drops ten degrees near a mountain stream. How smart these mountainfolk were to build their house facing the creek!

We are even smarter when, as Christians, we live not only with our house facing the mountain stream of Jesus, but also with our roots put down deep near its banks. When our confidence is in God, our faith is watered by His Son, and our hearts are refreshed by the Spirit, divine peace can blow through our days, drying the sweat on our brows.

If you've reached the end of a hard day, stop by God's creek.

God, thank You for Your cooling waters that refresh me after a hard day. Amen.

Standing Watch

Don't be anxious about things; instead, pray . . . And know that the peace of God (a peace that is beyond any and all of our human understanding) will stand watch over your hearts and minds in Jesus, the Anointed One.

—Philippians 4:6–7 VOICE

As the family walked up the dirt driveway to their house, they stopped to talk to the lone firefighter as he leaned against a post in the darkness of the night. They asked if he was waiting for someone, and he replied, "No, I'm posted here for the next four hours to watch your hillside while the others sleep. We've been fighting fires for thirty-six hours. Now we're going to take four-hour shifts and make sure the fire does not threaten you."

A few minutes later, the family was tucked into bed, at perfect peace in the situation. Just before turning out the bedside light, the wife said to her husband, "Isn't that just like our awesome God to give us a concrete example of His presence with us?"

Her husband smiled. "It's as if He is saying, 'I know you are weary and your faith has been tested. Rest assured that I am always watching over you. You are safe.'"

God, thank You for standing watch over me. Thank You that, in You, I can know safety, hope, and peace, whatever the circumstances. Amen.

Things Above

Set your mind on the things above, not on the things that are on earth.

—Colossians 3:2 NASB

The night sky with its countless stars and suggestion of endless space does a nice job of reminding us of how big a God we serve! We may walk outside in hopes of finding the Big Dipper or the Little Dipper and seeing Jupiter or Venus. And we may actually see those things, but we may also be humbled, completely awestruck by our God.

The Holy and Eternal One is far greater than we can describe, yet earthly cares can distract us from Him despite His great glory hinted at by the starry host. Daily responsibilities can keep us from looking to Him. That's why we need to be commanded to set our minds on God. Doing so doesn't come naturally to us. The world's problems and life's daily demands can keep our minds set on aspects of this temporary earthly existence. Solutions for those problems and strength for those demands as well as direction, comfort, and peace come when we set our minds on the things that are on God's mind. Let's give it a try!

Lord, teach me how to set my mind "on the things above," on things eternal and lasting, on You and Your amazing love and grace. Amen.

Strength That Grows

Our fight is not against people on earth but against the rulers and authorities and the powers of this world's darkness, against the spiritual powers of evil in the heavenly world.

—Ephesians 6:12 NCV

Gamers today spend hours upon hours doing battle in the computer game's alternate world. At each level of play in that virtual reality, characters can gain new powers, greater strength, and more sophisticated weapons; they are better prepared to defeat the enemy.

Can the same be said of us, though? The apostle Paul reminded us that we are fighting not only the darkness in this world, but also "the spiritual powers of evil," very real enemies from a real alternate world. And God has provided us with His Spirit as well as His armor of truth, righteousness, the gospel itself, faith, salvation, and Scripture (Ephesians 6). The Lord also enables us to gain new strength. That strength increases each time we resist temptation. That strength also grows as we study God's Word, as we pray, as we choose to put on peace and humility.

God, we know that light and truth ultimately win this battle against darkness and evil. Until then, may I be strong and bold for You! Amen.

Captive Thoughts

We demolish arguments and every pretension that sets itself up against the knowledge of God, and we take captive every thought to make it obedient to Christ.

—2 Corinthians 10:5 NIV

Too often a hostage situation makes the news. Intense negotiations between the police and the hostage taker can go on for days. There isn't always a happy ending despite everyone's best efforts.

We believers were once hostages, but our situation has a happy ending. The brutal hostage taker Satan hijacked our thoughts and feelings. He is a capable deceiver who knows God's truth and twists it. Satan also knows exactly how to make us doubt our good God. But we believers—we who recognize our sin and the forgiveness offered on the cross—don't have to stay hostages. The apostle Paul called us to act, specifically to "take captive every thought."

God wouldn't command us to do something we couldn't do. Relying on His power, let us stand strong against Satan and use that strength to take captive our own thoughts. When we round up our renegade ideas and surrender our thoughts and actions to God, we can live freely and in peace.

God, keep me vigilant about my thought life, aware of Satan's half-truths. I want my thoughts to be captive to You. Amen.

Remember the Equation

My dear children, you belong to God and have defeated them; because God's Spirit, who is in you, is greater than the devil, who is in the world.

—1 John 4:4 NCV

Do you remember any of the math equations you memorized in school? A basic is the formula for the area of the triangle: ½bh (one-half x length of base x length of height).

Today you may use equations without even thinking about them. You calculate the tip when you eat out; you figure out your car's miles per gallon when you refill the tank. Here's an equation from Scripture: God's Holy Spirit within you is greater than anything that may come against you. The Devil may appear to be mighty and strong, but the key word is *appear.* Again, remember the equation: you plus God are mightier and stronger than the Devil. When you feel weak and defeated, remember that equation and find peace. God is greater than anything you face, and He's on your side of the equation.

Lord, when I feel small and weak, help me to remember this equation: You + I > the Devil. Amen.

Right Things

Whatever things are true, whatever things are noble, whatever things are just, whatever things are pure, whatever things are lovely, whatever things are of good report, if there is any virtue and if there is anything praiseworthy—meditate on these things.

—Philippians 4:8 NKJV

Did you know that *thankful* and *to think* have the same Latin root? When our *thoughts* are on the right things, we are positive, happy, and *thankful* people. Tough circumstances are easier to face, grieve, and address when we think about what God instructs us to think about in Philippians 4:8. The converse is equally true. When our thoughts are on the wrong things, we are easily frustrated, focused on ourselves, and ungrateful.

What should we allow to occupy our minds? In Philippians 4:6 is the command to be anxious for nothing and to be thankful as we make our requests. When we choose not to worry but to be thankful, we will know the Lord's peace. Then comes today's verse: we are to think about whatever is noble, pure, lovely, and peace-producing.

When you choose to think on whatever is noble, pure, lovely, and peace-producing, thankfulness fills your mind and heart, and God's peace isn't far behind.

Lord, help me to think about the right things because obedience to You brings peace. Amen.

Oooh! Ahhh!

Without a doubt, His salvation is near for those who revere Him so that He will be with us again and all His glory will fill this land.

—Psalm 85:9 VOICE

Have you ever watched a fireworks show near water or the mountains? Over water, each burst fills the sky with dazzling beauty, which the water perfectly reflects, making the light and colors twice as spectacular. In the mountains, the boom of every explosion reverberates, making the fireworks an experience you feel in your body.

As you and those around you observed the amazing show, did you notice the "ooohs" and "ahhhs"? The child in all of us seems to respond to fireworks with awe and wonder, speechless except for the somehow inevitable "ooohs" and "ahhhs."

But you know what will be far more glorious than any fireworks show? Christ's return to this earth to take His throne! That event will make our hearts soar higher than anything manmade ever could. God's glory will fill this land, and peace and justice will reign forevermore.

The next time you watch a fireworks show, may the beauty and excitement remind you of how glorious that day will be.

Christ, with great anticipation I look forward to Your return, to the time when Your glory and peace fill the earth forevermore. Amen.

Catching Us

The minute I said, "I'm slipping, I'm falling," your love, GOD, took hold and held me fast.

—Psalm 94:18 MSG

Have you ever seen a child fall and then look around to see who's watching? If we run over quickly with a less-than-calm "Are you OK?" tears come. If we make eye contact and offer a thumbs-up, a smile, or even a "You're OK, big guy!" no tears.

Adult falls tend to be a more serious matter. A physical fall will break bones—and we don't heal like we used to! Emotional and spiritual falls can break hearts.

When our hearts break into a million pieces, God scoops us into His arms and puts us back together. When our minds spiral out of control, God draws us close in His loving embrace.

Falls happen without warning. We won't have time or the presence of mind to cry out to God, but we don't need to. God promises to be there for you.

God, in this world and because of my sinfulness, I know I will fall. I find great peace in knowing that every time I fall, You will catch me. Amen.

Satisfied!

Let them give thanks to the LORD for his unfailing love and his wonderful deeds for mankind, for he satisfies the thirsty and fills the hungry with good things.

—Psalm 107:8–9 NIV

A group of people from a church decided to serve the community by taking bottles of water to people working outside. Two of the men set out with just four bottles of water each, and they thought that giving them away would be easy. But after a couple hours of driving around, they had found no one.

Just as they were about to call it a day, the men drove by a laundromat and saw two women weary from the heat. When they gave the women the bottled water, they learned that the women were living with their families in vans parked out back. So the water-bottle missionaries helped the families find shelter and a meal.

God used these willing servants to help meet the physical needs of two families. God is concerned about our hunger and thirst, about safety and shelter. But God also meets the spiritual needs of His children. God satisfies our spiritual thirst with His presence and our spiritual hunger with His Word.

Thank You, Lord, for Your unfailing love. Thank You for satisfying my spiritual hunger and thirst with Your presence and Your Word. Amen.

The Doctor Is In

"I will bring health and healing to the people there. I will heal them and let them enjoy great peace and safety."

—Jeremiah 33:6 NCV

Everyone is a specialist, and nowhere is that more obvious than in the medical world. There seems to be a doctor for just about everything. There are foot doctors, heart doctors, skin doctors, bone doctors, ear/nose/throat doctors, eye doctors, and many others. Outside hospitals we find pet doctors, furniture doctors, and lawn doctors. Sometimes doctors can heal our ailment, fix what's broken, or find a solution for our problem. But sometimes they can't.

Some things break and can't be fixed. Diseases run rampant and can't be stopped. Our lives are bandaged, yet some wounds don't seem to heal. Sometimes that may be the Lord's will (remember Paul's thorn in his side? [2 Corinthians 12]), but sometimes maybe the great Physician simply hasn't acted yet. Continue to go to Him with whatever ails you or has caused you heartache and pain. We don't know exactly how or when He will heal, but we can trust Him to be with us as we wait for His perfect plan in His perfect time.

You are my Creator, the great Physician, my Comforter, my Rock. Thank You that I can entrust all of myself—body, mind, and spirit—to You. Amen.

Before and After

Do not be conformed to this world, but be transformed by the renewing of your mind, that you may prove what is that good and acceptable and perfect will of God.

—Romans 12:2 NKJV

Maybe you were in kindergarten, and you watched a caterpillar munch leaves. One day you got to school, and the caterpillar was gone. In its place was a cocoon, soon a butterfly emerged. How amazing!

Other transformations happen around us. We watch puppies become dogs, babies become adults, acorns become oaks. The concept of rebirth and transformation is truly fascinating. Deep in our hearts God planted a seed of our own transformation because He planned a rebirth of some kind for you and me. But too aware of our human (read "sin") nature, we cannot imagine being transformed into anything pure—and certainly not in our own power.

But God makes impossible transformations happen. Oh, we have a degree of responsibility: "Do not be conformed to this world" is a command we are to obey. "Be transformed" is what can result. God can do an amazing work of transformation in us just as He does in caterpillars.

God, the tiny caterpillar and the delicate butterfly remind me of this truth: in Your hands, my mind can be renewed, I can be transformed, and peace can flood my soul. Amen.

Automatic Downloads

"Who has known the mind of the Lord so as to instruct him?" But we have the mind of Christ.

—1 Corinthians 2:16 NIV

Have you ever set up to have automatic updates on your cell phone or computer? Just understanding the instructions can be a challenge. Then, during the setup process, you often encounter a number of steps to verify the steps—and then more steps to confirm those steps. About halfway through, you may begin to wonder exactly how "automatic" the process really is!

Growing in our faith isn't automatic at all. Even with the Lord's help, we can feel as though we take two steps forward and one step back in our efforts to discipline ourselves to pray and read the Bible. Oh, we want to do this because we love Him, yet putting that love into action isn't easy.

Christian maturity is not a simple download, but something else is. When we confess our faith in Christ, God downloads "the mind of Christ." We still have a new program to learn, but we have what we need to learn it. As we use that new program—as God refines our faith and purifies our hearts—the mind of Christ will become our default.

God, thank You for giving me the mind of Christ, which allows me to become more like Him and to live in peace throughout that lifelong process. Amen.

Choosing the High Side

Lay aside the old self, which is being corrupted in accordance with the lusts of deceit, and that you be renewed in the spirit of your mind.

—Ephesians 4:22–23 NASB

Corruption: we see it in government, in politics, in local communities, and even in ourselves. Wherever and whenever power and the underbelly of humanity come together, corruption easily takes hold. It happens at every level of society, from the rich and famous to the poor and unseen. The word *corruption* implies that at one time the person or group was good, but that's in the past.

At our creation, God declared us humans not merely good, but very good. Yet when power and control tempted us, we sinned; our hearts were corrupt. Because we have accepted Christ, we are able to lay aside that old, corrupted self. We can choose to change our ways and cooperate with the Spirit as He renews our minds. He will also empower us to continue to leave corruption behind, and that is key to living in God's peace.

God, thank You that I can leave my old, corrupt self behind and instead choose to live in peace, with a mind You have transformed and renewed. Amen.

A Jesus Attitude

Adopt the mind-set of Jesus the Anointed. Live with His attitude in your hearts.

—Philippians 2:5 VOICE

Attitude can make a huge difference. A good attitude regarding a miserable task ("I won't have to do this for another year—and at least I have help!") can make it less miserable. A teenage daughter's good attitude (can you say, "Respect"?) can make raising her less difficult. How we approach life with its challenges, question marks, and stress greatly impacts how those events affect us. Attitude can destroy or renew a person.

As followers of Christ, we are to adopt the attitude or mind-set of Jesus in our hearts. A Jesus attitude is loving, patient, and kind. A Jesus attitude does not hold grudges, but is instead forgiving and gracious. A Jesus attitude can give a struggling family hope and soften and heal a hardened heart. A Jesus attitude prays and trusts and therefore knows peace.

How much like a Jesus attitude is yours today?

Help me, Lord, to live with a Jesus attitude especially at home, but also in the neighborhood and at my job. Amen.

Ultimate Defense

Since we are of the day, let us be sober, having put on the breastplate of faith and love, and as a helmet, the hope of salvation.

—1 Thessalonians 5:8 NASB

Through the years defense contractors have improved body armor to better protect our military men and women. Vests, for instance, are more lightweight, and some even have a built-in cooling system that, in the heat of desert battles, is a welcome feature. The most important feature of a vest hasn't changed through the millennia: the armor must protect the body, specifically, the heart, lungs, and other vital organs.

When the arrows of life come your way, you need spiritual protection, and God provides the armor you need. Among the must-have features of this divine defense are mind protection, the choice to keep one's faith in God and His Word, ensuring sober and clear thinking; heart protection, provided by the choice to trust in God's love; and thought protection, accomplished by unshakable hope in God. Clearly, God's armor protects all the functions vital to keeping a Christian's faith in Him alive.

The battle rages, but God has issued you the armor you need. Will you put it on?

God, whenever the arrows come my way, remind me to put on the armor of faith, love, and hope that You provide. Amen.

Under Control

Let the peace that Christ gives control your thinking, because you were all called together in one body to have peace. Always be thankful.

—Colossians 3:15 NCV

In a baseball game, the umpire has an important and difficult job. From his vantage point, looking over the catcher's shoulder, he calls balls and strikes and sometimes fair balls, foul balls, and whether a base runner is safe or out. An umpire follows the rules of the game and uses his experienced professional judgment to make calls, then he stands by those decisions even when the fans yell their opposition. The umpire's job, though it may seem divisive, is necessary: someone has to control the game.

Interestingly, the word *control* in today's Scripture means "umpire" or "referee." So Paul was saying that peace is to serve as the umpire for our thoughts. For instance, when our emotions conflict with what we know we ought to do, we can allow peace to be the umpire that determines our behavior. Our feelings and other people may not be impacted by the umpire's ruling. But when peace enables us to do what Jesus wants us to do, that's all that matters.

Make peace the umpire that keeps your words, thoughts, and actions under control—God's control.

Lord, I need help controlling my words, thoughts, and actions. Thank You for the strength I get from both Your Holy Spirit and this written truth. Amen.

Shelter in the Shade

Indeed, he who watches over Israel will neither slumber nor sleep. The Lord watches over you—the Lord is your shade at your right hand.

—Psalm 121:4–5 NIV

If you know the South in the summer, you'll appreciate this observation: "You know you're in the South when you choose your parking spot based not on its proximity to the store entrance, but on where you can get the most shade for your car."

Whenever temperatures soar, we automatically search for shade. Leafy trees, the shadows cast by tall buildings, store awnings, and even a passing cloud all offer welcome relief. The sun can sap the life out of us, but even a little shade can revive us.

When the sun beats down, when you feel energy draining from you, God is the shade you seek. He will stand over you and block the damaging rays. He will shade you from the heat both night and day. In His care, you are revived, and you find peace.

If life is a little too hot today, seek shelter in God's shade and allow His Spirit to revive you and fill you with peace.

When the heat is getting to me, Lord, I know Your shade that revives and renews is near. Thank You for faithfully watching over and providing for me. Amen.

PEACE IN TIMES OF TROUBLE

The Battle Is Won

It pleased the Father . . . to reconcile all things to Himself, by [Jesus Christ], whether things on earth or things in heaven, having made peace through the blood of His cross.

—Colossians 1:19–20 NKJV

War is bloody. Through the millennia, on battlegrounds across America and around the world, millions of people have spilled their blood in war. These people fought for many reasons, among them land, power, and freedom. The blood—spilled by people willing to give their lives for the cause they believed in—represents precious lives.

Jesus was in a war, a cosmic battle between light and dark, truth and evil. The major battle of His life happened on an ugly wooden cross, and His blood spilled as He died. That excruciatingly painful and bloody death, though, ended the battle for your soul: Jesus defeated sin.

Jesus voluntarily fought this war, and He paid the ultimate price on Calvary. But as a result, you and I can live at peace with God. Jesus won the battle, and the spoils go to us!

Thank You, Jesus, for paying the ultimate price for my peace with God. Amen.

In a Hole

I am persuaded that neither death nor life, nor angels nor principalities nor powers, nor things present nor things to come, nor height nor depth, nor any other created thing, shall be able to separate us from the love of God which is in Christ Jesus our Lord.

—Romans 8:38–39 NKJV

From time to time you'll read about it in the news: out of nowhere a sinkhole will appear, swallowing everything in its vicinity. Though sinkholes rarely cause catastrophic injuries, the thought of being in a hole is justifiably terrifying.

I've never fallen into a hole in the ground, and you probably haven't either. But we've fallen into other kinds of holes—emotional and spiritual holes of loneliness, worry, fear, sadness, anger, confusion, indecision.

No matter how we feel, how utterly isolated and unloved, we can choose to hold on to the rescue line of God's promises. He has promised to be with us always (Matthew 28:20). His Word proclaims that nothing can separate us from His love (Romans 8:38–39). Our God blesses us with peace that passes understanding (Philippians 4:6–7).

Cling to promises like these, knowing there's no place God's love can't reach!

I believe in the promises You make, God. Help my unbelief when I'm stuck in an emotional or a spiritual pit. Amen.

Day of Trouble

May the LORD *answer you in the day of trouble! May the name of the God of Jacob set you securely on high!*

—Psalm 20:1 NASB

Unemployment, wars, terrorism, natural disasters, leaders' poor decisions—times are hard. But as our older relatives will tell us, hard times are nothing new. Flip through old family photo albums or history books, and see how difficult life was. Against the background of diseases, droughts, and financial depression, we see men and women of deep and abiding faith.

Turn in the Bible to the book of Psalms. There we hear the cries of God's people in times of trouble. We also hear echoes of our own frustration, our own fears, and our pleas for help from the only One who understands, the One who can best respond.

When the troubles of this world crash in around you, flip through the pages of that photo album to gain some perspective. Then open the Psalms and find words of encouragement and peace for your weary soul. God is faithful, He understands, and He hears your prayers.

God, thank You for believers in ages past who struggled in times of trouble yet held fast to their faith. Help me to be able to hold fast to my faith. Amen.

Better Than an Umbrella

Let all who take refuge in you be glad; let them ever sing for joy. Spread your protection over them, that those who love your name may rejoice in you.

—Psalm 5:11 NIV

Umbrellas used to be so simple. Have you noticed how sophisticated the lowly umbrella has become? No longer is the goal to simply shield you from the rain. Umbrellas have to be easy to open and close, so buttons automatically extend and retract, sometimes to a compact six or eight inches. Umbrellas are made of space-tested fabrics that dry quickly, and the steel parts are made to last even when gale-force winds come from every direction.

The temptations that Satan sends your way—his fiery darts—come with their own gale-force power, but you are protected by more than a sophisticated umbrella. Your almighty God protects you from head to toe, outside and in, with His shield and His peace. In times of trouble, you can count on God, rejoicing that Satan's arrows cannot reach your heart. In almighty God, you have complete protection.

Lord, I am grateful that You provide for me thorough and unyielding protection, for Your shield is better than the best umbrella. Amen.

Bodyguard

The LORD defends those who suffer; he defends them in times of trouble.

—Psalm 9:9 NCV

Most of us don't move through our days with a professional bodyguard working to protect us. These bodyguards are specially trained to protect a person—usually a wealthy or politically important person—from danger. A bodyguard can also double as a driver, serve as a close-protection officer, or be part of a unit that provides security clearance. Bodyguards carry weapons and use shields to ensure the safety of those they've sworn to protect.

God is an unseen Bodyguard for His people, for you and for me. If you suffer or are in trouble, your Bodyguard cares greatly, and He will protect you. When He sees that you need to be carried, He will carry you securely you in the palm of His hand. Your Bodyguard has provided the shield of His Word. Never hesitate to pick it up, for it can protect you from all dangers. Knowing that your Bodyguard is always with you and always on duty gives you peace.

Almighty God, I take great comfort in knowing that You are my Bodyguard and that You are ready to protect me whenever I need it. Amen.

House of Refuge

Trust in Him at all times, you people; pour out your heart before Him; God is a refuge for us.

—Psalm 62:8 NKJV

In 1876, the U.S. Lifesaving Service constructed ten houses of refuge, or lifesaving stations, along Florida's Atlantic Coast. The keepers and their families who staffed these houses found, rescued, and ministered to those who fell victim to Florida's treacherous reefs.

Prior to the construction of these houses, many shipwreck victims who managed to make it to shore would die of starvation and thirst. So the keeper and his family walked the sandy beaches looking for anyone who might have washed ashore. They carried bread and water, along with first aid supplies, in hopes they could save a life.

God is our house of refuge. God is the Keeper who searches day and night for those who are in trouble. When we find ourselves battered and beaten by the storms, washed up on shore, He will minister to our needs. We can count on Him.

God, when I'm battered and beaten, help me lift my eyes to You, my Rescuer, and find my place of refuge. Amen.

Peace and Quiet

[God's house is] the only quiet, secure place in a noisy world, the perfect getaway, far from the buzz of traffic.

—Psalm 27:5 MSG

How do you find rest in this crazy, noisy, and rushed world? Do you escape with a book, go for a run, or watch TV? Do you have a place where you go to revive your spirit, such as a garden, the beach, or a walking trail?

Trying to find rest isn't just a modern-day challenge. The author of many psalms, King David lived about a thousand years before Christ. Surely he, a king, could find a quiet place to get away and rest. Yet David struggled just as you and I do to find peace and quiet. Some of the noises and troubles of David's world were different from ours, but his shelter from them was the same as ours. David found shelter in God, in whom he could find peace.

If your noisy life has you longing for some peace and quiet, get away with God and step into the shelter of God's Word. There you will find rest and peace for your soul.

I am grateful, God, that I can escape this noisy world—that I can call to You in prayer, step into the shelter of Your Word, and find quiet, hope, and peace. Amen.

The Eternal One

Trust in the Eternal One forever, for He is like a great Rock—strong, stable, trustworthy, and lasting.

—Isaiah 26:4 VOICE

From Plymouth Rock to the Blarney Stone, certain rocks have been transformed from ordinary to famous, even to tourist attractions. People visit Haystack Rock, a natural formation caused by the erosion of ancient lava flows along the Oregon Coast. Virginia's Natural Bridge in Shenandoah Valley is one of the most famous natural rock formations, towering 215 feet high and spanning ninety feet across. Perhaps the most visited rocks are El Capitan and Half Dome in Yosemite National Park.

Yet another Rock is far more notable, more ancient, more significant, and more visited than all the others. This Great Rock is strong, stable, trustworthy, and everlasting. When trouble comes your way, you can trust this Rock to shelter you, anchor you, and stabilize you. In this great Rock—the eternal One—you can trust and find peace.

To remind you of this truth, place a rock or stone on your desk. May it trigger prayers of gratitude and moments of peace: almighty God is your Rock.

The next time I contemplate an amazing rock formation, may it remind me that You, eternal One, are the Rock in whom I can trust and find true peace. Amen.

Our Refuge

God is our refuge and strength, a very present help in trouble.

—Psalm 46:1 NKJV

If you travel in the wilder sections of our country, sooner or later you are likely to see a sign with a flying goose noting land that is part of the 150 million acres of the National Wildlife Refuge System.

In 1868, President Ulysses S. Grant acted to protect the Pribilof Islands in Alaska as a reserve for the northern fur seal. Today the Refuge System has designated sites all across the nation. These lands and waters are devoted to conserving wildlife and providing them a place of refuge so we are able to enjoy nature as God created it.

In the same way that the northern fur seal and other animals have been able to thrive under the protection of the National Wildlife Refuge System, we can thrive in this sin-wracked, fallen world by letting God be our refuge. The death and resurrection of Jesus opened that possibility to us. When we accept Jesus as our Savior and Lord, we become eligible to live in the refuge of the Almighty. We find in Him not only this safe, peaceful refuge from a polluted and sin-soaked world, but also strength and help for whatever trouble we face.

Thank You for offering me a place of refuge and peace, Lord. I know that privilege cost You greatly. I am humble and grateful. Amen.

You Called?

When I am in distress, I call to you, because you answer me.

—Psalm 86:7 NIV

Do you know people who are hard to reach? They never seem to have their cell phone with them, or if they do, it isn't turned on. Or if it is turned on, their voicemail is full. Other people don't return messages or rarely check their e-mail. What are we supposed to do? Drive to their house and knock on the front door?

Unlike these people, God isn't hard to reach. Our heavenly Father always has His ear tuned to our ringtone. He always answers His phone; He never screens His calls. He is always available: you can instant-message Him, and He will respond immediately. In a crisis, you can call on God and be confident that He will always answer. And when He does answer, you can be sure that His voice will offer you calming peace.

But you don't have to wait for distress to strike. He always enjoys hearing from you, so give Him a call.

Heavenly Father, thank You that when I call on You, You will answer, and Your peace will be among Your gifts to me. Amen.

Indestructible Shield

As for God, His way is blameless; the word of the Lord is tried; He is a shield to all who take refuge in Him.

—Psalm 18:30 NASB

In 1941, a superhero in the comic book world joined the military's fight against tyranny in World War II. The patriotic solider, named Captain Steven Rogers, received super-soldier serum that made him America's most effective special operative, Captain America. In the pages of Marvel Comics, Captain America wore a costume with an American flag motif, and—far more importantly—he was armed with a nearly indestructible shield that could not only be used to defend himself, but also to throw as a weapon.

We all want a Captain America on our side. We who know Jesus as Savior and Lord, however, have Someone even stronger, Someone even more reliable, Someone who offers greater protection on our side. Our almighty God has fought the tyranny of sin and death, and His victory was decisive for eternity. He is a holy God of justice. His ways are blameless, and His presence brings peace. The Lord has given us His Word as our greatest weapon, and He is our indestructible shield.

I praise You, Lord, for Your victory over sin and death and for Your empowerment and protection. I am glad You're on my side. Amen.

Lost in the Maze

"Don't get lost in despair; believe in God, and keep on believing in Me."

—John 14:1 VOICE

Have you ever had fun walking through a corn maze? In the fall, these mazes are popular attractions at pumpkin patches and family farms.

Corn mazes come in a variety of designs. Some are created to tell stories, while others are designed around a particular theme. Some lead explorers to the middle, and other mazes don't end the story until they guide the explorers out again.

Getting lost—in a corn maze or life—can bring on panic. Most corn mazes have spotters who go around looking for explorers who need help and then showing them the way out. Jesus does the same thing for us when we get caught in the maze of life, feeling lost in despair, hopeless, and alone. As Jesus said, believing in God is the way to get unlost. Choosing faith, whatever the circumstances, moves us along the path toward hope, and Jesus is our Companion along that path. Whether we cry out or, like a spotter, Jesus finds us, we can take His hand and keep on going.

Lord, when despair has me feeling lost, unable to find my way out, help me reach for Your hand and let You lead me. Amen.

When a Bucket's Not Enough

"I leave you peace; my peace I give you. I do not give it to you as the world does. So don't let your hearts be troubled or afraid."

—John 14:27 NCV

Imagine being in the middle of a lake. The boat you're sitting in has sprung a leak. The lake is deep, the shore is distant, and your boat is filling fast. You know what it feels like to be "troubled or afraid"!

What you need is a bucket to bail the water out—or do you? A bucket will only do so much. Sooner or later the water will come in faster than you can bail it out. You realize that if you want to stay afloat, you need to fix the hole in your boat.

When life is difficult, much is out of our control, and we feel ourselves sinking, we need to recognize that we aren't able to bail ourselves out. We won't find peace, much less our way back to shore, on our own. We need to fix the problem at its source—and only Jesus can do that. The peace as well as the guidance and help He offers will keep us afloat.

So the next time you reach for a bucket, consider reaching out for Jesus instead.

Lord, thank You that You give me not only the strength I need for the challenge, but also guidance, help, and peace when I'm sinking. Amen.

Our Trustworthy God

God's my strong champion; I flick off my enemies like flies. Far better to take refuge in God than trust in people.

—Psalm 118:7–8 MSG

The hurts can start in childhood: a parent doesn't come through on a promise. "I love you" isn't ever spoken in your home. Alcohol or abuse teach painful lessons about your lack of worth. Too early we learn what it means to be hurt by another, and too often that lesson is reinforced. Of course we try to protect our hearts, but then it happens again. Someone we trusted, someone we loved, someone we thought was a friend turns on us. The deep, throbbing pain makes us wonder if we will ever be able to trust anyone.

You can trust your heavenly Father. He has proven Himself fully trustworthy. He keeps every promise, He sent Jesus to die on the cross to show you His love and your worth, and He is always kind and compassionate. No matter how well intentioned, people will let us down and hurt us. God is different.

Join the psalmist's praise that God is your Champion; He is your Refuge; and you *can* trust Him. When you embrace that truth, you find comfort and peace.

Lord, though I've been deeply wounded by people I thought I could trust, help me learn that I can absolutely trust You. Amen.

Creator and Restorer

The God of all grace, who called you to his eternal glory in Christ, after you have suffered a little while, will himself restore you and make you strong, firm and steadfast.

—1 Peter 5:10 NIV

Restoration is big business today. We restore houses, cars, and photographs, to name a few. In order to restore something, though, we first need to know its original condition. Then, with that image in mind and patient precision, we can begin to repair what has been damaged.

Our gracious God is in this restoration business full-time. Warmly and without hesitation, He receives every one of us who looks to Him. Understanding our damaged state, He begins a careful and often painstaking process to return us to our former glory. He makes us once again "strong, firm and steadfast."

If you've been broken by life experiences—and all of us have been to one degree or another—know that God is in the process of restoring and redeeming you. That process probably won't be free of pain, but take comfort in the fact that God is the expert Craftsman who knows what He's doing. Your Creator is also your Restorer. You couldn't be in better hands.

Lord, I am damaged and need the restoration only You can provide. Thank You for restoring me for my good and Your glory. Amen.

In His Shadow

He who dwells in the shelter of the Most High will abide in the shadow of the Almighty. I will say to the LORD, "My refuge and my fortress, my God, in whom I trust!"

—Psalm 91:1–2 NASB

When we were children, it was fun to chase shadows. Late in the day we would try to find just the right place to stand so our shadows would grow. We played with a friend so our shadows could dance. When weather forced us inside, we performed shadow plays on the walls, and at night we used flashlights to make hand shadows in the dark. Shadows offered us hours of carefree fun.

In our life as Christians, we appreciate God's shadow for even greater reasons. First, His call to us to abide in His shadow communicates that He wants us near. And He wants us near because He loves us and He wants to take care of us. When we live in His shadow, we find ourselves sheltered under His wing, feeling carefree and at peace.

God, thank You for the shadow of Your wing where I can know Your love, care, and peace. Amen.

Cast Your Cares

Cast your burden on the Lord, and He shall sustain you; He shall never permit the righteous to be moved.

—Psalm 55:22 NKJV

So how many egg tosses have you participated in this summer? If you're not familiar with this contest, it involves two partners tossing a raw egg back and forth. With every successful (the egg did not break) catch, the teammates take another step away from each other. The farther away you get, the harder you have to throw the egg—but you still have to catch it gently. The competition doesn't end well for the egg!

And what does an egg toss have to do with Psalm 55:22? It's an example of the opposite kind of mind-set we should have when we cast our cares on the Lord. In other words, there should be nothing at all gentle about our getting rid of our cares. We are to fling, toss, and hurl with all our strength those worldly things, current concerns, and possible events that distract us from God, from serving Him and praying to Him. We are to fling, toss, and hurl all our anxiety about what to eat and drink. We are to instead trust our heavenly Father to care for us.

Lord, help me to give You everything that weighs me down mentally, emotionally, and spiritually. I want to leave these concerns in Your capable hands. Amen.

A Twig at a Time

When people are tempted and still continue strong, they should be happy. After they have proved their faith, God will reward them with life forever. God promised this to all those who love him.

—James 1:12 NCV

What a picture of perseverance God gave me in a mama mockingbird! It was nest-building time for her, and from morning until night, I watched her work—and it was work! She had to build her nest one twig at a time. She persevered. Yes, the work was tedious and the progress, slow. But she had a higher calling than living an easy life. She had a bigger goal than dodging hard work. This mama mockingbird knew her baby was coming, so she persevered.

Perseverance is not something we tend to readily volunteer for. It means gritting our teeth and pushing ourselves to trudge through tough circumstances, choosing to trust the Lord's faithfulness when nothing around us encourages such faith. But God wants us to persevere just like that mama bird did. Being tested under tough circumstances produces in us a steadfastness of faith in God that will strengthen our trust and give us a deep sense of peace. And the next opportunity to persevere just may be a bit easier.

God, I'm glad that I can call out to You for strength to persevere and that You bless me with peace and hope as well. Amen.

The Great Escape

Any temptation you face will be nothing new. But God is faithful, and He will not let you be tempted beyond what you can handle. But He always provides a way of escape so that you will be able to endure and keep moving forward.

—1 Corinthians 10:13 VOICE

March 24, 1944, was a moonless night. It was eerily dark; eerily still . . . above the ground. Underneath the German prison camp Stalag Luft III, seventy-six Allied prisoners were crawling through a deep tunnel that more than two hundred fellow prisoners had dug. This breakout from the reputedly most secure German facility came to be known as the Great Escape.

As daring as this attempt to gain freedom was, God's plan to give us freedom is even more amazing. His plan has been in the works for millennia, and He gives us the tools of escape—God's Word and His presence. With these tools we can endure life's challenges to our faith and escape the prison of sin and doubt Satan keeps us locked in. We can keep moving forward toward a life of freedom in Christ, hope for the eternal future, and peace with God and within our restless hearts.

God, I am grateful for Your escape plan that frees me to know peace with You. Help me continue to use the tools You provided—Your presence and Your Word—to glorify You with my life. Amen.

Holy Correction

No discipline seems pleasant at the time, but painful. Later on, however, it produces a harvest of righteousness and peace for those who have been trained by it.

—Hebrews 12:11 NIV

Discipline in the sense of punishment is often painful, embarrassing, and humbling. A loving parent disciplines a child in order to train that child in character, obedience, and godly living. The child is not always happy about the parent's rules or the consequences of breaking those rules, and the parent is even less happy about needing to follow through on those consequences. But most parents know—as God our Father does—that discipline is necessary: it produces maturity.

When God disciplines us, He does so because He loves us enough to want to train us in holy living. The fact that He needs to correct, rebuke, chasten, and let us suffer consequences is probably not the favorite part of His job, but He knows He must if we are to be fit for His purposes in this world and the next.

Let us thank God today for His discipline that "produces a harvest of righteousness and peace" and holiness for our good and His glory.

I don't like to be disciplined, but I know that when You correct me, Father God, it is because I need it. I know that You are using it to grow me in holiness. Amen.

Hide-and-Seek

I love you, God . . . My God—the high crag where I run for dear life, hiding behind the boulders, safe in the granite hideout.

—Psalm 18:1–2 MSG

Do you remember playing hide-and-seek on warm summer nights? The best time to play was at dusk because you could still see well enough to find the right hiding place, but the growing darkness made it difficult to be found.

When David ran from Saul, he hid in the caves and steep cliffs near the Dead Sea. If you visit this place today as the sun is setting, you can see how easily David could have used the shadows of the waning sun to find just the right cave in which to hide. We read in the book of Psalms, however, that David eventually learned that his real hiding place was in God.

When trouble seems to chase you just as Saul pursued David and you are running for your life, climb the mountain of God and find refuge behind the boulders. There in His presence, evil cannot stand. There in His presence, you will be safe. There in His presence, you can know peace.

God, thank You that I can run to Your mountain, hide in Your caves, and find in Your presence safety and peace. Amen.

A Trust Fall

The LORD is good, a stronghold in the day of trouble; and He knows those who trust in Him.

—Nahum 1:7 NKJV

Corporate team-building experiences have become popular. The thinking is that a staff will be more effective and productive if the employees view themselves as interdependent members of a team instead of as individual workers. That's why many exercises done at conferences and retreats are designed to develop trust among employees. One exercise is a trust fall: a person is to fall backward, trusting that his teammates will catch him.

Such *interdependence* has always been part of the Lord's thinking. In the New Testament the church is described as a human body. No matter how hard we try, we are never truly acting independently. Yet at the same time we need to be deliberate about acting interdependently, especially when a fellow believer is in trouble. We are to come alongside with practical help as well as prayer. Being at our brothers' or sisters' sides can strengthen their faith. We help them do a trust fall into God's arms. Our strong and good God will always catch us.

God, interdependence grounded in dependence on You means a life of trust, hope, and peace. Thank You for calling me to be part of Your body. Amen.

Take Heart!

"I have told you these things, so that in me you may have peace. In this world you will have trouble. But take heart! I have overcome the world."

—John 16:33 NIV

The anthem of the Civil Rights Movement of the 1960s was "We Shall Overcome," probably derived from the hymn "I'll Overcome Someday" by the Rev. Dr. Charles Tindley of the Methodist Episcopal Church. The title, words, and tune differ today, but Tindley's hymn—published in 1901—captures the spirit of the 1960s: "This world is one great battlefield, with forces all arrayed. If in my heart I do not yield, I'll overcome some day."

The slaves who sang songs like this certainly knew the trouble Jesus promised His followers. These slaves knew the world's battle between justice and injustice, freedom and captivity. They also knew personally that Jesus was their only hope for enduring and overcoming the atrocities they suffered. Any peace they knew, they found in Jesus. Their hope for eternal freedom and joy with Him sustained them.

You, too, can find peace in Jesus. Look to Him, confident that He who has indeed overcome the world will come again to reign as King of kings.

Almighty God, troubles can seem overwhelming, but help me find peace because You have overcome the world. Amen.

Real Comfort

He consoles us as we endure the pain and hardship of life so that we may draw from His comfort and share it with others in their own struggles.

—2 Corinthians 1:4 VOICE

Platitudes like "There must be a reason" or "God doesn't give us more than we can handle" are the last thing we need or want to hear when something terrible happens. Yet, sadly, that is often what we get even from well-intentioned people who love Jesus and love us. When our hearts are breaking, we want to be with people who have known pain and asked hard questions. Even if our experiences aren't exactly the same, someone who has suffered loss brings comfort like no one else can, even if the person simply sits with us and doesn't say a word.

God doesn't offer platitudes. He has experienced every kind of pain that we've experienced, and He understands our sufferings because He watched His own Son die on the cross. God's comfort is real because He suffered the loss of a child, He knows betrayal, and His heart has been broken.

Just as God comforts you in your brokenness, He can use you as a source of real comfort for others.

Redeem my pain, Lord, by using me to bring comfort and peace to those who hurt. Help me to know when words aren't necessary, when being present is enough. Amen.

Good Medicine

[The Lord's] anger is but for a moment, His favor is for a lifetime; weeping may last for the night, but a shout of joy comes in the morning.

—Psalm 30:5 NASB

The novelty of winter snow wears off faster for some of us than others, and we are the ones who complain about the long, dark days and the icy cold weather. Millions of people suffer to varying degrees from seasonal affective disorder, with symptoms such as loss of appetite, sleep deprivation, daytime fatigue, and depression. The hopeful news for those suffering from this disorder is that bright spring sunshine always follows dull winter days, and that warm sunshine is indeed good medicine.

The picture of winter giving way to spring is enriched when we think of wintry darkness being the absence of God's favor. When we experience trials and struggles, it feels as though God has turned His back on us, but feelings can lie. God is always present with us, even in the darkest winters of our lives. However suffocating the darkness, we can and must hold on to the promise of joy coming in the morning. The glorious light of God's love will break through the darkness.

When the darkness seems endless and You seem far away, help me hold to the beliefs that, in Your timing, You will cause the darkness to flee and that You are near me. Amen.

Sour Grapes

The LORD has mercy on those who respect him, as a father has mercy on his children.

—Psalm 103:13 NCV

M*erriam-Webster* defines *sour grapes* like this: "unfair criticism that comes from someone who is disappointed about not getting something; disparagement of something that has proven unattainable." I'm pretty confident every human who has walked this earth knows sour grapes. When we want something we don't get, we find a degree of comfort in criticizing that something or trying to convince ourselves that, after all, we didn't really want the something we can't have.

How often do you munch on sour grapes? You may feel that life is unfair or that God blesses others more than He blesses you. God not only forgives such sour-grapes attitudes; He also helps us remember that there is more to the story than we can see. That truth brightens our spirit and our attitude. Life is more peaceful when we don't snack on sour grapes.

God, forgive my me-focused sour grapes. Who am I to question Your ways or suggest that You are being unfair? I am grateful for Your great mercy. Amen.

The Quicksand of Despair

He also brought me up out of a horrible pit, out of the miry clay, and set my feet upon a rock, and established my steps.

—Psalm 40:2 NKJV

You've undoubtedly seen it at least once. A movie's protagonist—or maybe his girlfriend—falls into quicksand, which sucks its hapless victims down into a bottomless pit. In reality, quicksand is just sand that has absorbed so much water that there's not much friction between the grains. This mushy mixture can't support a lot of weight. So here's your survival tip: you'll sink faster in quicksand if you struggle; you'll float if you relax because the human body is less dense than quicksand.

Rather than quicksand, the psalmist had been stuck in "miry clay," and maybe your despair seems like miry clay or quicksand. You feel stuck. How quickly you cry out to God for help getting unstuck depends on many factors (your pride, experience with quicksand, knowledge of the Lord, etc.). When you do cry out and God responds, He will lift you out of the sticky mud or slippery quicksand and set your feet upon a solid rock.

The quicksand of despair is not forever; Jesus, our Rock, is.

God, thank You for lifting me out of quicksand and setting my feet on firm ground, giving me peace. Amen.

The Most Important Roster

So, what do you think? With God on our side like this, how can we lose?

—Romans 8:31 MSG

What has your experience in the world of sports been? Maybe you got a taste of Little League or softball and have yet to put your glove down. When you were on a team, maybe you liked the camaraderie and sense of belonging, but there were pressure-filled moments that you don't miss at all. And if one of those pressure-filled moments didn't go your way, you remember it all too well.

Pressure comes for various reasons. We want to glorify God with our skills. We don't want to let the team down. We want Dad to be proud. We don't want to be embarrassed. And—bottom line—we want to win!

If you have named Jesus your Savior and Lord, you can be sure that you are already on the winning team for life—and for eternal life. Also, whether you have two left feet or you can dunk better than anyone on the court, your place on the roster is assured. So when you're on the court, relax! Give your best effort to honor the Lord, but enjoy playing the game.

Jesus, thank You for Your victory on the cross, guaranteeing me the joy of being in heaven with You. Amen.

The Eyes of God

"Are not two sparrows sold for a penny? Yet not one of them will fall to the ground outside your Father's care."

—Matthew 10:29 NIV

As a child, no fear was too big to handle as long as you had your beloved stuffed toy with you. As you grew older, its fur rubbed off, and the stuffing was not so fluffy anymore. One of its two beaded eyes hung by a thread, but you didn't care. You loved that stuffed toy and set it in a place of honor on a shelf. Its presence was somehow heartwarming and reassuring.

Adulthood brings different fears, but we still have One with us to help us feel safe and secure. Our all-powerful, everywhere-present, and always-loving God watches over us night and day.

When life starts getting a little dark and scary, know that God's eyes are on you. Be sure to turn your eyes toward His. Be reminded and encouraged: He has all that you need.

Thank You, God, for providing me safety and peace and for always welcoming me to You when I'm nervous or afraid. Amen.

Unburdened

"Come to me, all of you who are tired and have heavy loads, and I will give you rest."

—Matthew 11:28 NCV

Isn't it ironic that all our time-saving devices and technologies have made us more tired, not less? Statistics indicate that we are working longer hours than previous generations and that stress is the leading cause of health problems. Many of us do okay eating right and exercising, but how are we doing with sleep?

God created the human body to need a certain amount of rest. In addition to getting adequate sleep, we are to rest from our work, take a break from the sources of our stress, and put down those heavy burdens. Jesus' words in today's verse allude to the rest a pack animal gets when its load is removed for the night: it sleeps soundly. Then, in the morning when the burden is again strapped to its back, that donkey or camel can carry on.

After we get a good night's sleep or take a vacation, the burden seems lighter when we next pick it up, and because of the rest and refreshment we experienced, we are able to carry on. Jesus is there to take our heavy loads and to give us rest. Let Him.

Lord, teach me to get the rest I need, and help me hear Your voice when You call me, wanting to take my heavy load and give me rest. Amen.

A Bucket List

"So do not worry about tomorrow. Let tomorrow worry about itself. Living faithfully is a large enough task for today."

—Matthew 6:34 VOICE

A bucket list is a list of things we want to do before we die, before—as the saying goes—we kick the bucket. Websites and mobile apps help people make their lists. Some people hope their bucket list items will help them find meaning and purpose. Others discover that their list helps them to focus right now on what is important and to let the less important items go. Still others find the whole idea of trying to do certain things before they die rather morbid.

Even the phrase *before they die* is something of a wake-up call. None of us knows when that day will come. None of us knows when a today is our last. We Christians know the comforting truth that dying in this world is actually going home to our heavenly Father. Still, when we do, we will be asked to account for our life.

Living in a way that honors our gracious God is not something we should ever put off until tomorrow. If you should kick the bucket tomorrow, will you be able to say that you lived faithfully today?

God, since no one is promised tomorrow, enable me to live each today being faithful to You. Amen.

Stick to It

We give thanks to God . . . remembering without ceasing your work of faith, labor of love, and patience of hope in our Lord Jesus Christ in the sight of our God and Father.

—1 Thessalonians 1:2–3 NKJV

We get misty-eyed at the wedding; the bridegroom and bride are so much in love. We also get misty-eyed when we see a couple walking hand in hand, very much in love after fifty-plus years. The newlyweds' rings are shiny; the other couple's have the warmth of age. They also have something more precious: years of stories to tell about God's great faithfulness to them in all seasons of their marriage.

God is glorified when a husband and wife prove faithful to their marriage vows. The phrase *work of faith* describes someone who lingers or stays. The love of *labor of love* is a love that stays and works through tough times. And *patience of hope* is endurance inspired by hope and expectation rooted in love for Jesus. God will bless those who choose to linger in their marriages, to be true to the vow they made to Him and to each other. And God has great rewards for those who choose faith through thick and thin.

Lord, the longer I live, the more of Your grace I receive, the more often I see Your hand in my life, and the sweeter the lingering with You is. Amen.

Glory Be!

I consider that the sufferings of this present time are not worthy to be compared with the glory that is to be revealed to us.

—Romans 8:18 NASB

"Glory be!" was once a common phrase spoken by the faithful. When learning of a friend's cancer diagnosis, discovering buds on a rosebush thought dead, or confronted with one's own shortcomings, the reply might have been "Glory be!" Often those words expressed surprise, wonder, and joy, yet they also pointed to the eternal glory to come. That future puts events in our lives, whether good or bad, into the perspective of eternity.

We don't hear "Glory be!" today, but it wouldn't be bad to revive it. All of us would benefit from its simple reminder that the depth of the pain we or our loved ones suffer cannot compare to the indescribable glory of King Jesus' return. "Glory be!" indeed.

So the next time you receive bad news, something surprises you, or you see God work in ways far greater than you would have imagined, respond in your heart and mind with "Glory be!" May that phrase fill you with peace as it reminds you of our glorious heavenly future.

Lord, today's sufferings are nothing compared to the glory You've promised. What a lifeline to hold on to! Amen.

A Refiner's Fire

Pure gold put in the fire comes out of it proved pure; genuine faith put through this suffering comes out proved genuine.

—1 Peter 1:6–7 MSG

Picture a craftsman sitting next to a fire so hot that the gold he works with is molten or liquid. The temperature of those flames approach 2000 degrees Fahrenheit, yet there sits the refiner, stirring the gold and skimming off impurities as they rise to the top. The refiner's efforts to get the purest gold possible mean sitting at that fire—an extremely hot and therefore risky and uncomfortable task.

Just like this craftsman, God wants any good in us, His children, to be separated from the impure and the unholy. The impurities that bubble up from within us makes us unsuitable for His purposes. In order to be fully used by Him, we need refining, transforming, and purifying. The suffering in this life works like the craftsman's flames: it brings impurities and sin to the top to be skimmed away. And like that craftsman, our God is never far away from us even as the fire rages. Only as we are refined will we be able to best reflect His love and peace in this dark and hurting world.

Lord, enable me to submit to Your refining process so You can remove my impurities and use me for Your good work on this earth. Amen.

Character Counts

We also glory in tribulations, knowing that tribulation produces perseverance; and perseverance, character; and character, hope.

—Romans 5:3–4 NKJV

Some things—maybe most things—are learned by doing. We begin by reading how to multiply fractions or by watching someone swim. But the point comes when we have to do the fractions worksheet or jump in the pool. Reading and watching take us only so far in our academic pursuits, athletic interests, or character development. Reading about patience doesn't teach us to be patient the way dealing with a certain coworker does. Nor does reading a self-help book on loving transform our hearts and enable us to love selflessly.

The Word of God explains why: character develops as we persevere in tough times. Perseverance can't be learned by reading about it or watching someone else persevere. We learn to persevere . . . by persevering. And we aren't persevering when life is easy; we persevere in the rough patches of life. So instead of protecting ourselves from difficult times, we need to acknowledge the hardship and pain but also accept the bumpy stretch as a time for us to learn perseverance and develop character.

Lord, tribulation isn't the path I'd naturally choose, but help me to embrace it because I know You are building my character and making me more like Jesus. Amen.

Happy Endings

The eternal God is your refuge, and underneath are the everlasting arms. He will drive out your enemies before you, saying, "Destroy them!"

—Deuteronomy 33:27 NIV

It was a regular summer-evening occurrence: the good guys in the neighborhood chased the bad guys in the neighborhood during a spirited game of cops and robbers. Sometimes we wore black hats and white hats, sometimes we donned bandannas, and other times we dressed in full costume. In our reenactments, which always ended when the streetlights came on, the bad guys were always caught and the good guys always won. We liked happy endings when justice prevailed.

Life is not so neat and simple. The bad guys don't always wear black, and the good guys don't always win. Yet the Bible enables us to have absolute confidence in the fact that the good guys win in the end, ultimately and for eternity. Even in the Old Testament we read that God's voice will cry out, "Destroy them!" and the bad guys will quake. The sinless Jesus Christ, the King of kings and Lord of lords, will prove victorious. Goodness and justice will reign forever!

What peace comes with knowing that history will have a happy ending! Jesus, may Your righteous kingdom come—and come soon! Amen.

The Fire Boss

I will stand on my guard post and station myself on the rampart; and I will keep watch to see what He will speak to me.

—Habakkuk 2:1 NASB

Do you know what the fire boss's very important job was at the coal mines? He was the first man to enter the mine to check the gas levels. He did this by watching the flame in the lantern he carried. If the flame changed in color or started to burn brighter, the fire boss knew the mine needed more ventilation. Throughout the day the fire boss continued his job, testing the air and keeping watch. He was well aware that the well-being—the very lives—of hundreds of miners depended upon him.

In a sense, the prophet Habakkuk was a fire boss for the people of Israel. He stood watch, holding a lantern in his hand to help light the people's way and listening for a whisper from God.

In our day, we might be something of a fire boss too. As we walk in God's light, we notice both the church's waning fire for God and the world's decreasing interest in Him. May we remember that both the well-being and the lives eternal of lost mankind depend on the strength of our light, our love, and our peace as God's people.

I want to stand guard, Lord, listening for Your voice and being willing to speak Your truth to a darkened culture whose well-being is at stake. Amen.

A Song of Deliverance

You are my hiding place; you will protect me from trouble and surround me with songs of deliverance.

—Psalm 32:7 NIV

Getting a song stuck in our heads is a curious phenomenon. It doesn't bother us when a song from the worship service sticks, but it's annoying when a radio jingle plays on an endless loop in our minds. Sometimes we have to choose a different song and focus on that until the other is silenced. But there's nothing better to have at the forefront of our minds than one of God's songs of deliverance.

As we read in today's verse, when trouble threatens, God protects us and surrounds us with His songs. These aren't songs randomly pulled from God's playlist. He chooses them strategically and specifically for you. These are songs of deliverance, songs that will encourage you and offer a degree of spiritual and emotional protection from trouble. Strength comes as God's songs remind you of His great power, faithfulness, love, and presence with you. Strength comes as you respond to His invitation to find your life's rhythm in His chords, peace in His lyrics, and hope in His songs of deliverance.

God, give me ears to hear Your songs of deliverance so that I might find my life's rhythm in You and know Your peace. Amen.

My Deliverer

I sought the LORD, and He heard me, and delivered me from all my fears.

—Psalm 34:4 NKJV

If you've ever lost power in the middle of the night, you know how unnerving it can be. You stumble and fumble around in the dark, reaching for your cell phone that isn't where it's supposed to be. You make your way down the hall to try to find a flashlight, stubbing your toe on just a few stray toys and bumping your head on the doorframe. It only takes one such experience to encourage to keep a light source within easy reach in the dark.

When troubles thrust us into the darkness of despair, we can stumble and fumble around looking for a source of light, a source of comfort or direction or peace. We can stub our toes and bump our heads on many of the options the world offers before we reach for the only Light that can deliver us from our dark despair. Only the Lord hears our cries when the power goes out.

The next time you find yourself in thick darkness, reach first for the only Light that's always close at hand. Only He—only Jesus Christ—can deliver you.

Lord, thank You for being my Deliverer. You hear my cry in the darkest of nights and then shatter that darkness with Your Light. Amen.

Hush, Little Baby

When the upright need help and cry to the Eternal, He hears their cries and rescues them from all of their troubles.

—Psalm 34:17 VOICE

Talk with any new mom, and one of her questions will be how to discern what her newborn needs when he cries. Is he hungry? Is he tired? Does he need a diaper change? After the mom meets all these needs, her baby may still be wailing. She may walk or rock or hum or sing or drive him around in the car. She may call Mom or girlfriends for tips and—ideally—solutions.

Sometimes when trouble comes our way, we can be like that baby—still wailing after friends and family have done everything possible to comfort and console us. The home-cooked meal, the wonderful nap, the willing listener—all these help, but sometimes the tears still don't stop. Then we eventually cry out to the only One who has all the answers. Our heavenly Father hears our cries and gently takes us in His arms. He quiets our spirits, comforts us as the tears slow to a stop, and gives us peace.

When my tears won't stop, Lord, I ask You to make Your presence with me very real so that I may know Your peace. Amen.

A Really Good Thing

"The mountains may disappear, and the hills may come to an end, but my love will never disappear; my promise of peace will not come to an end," says the LORD who shows mercy to you.

—Isaiah 54:10 NCV

"All good things must come to an end," as the saying goes. Beautiful sunrises do turn into day, and gorgeous sunsets into night. Youth ages and wisdom fades. You can't hold on to that perfect moment or that feeling you never want to lose. Try as you might, you can't make time stand still. Yes, good things must come to an end, but not all good things.

God's love for you—and that is a very, very good thing—will never fade; it will never disappear. As Isaiah so boldly proclaimed, although the mountains surrounding you may crumble into dust and the earth beneath you may quake, you can count on God's promises to be solid and unshakable. Among the Lord's promises are His love that will never disappear and His peace that will not come to an end.

So perhaps the saying could be amended: "All good things must come to an end—except those really good things that come from God."

God, the next time I'm saddened by the thought that all good things must come to an end, help me remember that the best things—Your love and Your peace—will never end. Amen.

Victory Assured!

"You need not fight in this battle; station yourselves, stand and see the salvation of the LORD on your behalf, O Judah and Jerusalem." Do not fear or be dismayed; tomorrow go out to face them, for the LORD is with you.

—2 Chronicles 20:17 NASB

No one goes into battle without a plan, and war buffs often describe when and where an army used a particular maneuver and how successful it was . . . or wasn't.

God's strategy for defeating Satan included a few key elements: a baby in Bethlehem, a toddler fleeing to Egypt, a carpenter-turned-itinerant-minister-teacher-and-healer, a denial, a betrayal, and a death on a criminal's cross.

So, when you are battle-weary and feel as though you can't go on, look to Calvary, where the decisive battle against darkness, sin, and evil was won. Keep in mind Jesus' act of surrender to God and love for you when you face life's troubles. Allow God's peace to wash over you because—as the empty tomb and the book of Revelation testify—this battle against Satan is already won.

Finally, the charge in 2 Chronicles 20:17 is a charge to you: "Do not fear or be dismayed. . . . for the LORD is with you" (NASB).

Lord, because of Your once-and-for-all provision for my salvation, I can know peace with You and peace for my journey through this life. Amen.

Stand Firm!

Moses answered the people, "Do not be afraid. Stand firm and you will see the deliverance the LORD will bring you today. The Egyptians you see today you will never see again."

—Exodus 14:13 NIV

In a beach game named Last Man Standing, children line up where the ocean waves break. As each wave washes in and out, some lose their footing while others hold steady. Those who stand firm play the next round. Still in line, they take a step deeper into the water. Standing firm becomes more difficult with each round. Finally, everyone has fallen except the winner, the last one standing.

Like the players at the beach, the Israelites needed to do their best to keep standing. They were pursued by an army that greatly outnumbered them. As their leader, Moses encouraged them to stand firm and pointed them to and promised "deliverance [of] the LORD." Does that promise mean that standing would be easy, that their knees wouldn't buckle, or that they wouldn't be afraid? Absolutely not. Moses simply said, "Stand firm," and in the end, they would—by God's grace and in His power—still be standing.

God will also help you stand firm and see His deliverance.

When the waves crash in around me, Lord, it's hard to not lose my footing. Thank You for helping me to stand firm. Amen.

A Sure Lifeline

"If you'll hold on to me for dear life," says God, "I'll get you out of any trouble. I'll give you the best of care if you'll only get to know and trust me."

—Psalm 91:14–15 MSG

The woman had managed to get on top of her car as the floodwaters rose. The man had been swept downstream but had been able to grab hold of a tree limb. The child had fallen into an old, unmarked well. And you've encountered a spiritual darkness that threatens to suffocate you.

The first three incidents can mean dramatic footage of daring rescues by brave men and women trained to do exactly that. In each case, after methodically preparing, they were ready to throw the lifeline. Cameras caught the happy endings.

The fourth scenario also requires a lifeline, and God will provide. First, He provides Himself: "Hold on to me . . . I'll get you out of trouble." Holding on to Him is made easier by the Holy Spirit, also known as the Comforter, and by God's written Word, which is a light of hope, truth, and promises. Both are lifelines for a soul in the dark.

If my world were always sunshiny and bright, I wouldn't need to trust You for much. Please use this dark time to grow my trust in You. Amen.

My Tower

The name of the Lord *is a fortified tower; the righteous run to it and are safe.*

—Proverbs 18:10 NIV

Did you immediately picture a medieval castle when you read "fortified tower"? That tower was the most defended area of the castle and therefore the safest spot for the nobleman who owned it. Castles eventually added two more defensive elements. First, walls around the top of the castle called battlements had regular spaces through which the people inside could shoot. The other innovation was arrowslits, narrow vertical openings in walls through which the people inside could shoot. The tower's structure and these two reinforcements made it difficult for attackers to harm to the defenders inside.

With these images in mind, consider that "the name of the Lord is a fortified tower." God's very name provides protection and safety. So when trouble surrounds you, say His name out loud or whisper it in your prayers, and you will know the safety of the Lord's tower surrounding you. Within the fortified walls of this mighty tower, you are safe from the arrows of the Enemy.

Sometimes I forget how powerful Your name is, Lord God. Thank You that the next time flaming arrows fly toward me, I can whisper Your name and know safety and peace in You. Amen.

The Noose of Fear

The fear of man brings a snare, but he who trusts in the Lord will be exalted.

—Proverbs 29:25 NASB

A snare is a certain kind of animal trap that we twenty-first-century city slickers probably don't know much about. A quick Internet search of "snare" reveals variations on this basic feature: a noose catches an animal by its neck, and as the animal keeps walking, the noose tightens.

When fear fills our hearts and minds, we can feel as if a noose is around our souls. When caught in this snare and feeling as though we're being strangled, the more we wiggle and squirm, the tighter the noose becomes. We loosen that noose when we make the choice to trust God. Trust is the opposite of fear, and trust brings a sense of peace.

So the next time you are caught in fear's trap, turn to God and trust that He will rescue you. The noose of fear will loosen, and the Lord will bless you with peace.

This day, instead of choking in the noose of fear, I will choose to trust in You, Lord. Amen.

Don't Wait!

O Eternal One, You are my strength, my fortress, my sanctuary in times of trouble.

—Jeremiah 16:19 VOICE

It's not easy to be the bearer of bad news. We've all been in that role at some point, but probably never to the degree that the Old Testament prophet Jeremiah found himself. He was to tell Israel that even at its lowest, even when Israel was at the bottom of the well, it was not too late for them to call out to God. Jeremiah reassured Israel that God would hear their cry and lift His repentant people out of their claustrophobic, sinful existence.

God's people had indeed fallen deep into idolatry and evil ways. Jeremiah foretold their eventual humble return to God, but first—he told them—they would one day come to the end of their own abilities and realize how much trouble they were in. Only at the bottom of the well would they realize their need to call out to God, their only hope. And because of God's mercy, He would receive His wayward people back.

He will do the same for you. And you don't have to wait until you're at the bottom to cry out.

Whenever I hit rock bottom—and even before I get there—I need Your mercy. Thank You for the rescue, peace, hope, and redirection You will mercifully give. Amen.

PEACE TO CALM THE STORM

Stormy Waters

"When you pass through the waters, I will be with you; and through the rivers, they shall not overflow you."

—Isaiah 43:2 NKJV

It takes more than an adventurous spirit to enjoy whitewater rafting, but an adventurous spirit is a good starting point. Whitewater rapids are rated for difficulty from Class I to Class V. Class I rapids are the easiest: with no waves or obstructions, "rapids" may be a misnomer. At the other end of the spectrum are the intense Class V rapids with their powerful currents, turbulent crosscurrents, and large drops. A raft guide who has been trained to read the river, navigate the hazards, and call out instructions is essential for safety and fun, especially on a Class V adventure.

Life also offers stretches that range from Class I to Class V, but we don't always know when the rapids will become more intense. A fast-moving but easy Class I stretch may quickly become an intense Class V with hazards at every turn. The good news is we have a Guide who can read the river, knows how to help us navigate those hazards, and calls out instructions and reassurance in His Word. So when you pass through those stormy waters, listen to your Guide and trust Him.

When the river of my life is filled with hazards, I am grateful You are my Guide who will keep me safe and bring me to a peaceful shore. Amen.

A Refuge in the Storm

Take my side, God—I'm getting kicked around, stomped on every day. Not a day goes by but somebody beats me up.

—Psalm 56:1–2 MSG

Mention an approaching hurricane to anyone living on the coast, and you may get a glimpse of fear in their face. Maybe only the outer edges will impact the coastal residents. That would be a relief, for they know that the worst of the storm occurs at the eye wall, the ring of powerful thunderstorms that encircles the eye. According to experts, the most dangerous part of that eye wall is where the wind blows in the same direction that the storm is moving.

The eye wall of a Category-3 or higher storm can rip houses from their foundations and turn trees into torpedoes. Just inside this frightening eye wall is the actual eye, or center, of the hurricane. Deceptively, in the eye of the storm are light winds and clear skies—until the opposite part of the eye wall passes by.

Perhaps you are experiencing the eye wall of a hurricane right now. The wind and rain are intense, and you worry about being lifted from your foundation. Go to the Refuge as the storm rages—and know He'll be there whatever the weather.

Help me center myself in You—the peace and calm in the eye of the storm, and the peace and calm when the rest of the storm passes. Amen.

Smooth Sailing

Give Him the credit for everything you accomplish, and He will smooth out and straighten the road that lies ahead.

—Proverbs 3:6 VOICE

Every sailor hopes for smooth sailing—for calm seas free of high winds, big waves, and rough waters. But a good sailor needs to know how to sail in high winds with big waves and rough water. Too often, novice boaters head out on a calm and sunny day only to have conditions change suddenly and radically. Their day of smooth sailing has turned into a seaman's nightmare. If they haven't been well trained, those sailors are in trouble.

All of us want a life of nothing but smooth sailing, but this is not reality. Still, we pray for smooth sailing and thank God for those calm days. But when the waters turn rough, remember His promise to go ahead of you even as He is with you. Give God credit for the rough seas He has guided you through before, and thank Him for the training He has given you through His Word. Call on God, for He alone can help you navigate life's rocky shoals. He alone will bring you safely to that peaceful shore.

Lord, thank You for helping me navigate the stormy waters in my life until there is smooth sailing once again. Amen.

Calm for the Storm

May the God of peace Himself sanctify you completely; and may your whole spirit, soul, and body be preserved blameless at the coming of our Lord Jesus Christ.

—1 Thessalonians 5:23 NKJV

We are all devastated when a natural disaster occurs or a calamity befalls a family in our church or neighborhood. The presence of evil can be hard to come to grips with. Some people avoid the matter by saying that a natural disaster is God's judgment on a particular group of people because of their godless behavior. (All of us are guilty of godless behavior!)

Another possibility is that natural disasters are one result of sin's presence in the world. Sin has taken its toll on the natural order, but God redeems the disasters by using the resulting pain and suffering to—as counterintuitive as it sounds—draw us to Him and teach us about faith. God is never happy when people suffer.

The next time you hear of a tragedy on any scale, pray that God will indeed use it to make Himself more real to those impacted. He does indeed use loss, pain, and hardship to get our attention, show us our need for Him, and sensitize us to His comforting presence with us.

You are a God for whom nothing is impossible. You bring good from our loss, pain, and hardship. All glory to You! Amen.

Sea Monsters

From deep in the realm of the dead I called for help, and you listened to my cry.

—Jonah 2:2 NIV

Reports of unknown monsters of the deep have been a part of sea lore for hundreds of years. From the description of Leviathan in the book of Job, with its "terrifying" teeth and scales like rows of shields, to the legend of the Loch Ness Monster, first described by a monk from the Scottish Highlands in the sixth century, we have been fascinated and curious. We aren't afraid, but we want to know what lies beneath!

The runaway prophet Jonah—who headed in the exact opposite direction of what God had commanded—learned something about what's down there when he encountered a big fish that swallowed him whole. As frightening as that would have been, he called for help, and God heard him. God demonstrated for Jonah and for us His command over stormy seas and sea monsters alike. God hears your cries for help when you feel like you've been swallowed whole. He will rescue you. Simply cry out God's name.

Whatever stormy seas and sea monsters life brings my way, replace my fear with Your peace, and set my feet on dry land. Amen.

Look to the Lighthouse

The Lord is near to the brokenhearted and saves those who are crushed in spirit.

—Psalm 34:18 NASB

Located in northwestern France is a lighthouse named La Jument, and it became famous when, during a 1989 storm, a photographer circling it in a helicopter got an amazing shot. The dramatic moment he captured was when the lighthouse keeper, hearing the helicopter, stepped into the doorway and looked up at the sky. At exactly that moment, a huge wave encircled the rock on which La Jument stood.

Clearly, such raging waves can be deadly for vessels unaware of the reefs and rocks along the shore. A lighthouse not only warns ships of the danger, but also helps guide ships seeking safe harbor. No wonder lighthouses have become a favorite symbol for believers. God also warns us of danger and helps guide us to safe harbor. And like La Jument standing in the middle of a stormy sea, God is right there with us whenever the swells of life crash down around us. When crushing waves threaten, look to the lighthouse for God's guidance to safe harbor.

God, thank You for using Your immeasurable strength to protect me and guide me to a peaceful harbor. Amen.

Going Deep

My flesh and my heart fail; but God is the strength of my heart and my portion forever.

—Psalm 73:26 NKJV

Many dangers await the deep-water diver, but the biggest is nitrogen narcosis—a feeling of intoxication and impaired judgment and coordination that can happen at depths of one hundred feet or more. To prevent this problem, divers wear atmospheric suits that allow them to remain at normal atmospheric pressure no matter how deep they descend. This second skin compensates for a diver's physical weakness.

Maybe at times in your life God has been like your atmospheric suit. Your flesh was weak and your heart seemed apt to fail until, like a second skin, God's strength and comfort blanketed you. The atmospheric suit God has for you provides you with a keener sense of judgment, sharper focus, and the ability to make wise decisions.

With God, therefore, you can go deep into the ocean waters and experience the wonders it has to offer in its mysterious depths. There in the deep, with God, you will know peace.

God, thank You for giving me strength and comfort, for enabling me to focus well and make good decisions, for always accompanying me into the depths of life's challenges. Amen.

First Aid

He heals the brokenhearted and binds up their wounds.

—Psalm 147:3 NIV

All of us had our share of scraped knees, bee stings, and splinters when we were growing up. Our parents, though, always had a big enough lap for us to crawl into. In these simple moments, with the help of a first-aid kit and that magical kiss that made the booboo better, we experienced something of what it might be like to have God pull us into His lap.

As we got older, the rough-and-tumble world got rougher and the hurts, deeper. When life bangs up us adults with betrayal, wandering children, job issues, unfulfilled dreams, and broken hearts, we can be sure that our heavenly Father's lap is plenty big. In addition, God's first-aid kit contains the bandages of His holy Word that He uses to bind up our wounds and the ointment of peace that comforts an aching heart.

If you need healing and comfort after bruises sustained in this world, allow God's tender, loving care to soothe your pain. Through your tears, watch as He pulls out His first-aid kit; it contains all you need to experience comfort and feel at peace.

God, I feel bruised and achy from life, but Your presence in my life brings such healing and peace. Thank You. Amen.

Steady as She Goes

You will keep in perfect peace those whose minds are steadfast, because they trust in you. Trust in the LORD forever, for the LORD, the LORD himself, is the Rock eternal.

—Isaiah 26:3–4 NIV

The job of a helmsman or skipper is to steer the ship—to maintain a steady course, execute all rudder orders, and communicate to the bridge the ship's location and heading. A skipper relies on visual references, a compass, and something called a rudder angle indicator to steer a steady course. The phrase "steady as she goes" is the instruction given to the helmsman when the captain wants to keep the ship on its current course.

As we sail the waters of life, we are blessed to have Jesus as our Helmsman. He reads the waters, He knows our location and, above all else, He steadies us as He steers us through shallow waters and stormy seas. When God, the Captain, calls out, "Steady as she goes," Jesus knows how to calm our minds and steady our hearts so that in the end we will sail into the safe harbor of God's arms.

If seas are stormy right now or you see dark clouds in the distance, find peace in knowing that your Helmsman is at His post: He will steer you into safe harbor.

Jesus, thank You for being my Helmsman, for calming my mind and steadying my heart when storms rage. Amen.

A Firm Grip

"Don't panic. I'm with you. There's no need to fear for I'm your God. I'll give you strength. I'll help you. I'll hold you steady, keep a firm grip on you."

—Isaiah 41:10 MSG

When we're in an emergency situation, we can sometimes find it difficult to think clearly. Our minds become a jumble of thoughts, fears, "what ifs," panic, and maybe even prayer. First responders recognize the look of panic on people's faces; they can identify someone who appears to be struggling to organize his or her thoughts. First responders know that panic can be deadly, so their first course of action is to help the person rein in those powerful emotions by giving him or her a task to do.

Likewise, God knows that when we panic, we may not be able to think clearly. His first course of action, by the power of His Spirit within us, is to comfort us, calm our fears, and reassure us of His presence with us. Then, like the first responders, He gives us a job: He tells us, *I have a firm grip on you; now you get a good hold on Me*.

When feelings of panic arise—whatever the reason—get a firm grip on God. Hold fast to Him, and your fear will subside.

Thank You that when I panic, You are there to calm and comfort me. Thank You for having a firm grip on me, the kind I want to have on You. Amen.

Targeted

"Blessed are those who are persecuted because of righteousness, for theirs is the kingdom of heaven."

—Matthew 5:10 NIV

When we are doing something good—when we are choosing wisely, doing the job that no one else will do, helping someone at a substantial personal cost of time, energy, or finances—why do we suffer? It doesn't seem fair that the people who treat others as they themselves would like to be treated are the ones with a target on their backs. But persecution doesn't care about fair.

Jesus taught that His followers who are persecuted for His sake and because they are living according to His ways are blessed. Yet when we experience persecution because of our faith, we feel anything but blessed. When we're lied about, framed, betrayed, or mistreated, we can still find peace in God's presence with us and peace as we look to the future. After all, His promise is that those who suffer for Christ's sake possess the riches of God's kingdom.

So take comfort, for the result of this battle is sure: God wins. And when He does—when Jesus returns as King of kings—the Lord will bless you greatly and give you an abundance of peace.

I hardly feel blessed or at peace, but I cling to the Matthew 5:10 promise: Your kingdom is mine because I've suffered for Your sake. Amen.

Why Worry?

"Which of you by worrying can add a single hour to his life's span?"

—Luke 12:25 NASB

Are you the type of person who will be late for her own funeral? Latecomers are too readily judged as lazy slackers who insensitively disregard the needs and feelings of others. But most folks who struggle with being late *do* want to be punctual because tardiness adds to their stress. Studies show that people who are consistently late don't mean to be inconsiderate or rude. They simply underestimate how long it will take to do something.

When we worry, we aren't—as Jesus Himself explained—adding any time to our day. Actually, when we worry, we are wasting time. Worrying takes up time that we could focus on more productive thoughts. Like the perpetually late person who can't will himself to be on time, however, the worrier can't will himself to stop worrying. But he can take steps to replace every worrisome thought with praise for God's provision and faithfulness.

All time is in God's hands. When you've forgotten that basic truth and are stressed and crunched for time, focus on Him so He can quiet your inner storm.

For me, Lord, worry, stress, and exhaustion form an unholy trinity. Help me replace that worry with praise for Your provision so I might also know Your peace. Amen.

Storm-Weary

Anxiety in the heart of man causes depression, but a good word makes it glad.

—Proverbs 12:25 NKJV

In 2006, the State of Florida experienced four back-to-back storms. In a six-week time frame, three hurricanes passed over the peninsula and caused severe damage. Then, two weeks later, a low-pressure cell sat over much of the state, dumping two feet of rain in less than a week. The people of Florida were storm-weary. As people began to realize just how extensive the damage was, the state saw an increase in the number of individuals seeking treatment for depression.

Life can bring a series of back-to-back storms as well, and maybe you're emerging from or even in the middle of such a season. If so, you, too, may be storm-weary. If you are struggling—and that's understandable—don't hesitate to seek professional help. Also follow God's advice: spend time regularly with a friend whose good words can make your heart glad and your spirit peaceful. This is God's prescription for the storm-weary, and getting that prescription filled truly will make your heart glad.

When I am storm-weary and blue, please guide my thoughts to someone who loves You and will speak words of life, hope, joy, and peace to my soul. Amen.

God's Emergency Plan

Be humble under God's powerful hand so he will lift you up when the right time comes.

—1 Peter 5:6 NCV

In communities across the country, emergency management teams come together to make plans for helping the most vulnerable among us when disaster strikes. Assisting the homebound and hospitalized, those in nursing homes, and people needing oxygen or other medical assistance requires a plan.

Note, however, that the plan addresses the humble and the weak; the self-sufficient are apparently left to fend for themselves. We who fall into this latter category might be frightened by the storms of life, but if we profess self-sufficiency to God, we don't give Him a chance to help us during these storms. Yet these will be the first to claim that God abandoned them. Not true! God did not leave them; they abandoned their need for God.

Yet, Scripture promises, if we humble ourselves under God's powerful hand, He will implement His emergency management plan for us. That plan includes, among other blessings, His lifting you high above the storms and giving you a heart that is at peace.

Lord, I know I need of Your mighty hand to both lift me up and give me peace. Amen.

Death Valley

Even when the way goes through Death Valley, I'm not afraid when you walk at my side. Your trusty shepherd's crook makes me feel secure.

—Psalm 23:4 MSG

Only a few statistics from the National Park Service are needed to show how aptly named this Southern California/Nevada desert spot is. The highest ground temperature ever recorded was 201 degrees Fahrenheit. During the summer of 1996, temperatures exceeded 120 degrees for 40 days and 110 degrees for 105 days. The 100-year average rainfall was just under two inches. No one volunteers to walk through Death Valley.

Similarly, we don't look forward to our inevitable Death Valley times when someone we love dies. Regardless of the circumstances, an encounter with death can be the lowest point in your life. Yet, despite the scorching heat and parched dryness of those times, you can hold confidently to the promise that you will one day see your loved ones again.

So, when you walk this lonely path, lean into and breathe deeply of the presence of your Good Shepherd, who is with you each step of the way to bless you with His comfort and peace.

Lord, thank You for being the Good Shepherd by my side, providing comfort and peace. Amen.

Hunker Down

I lift up my eyes to the mountains—where does my help come from? My help comes from the LORD, the Maker of heaven and earth.

—Psalm 121:1–2 NIV

Of the ten thousand people who attempt to climb the 11,250 feet of Oregon's Mount Hood each year, twenty-five to fifty must be rescued. One of the worst accidents occurred in May 1986 when seven students and two faculty members froze to death during a school's annual climb. Four climbers survived and described how they were caught completely unprepared for a blizzard.

Blizzards are snowstorms with winds in excess of thirty-five miles per hour. The driving snow can greatly reduce visibility, quickly making a mountain climber completely disoriented. Survivors say that the best plan if you're caught in a blizzard is to hunker down and wait for help. Similarly, sometimes we must simply find shelter, hunker down, and wait out the storms of life as well. When a storm hits, rest assured that your Maker and Creator knows where you are, and He will get you safely off the mountain.

I wasn't prepared for this blizzard, but I know to hunker down and wait out this storm. Thank You for being here with me. Amen.

A Pillar of Cloud

[The Lord] said [to Moses], "My Presence will go with you, and I will give you rest."

—Exodus 33:14 NKJV

As the warm, moist air of thunderclouds moves upward, it cools, condenses, and forms cumulonimbus clouds that can be more than twelve miles high. As the rising air reaches its dew point, water droplets and ice form and begin falling the long distance to the earth's surface. Storm watchers know the greater the towering cloud, the more powerful the thunderstorm.

God called His people out of Egypt on a long journey into an unknown future. During this trek, God manifested His presence among His people in a pillar of cloud by day and a pillar of fire by night. His continuous presence with them enabled them to persevere to the very end.

When an intense thunderstorm—with its crackling lightning, clapping thunder, and howling winds—enters your life, remember your all-powerful God. In the wilderness, He made His calming presence with His people evident in the giant pillar of clouds. Even today He will make His presence known by the power of His Spirit, and you will find the peace and rest you need to complete your journey.

When thunderstorms surround me, I will look to You and there find the guidance and hope, the peace and rest, I need to go on. Amen.

Noticed

You have made [man] a little lower than God, and You crown him with glory and majesty!

—Psalm 8:5 NASB

Nature has a way of making us feel small. When the earth shakes and the heavens release claps of thunder and lightning, we are reminded how big the world is and how insignificant we are. Looking at an endless range of mountains, plains stretching to the horizon, or at countless stars, we can indeed feel very unimportant, maybe even unnoticed.

Similarly, medical problems, financial calamity, or family matters can make us feel small and insignificant. We wonder if anyone—if God—even notices our pain and suffering. Does anyone—does God—care? Psalm 8 answers in the affirmative: God made us, of all created things, a little lower than Himself and far above all else in creation. In fact, God crowns each man and woman with His glory and majesty, making us anything but insignificant.

So, yes, God notices you—to the point that He counts the very hairs on your head—and He is aware of your pain. Go to Him and find peace, the peace of knowing how valued you are in all of His creation.

I often feel insignificant and overlooked. May I remember the truth from Your Word that I am crowned in glory and majesty because I am created and valued by You. Amen.

Shelter in Place

Let me live in your Holy Tent forever. Let me find safety in the shelter of your wings.

—Psalm 61:4 NCV

After several mass evacuations across the nation that resulted in clogged thoroughfares and roadways blocked by abandoned vehicles, protocol has changed. Today the instruction is quite different. Rather than evacuate when danger comes, most of us are told to take shelter where we are. In fact, we are to be able to survive without emergency assistance and to be self-sustaining for three to five days without water or electricity. That's definitely counter to our "fight or flight" human instinct!

The Bible does not advise running from danger. Instead we are to seek "the shelter of [God's] wings." There we can experience safety and security unlike anything the world offers. In God's holy tent we will not merely survive whatever the danger is, but we will also find peace and rest for our weary souls. And in God's tent we don't have to be self-sustaining. There, as we settle in the shadow of His wings, God provides for all of our needs. No wonder the psalmist cried out, "Let me live in your Holy Tent forever!"

God, when danger threatens, my first instinct is to run. Teach me to instead find shelter in You, where all my needs are met. Amen.

Like a Freight Train

[God] will be leading you. He'll be with you, and He'll never fail you or abandon you. So don't be afraid!

—Deuteronomy 31:8 VOICE

Have you ever been in a tornado? Most Americans haven't, even though tornadoes have been spotted in every state. Tornadoes come in various intensities, with an F5 rating signifying the strongest tornado. When tornadoes come—and you know this if you've seen *The Wizard of Oz*—they can lift houses, kill people, and generally wreak havoc.

When Moses handed the leadership reins over to Joshua, he knew Joshua would experience his share of tornadoes. Some of those swirling storms would be intense, but Moses knew Joshua would do fine—actually, better than fine because, just as Moses did, Joshua had Someone leading him, Someone who would be with him at every blind turn. Moses knew God would never fail Joshua or abandon him. God had been through tornadoes—He had created tornadoes!—and He would get Joshua through it.

Your heavenly Father will also help you when a sound like a freight train shatters the night. He will lead you just as He led Moses, just as He led Joshua.

God, tornadoes scare me, but the fact that You will be with me as the winds swirl gives me peace. Amen.

Pollyanna Thinking

I have learned the secret of being content in any and every situation, whether well fed or hungry, whether living in plenty or in want. I can do all this through him who gives me strength.

—Philippians 4:12–13 NIV

She gets a bad rap for being over-the-top happy, but we can learn from Pollyanna. Consider, for instance, the game she plays with her father. He told her to look at every situation for something to be thankful for. One time she was hoping for a doll, but instead she got a pair of crutches. So Pollyanna chose to be thankful that she didn't need them! Pollyanna thinking is not simply seeing the good, but seeing the good in spite of the bad.

Bad comes. There's no denying that—and it's not healthy to try to deny or ignore it. We can't stop storm clouds from forming. We can't prevent hurricanes or tornadoes, but we can learn to be content regardless of the life storms we experience. Again, contentment is not ignoring the storm or pretending it isn't as bad as it really is. Contentment is choosing to trust God despite knowing full well how bad circumstances are. God can help us learn contentment and bless us with His peace with each baby step we take.

I am still learning to be content in all circumstances, for my contentment is fertile ground for Your peace. Teach me, heavenly Father, to see Your good in spite of the bad. Amen.

SEPTEMBER 21

Wind-Whipped Waves

People who "worry their prayers" are like wind-whipped waves. Don't think you're going to get anything from the Master that way, adrift at sea, keeping all your options open.

—James 1:6–8 MSG

If you stand at a marina as a severe storm is approaching land, you'll see a strange sight: owners are unmooring their expensive boats and taking them out into open water. That's where they will anchor their boats, out of harm's way. When the storm rages, the harm will actually be in the harbor. There wind-whipped waves could drive the boats into the dock or impale them on pilings.

We are like those wind-whipped waves when we "worry" our prayers. Wind-whipped waves toss yachts, driftwood, and debris randomly around. We are tossing about thoughts, concerns, and ideas randomly around when we "worry" our prayers. Praying our prayers is a much better alternative. Standing firmly before God, our heavenly Father, we are to boldly present our requests, confident that He will answer and always deferring to His will.

God, I want to be firmly moored to You when I'm praying and whatever I'm doing. Amen.

A Paradigm Shift

"Have I not commanded you? Be strong and of good courage; do not be afraid, nor be dismayed, for the LORD your God is with you wherever you go."

—Joshua 1:9 NKJV

If you have a younger sibling, especially a much younger sibling, then you know what it's like to always be expected to be the responsible one. Anywhere you went, Mom or Dad would ask, "Where's your sister?" And then there was the fact that you couldn't do anything without your brother tagging along. Your little shadow was always with you. Does the phrase *brother's keeper* come to mind as you think back?

Some people feel this way about God. They believe His presence with them and His rules for them are too confining. A paradigm shift is in order! God's presence and His rules offer us safety and therefore peace. After all, God would not tell us hundreds of times in Scripture to "Fear not!" if life didn't provide many reasons to fear. And what are we to do in our fearsome world? We are to lean into our strong Lord, who is with us always. His presence with us is for our good!

Lord, show me any false ideas I have about You. I want to live in Your truth; I want to thrive in Your presence with me; I want to glorify You in all I do. Amen.

Stronger Because It Happened

You will forget your trouble and remember it only as water gone by.

—Job 11:16 NCV

Flooding is storm damage that keeps on giving. The initial damage is horrific and overwhelming enough as rivers of water cascade into houses and take furniture with it as it passes through. Once the water recedes, the wet, muddy, soggy, sad cleanup begins. Mourning the loss of things, some irreplaceable, battling stains from the mud, deciding what furniture and clothes to try to salvage, hoping to avoid mold—these are some of the ways that storm damage keeps on giving.

Some storms in life also keep on giving. Oh, there are those life storms that come and go and are gone. But some storms leave a big mess, require a major cleanup, and, too often, result in mold. When mold takes over, we sometimes need help with our cleanup. Ask God to guide you to good counsel, to give you courage to address the mold, and sustain you with hope of healing and wholeness.

Lord, I still have cleanup work to do. Please make me whole and stronger because the storm came. Amen.

Waiting for Your Call

Suddenly a furious storm came up on the lake, so that the waves swept over the boat. But Jesus was sleeping.

—Matthew 8:24 NIV

"Did we have a good night?" the new father asked his wife as he awoke from a solid night's sleep. He had slept through three wakings of his hungry son; she hadn't. Some people—like this dad—can apparently sleep through anything. Other people—and not just moms of newborns—are light sleepers. They hear things at night that most people don't hear when they're awake! In today's verse we see that, at least in this instance, Jesus was able to sleep through a lot.

Jesus and His friends were crossing the sea when a raging storm suddenly arose. The friends, some of whom were experienced fishermen, were busy tying off the nets and bailing water—while Jesus slept. What are we to make of that? Perhaps that when Jesus isn't acting as we wish—when He doesn't seem to notice that we are about to drown—all we need to do is simply call His name. He isn't asleep on the job; He's just waiting for our call.

You know I get frustrated and even angry when it looks like You are sleeping through a storm. Thank You that all I have to do to get Your help is call Your name. Amen.

Peace, Be Still

He caused the storm to be still, so that the waves of the sea were hushed.
—Psalm 107:29 NASB

Will satellites one day help us prevent the formation of a tornado's funnel cloud instead of just reporting its arrival and the aftermath? Researchers are trying to determine ways to control the weather, particularly destructive tornadoes and hurricanes. One idea is to blast a storm's beginnings with beams of microwaves from satellites. Another idea is to alter a storm's path by using a giant orbiting mirror that, reflecting the sun's energy, heats up the air in front of the hurricane. Sound like science fiction? All are only theories right now.

Jesus demonstrated that He could control weather. With a few simple words, Jesus calmed a raging storm—and people today wonder why He doesn't calm the storms in their lives. Perhaps He is addressing internal storms they aren't as aware of as that circumstantial storm raging in their lives. Often, the more important storm to calm is the storm that rages within. To those violent winds and crashing waves, Jesus simply says again, "Peace, be still" (Mark 4:39 KJV).

When Jesus speaks, storms listen and obey.

I too easily focus on the situational storms in my life, when the storms in my heart and mind are where I most need You to speak Your words of peace. Amen.

Hope Returned

"Mister, if you took him, tell me where you put him so I can care for him." Jesus said, "Mary." Turning to face him, she said in Hebrew, "Rabboni!" meaning "Teacher!"

—John 20:15–16 MSG

All of us grieve in different ways. All of us are on different timetables. And all of us need to give ourselves and one another grace. No one's grief is exactly like another person's. Yet there is one thing every grieving person needs.

Jesus died a horrifying and excruciatingly painful death. But with His death, His family and friends suffered an even greater loss than their Friend, Messiah, Teacher, Lord. With Jesus' death came the death of their hope. They had hoped that one day He would change things, and at the crucifixion that hope vanished.

When Jesus appeared to Mary after the resurrection, He simply spoke her name. In that moment, she felt hope return. What every grieving person needs to hear is Jesus tenderly say his or her name.

If you are currently dealing with grief, listen to Jesus say your name and receive His peace. And don't hesitate to do this again and again.

Jesus, I'm grieving, but when I hear You call my name, Your peace floods my soul and hope burns brighter. Amen.

PEACE WITH OTHERS

The Welcome Mat

Keep on loving one another as brothers and sisters. Do not forget to show hospitality to strangers, for by so doing some people have shown hospitality to angels without knowing it.

—Hebrews 13:1–2 NIV

Sometimes family members are the hardest to love. First, family can hurt us in the deepest part of our souls. Second, we aren't always on our best behavior with family members. And, third, there's the reality that we know one another better than we know anyone else.

So what does this command mean, to love people in the church "as brothers and sisters"? Loving others with brotherly love is loving with an in-spite-of kind of love, which is the kind of love with which our holy God loves us sinners. Essentially, God's call to brotherly love is a call to set out a welcome mat for our family, friends, fellow believers, neighbors, and coworkers and to accept them unconditionally and just as they are. We are to love them *in spite of* their hang-ups, *in spite of* how they've hurt us, *in spite of* their sin, and *in spite of* their judgment of us. We can and always should welcome people with loving, open arms. When we obey, we will enjoy the Lord's peace.

Thank You, God, for loving me with brotherly love *in spite of* my sinful wanderings and decisions. Enable me to extend brotherly, *in-spite-of* love to those in my path today. Amen.

SEPTEMBER 28

For Argument's Sake

Try to live in peace with all people, and try to live free from sin. Anyone whose life is not holy will never see the Lord.

—Hebrews 12:14 NCV

Some people don't seem to have as a goal "[living] in peace with all people." If you say the sky is blue, they'll say it's gray. If you suggest A, they'll push for B, C, or D. If you smile a greeting, they'll frown. They seem to thrive on creating disharmony and living with tension.

The writer of Hebrews was not addressing people like this who sparked conflict, but to people who faced opposition at every turn. The letter encouraged them to not return insults with harsh words nor respond negatively to the prodding. That is not an easy assignment, and the assignment is ours as well.

When we grow weary of difficult people and their needling, we can take courage from the way these faithful people lived. If they had fallen to the temptation to respond negatively, we would not be reading about them today. Instead, they remained faithful to God—and to loving others the way they themselves wanted to be loved. Because of the Hebrews' faith, we know that we, too, can live in peace with even the most difficult among us.

Lord, teach me not to respond to harsh words with harsh words, not to be oppositional just because I can. Help me to choose peace. Amen.

Stand Up to Evil

He must turn away from evil and do good; He must seek peace and pursue it.

—1 Peter 3:11 NASB

School yard bullies have always been with us. A wise response is to avoid the bully. Some people who can't avoid the bully join him in his cruelty. Still others want the bullying to end. Eventually, someone decides the bully must be stopped and stands up for the children being bullied. The message is that evil won't go unanswered.

That same message applies to all of history as much as it does to playground interactions. Evil will not go unanswered, but it takes courage to stand up to it. Sometimes our silence and inaction allow evil to flourish. The Bible advises turning away from evil, but it doesn't stop there. Peter encouraged believers to turn from evil and do good. He is not at all encouraging us to turn a blind eye to evil. The Enemy wins if we do nothing. And Peter told us something we can do: we are to seek peace. We are to stand up to evil and stand with the oppressed.

Look around. In what situation could your involvement make a difference for the cause of peace? Decide you won't turn a blind eye. Stand up to the bully.

Lord, show me how doing good and seeking peace sometimes means confronting evil. Amen.

Walking the Talk

If one of you says to them, "Go in peace; keep warm and well fed," but does nothing about their physical needs, what good is it?

—James 2:16 NIV

Most of us have known someone who is all talk. This person can always top our story and always turn the focus of the conversation to him. And once he's the focus, it's amazing how many causes he is passionate about and how many ideas he has for resolving the world's problems. He never seems to be without words, but if you listen closely, you don't hear anything about actions.

James pointed out that we can talk about helping people, believe in helping people, and support causes that foster helping people, but such talk is hollow. It is easy to say we believe in helping people, but if we really believe, we must go a step further and do something to actually help people. This same principle applies to peace. We must support our words with actions.

I don't want to just talk about living in peace and helping others. I want my actions to match my talk. Help me to make a difference for You, Lord. Amen.

Wisdom and Peace

The wisdom that is from above is first pure, then peaceable, gentle, willing to yield, full of mercy and good fruits, without partiality and without hypocrisy.

—James 3:17 NKJV

What kind of person makes a good leader? As children, we quickly saw the most popular and the most persuasive step forward as leaders, but we learned that following them is not always best. As we grew older, we saw the sweet-talker and the most attractive step forward. As adults, we saw that the smartest or the oldest aren't always the best leaders. So how are we to choose capable and effective leaders?

No simple answer exists, but the book of James gives us a guideline: good leaders will be wise. Today's verse describes wisdom as being "first pure, then peaceable, gentle, willing to yield, full of mercy and good fruits, without partiality and without hypocrisy."

So, when choosing a leader, may we not look for the most popular, the most persuasive, the best talker, the most attractive, the smartest, or the oldest. May we look for someone whose wisdom is evident, whose wisdom can help us live in peace.

Lord, enable me to be discerning about character when I choose leaders—and please grow in me the wisdom James described. Amen.

Bringing Out the Best

Look for the best in each other, and always do your best to bring it out.

—1 Thessalonians 5:15 MSG

Read this question and answer with the first person who comes to mind: who brings out the best in you? Maybe it's a long-time friend or someone God just brought into your life. Maybe it's a relative, a parent, or a mentor. In what ways does this person bring out the best in you? My guess is that this person is an encourager, a prayer warrior, and a fellow believer who has wisdom and God's big-picture perspective on life, who speaks the truth in love, who softens your rough edges, and who strengthens your faith.

What a blessing to have such a person in your life—and may there be more than one! And it's a blessing to be such a person in other people's lives. What a picture of God's love we would give the world if we believers always brought out the best in one another!

Thank You, Lord, for the people in my life who bring out the best in me. Use me to bring out the best in people so we may live together peacefully. Amen.

Speaking Truth

"Speak the truth to one another; judge with truth and judgment for peace in your gates."

—Zechariah 8:16 NASB

It is classic Mary Poppins wisdom: "A spoonful of sugar helps the medicine go down!" When the medicine is hard-to-hear truth, a bit of sugar, a heart of love, and even a touch of humor can help that truth be heard.

Have you ever listened to a Christian comedian? He will have you laughing so hard you're crying—and then *wham*! You've just been hit between the eyes with a point that penetrates your heart and just might change your life. A book can have the same impact. You're reading along, laughing out loud on a crowded airplane, and then comes a whack on the side of the head. Again, humor helped you hear a heart-changing story.

Jesus' storytelling was like that. He held His audiences spellbound and then delivered truth that touched their hearts. When you must speak a difficult truth to someone you care about, humor might be just the spoonful of sugar you need. Truth spoken in love like that brings peace to both the speaker and hearer.

Enable me, Lord, to speak truth humbly, carefully, with love, and maybe even with a touch of humor. Amen.

Peace Treaty

It was the Father's good pleasure for all the fullness to dwell in [Jesus], and through Him to reconcile all things to Himself, having made peace through the blood of His cross.

—Colossians 1:19–20 NASB

We sign peace treaties and make peace accords. We call a truce and then shake hands to confirm our intent. We declare, decree, and proclaim peace. We strive to avoid war, and we work for peace. When we experience peace, we seek to maintain that too-fragile and very precious state. Peace is hard to craft and even harder to sustain.

Yet Jesus came to bring peace—peace between sinful human beings and a holy God; peace with others; and peace within ourselves. When Jesus died on the cross, He signed the peace treaty with His blood and ended for eternity the war between humanity's sin and God's holiness. Sin has been defeated! Now we can be at peace with God, with others, and within ourselves.

Notice that last sentence: "We *can* be." Peace is not automatic. We need to confess our sin, acknowledge Jesus' death on the cross as payment for that sin, and then in gratitude surrender our life to Him as our Savior and Lord. Have you done so? Have you accepted Christ's peace?

Thank You, Jesus, for defeating sin. As skirmishes with sin continue, strengthen me to stand strong in You. Amen.

Doing

Whatever you have learned or received or heard from me, or seen in me—put it into practice. And the God of peace will be with you.

—Philippians 4:9 NIV

How many things can the human brain remember at once? How many items for the grocery store can we remember? How many tasks can we remember if we don't make a to-do list? Science used to think seven (hence the seven-digit phone number), but now scientists believe three or four (hence the success in memorizing phone numbers back in the day: the number is broken into three digits and four digits). If you just survived one of those running-around-in-circles days, you may have no trouble agreeing that our memory is limited.

In Philippians 4:9, the apostle Paul gave us just one thing to remember: we are to do what we know. It is not enough that we hear good sermons on Sunday morning or that we know that God is love. We must put into action those commands we hear and those principles we know we are to live by. It is in the hearing *and* the doing of God's will that we know peace. If we do nothing with God's truth when we hear it, what was the point of hearing it in the first place? May God's truth compel us to act.

I confess, Lord, that sometimes I hear but don't do. Hearing is only the first step; doing Your Word makes that hearing count. Amen.

A Three-Legged Race

You are joined together with peace through the Spirit, so make every effort to continue together in this way.

—Ephesians 4:3 NCV

Maybe it's been awhile, but you've probably participated in a three-legged race at some point in your life. You may have used a rope or bandanna to tie your right ankle to someone's left ankle. Then the two of you ran to the finish line. And as you ran your first three-legged race, you realized the secret: running *together.*

That lesson from a three-legged race can be applied to our peacemaking efforts. When we gave our lives to Christ, we became members of His body, of believers around the world, throughout time. As a follower of Jesus, you are not running a solo race. You need to run *together* if you want to obtain peace. More specifically, we believers will only cross the finish line in this three-legged race for peace if we run not only in the same direction but also at the same pace. You and your brothers and sisters in Christ are in this race together, tied together by the Holy Spirit, and ideally running as one.

Living in community—even a community of believers—is hard. Holy Spirit, help us live the Christian life and run the race toward peace *together* for our good and God's glory. Amen.

Taking Sides

By one Spirit we were all baptized into one body, whether Jews or Greeks, whether slaves or free.

—1 Corinthians 12:13 NASB

In the musical *West Side Story*, two rival gangs—the Jets and the Sharks—struggle to control the west side of New York City. The conflict intensifies when two teens—one Jet and one Shark—fall in love. They end up (spoiler alert) getting caught in the crossfire, and in the closing scene, Maria holds Tony as he dies. When the gangs turn on each other to continue the fight, Maria stops them. In a heart-wrenching scene, she screams to the members of both gangs that they all had killed Tony because of their hatred for each other.

The Jews and the Gentiles were the Jets and the Sharks of biblical times. Today we can name twenty-first-century religious groups that are also pitted against each other. In a vicious cycle, hatred and suspicion lead to an "us versus them" mentality, which fuels even greater hatred and suspicion. Beware of any hints of division and taking sides. We believers are all on the same side: we're all on Jesus' side.

God, we in Your church, we who name Jesus our Savior and Lord, need to all be on Your side, living in peaceful unity. Amen.

Alone in a Crowd

The Great Preacher of peace and love came for you, and His voice found those of you who were near and those who were far away.

—Ephesians 2:17 VOICE

Have you ever felt alone in a crowd? It's odd that we can be walking down a city street, sitting in a crowded movie theater, or even worshipping at church and, despite being surrounded by a lot of people, feel very much alone. That feeling of being alone can be hard to shake, but juxtaposing it with truth may help.

Consider the truth of today's verse. Listen to that first part: "The Great Preacher of peace and love came for you." Jesus Christ is that Great Preacher, and He preached not just with words but with His very life. He loved you before you loved Him. He called your name with a voice both gentle and strong, and by His grace you responded. In that moment you knew you would never again be alone. And that's true: never will Jesus leave you. He will walk as close to you as you let Him.

Lord, may I grow in my awareness of Your loving presence with me. Thank You that I am never really alone. Amen.

The Wet-Blanket Maneuver

Be like-minded, be sympathetic, love one another, be compassionate and humble.

—1 Peter 3:8 NIV

The command to love one another can feel like a pretty lonely assignment, especially (as you undoubtedly remember) at school, in the office, during children's sporting events, and sometimes even at the grocery store. Anywhere we go, we can find mean people—or, perhaps more accurately—people having a bad day. You've probably heard the truism that hurt people hurt people—and the Lord wants you to respond to their hurt with . . . love.

I recently heard of some creative parents who encouraged their child to try the "wet-blanket maneuver." Often our reactions to someone's meanness and teasing can encourage that person to continue, but if we respond with love, we throw a wet blanket on the heated exchange. These parents encouraged their child to respond to cruel intentions with blessings. Easier said than done, but it's not fun to tease someone who doesn't get angry in response!

This strategy works for adults too. Who in the office, on the PTA board, at pickup from the after-school activity can you use the wet-blanket maneuver on today?

God, help me master the wet-blanket maneuver so I can foster true peace and harmony with hurting people who want to hurt others. Amen.

Rejoicing for Others

If we live in the Spirit, let us also walk in the Spirit. Let us not become conceited, provoking one another, envying one another.

—Galatians 5:25–26 NKJV

Do you know someone with more talent than any individual should be allowed to possess? Or someone whose life seems charmed in every way imaginable? Or someone who has excelled in business or raised kids who never rebelled? Initially we may stand in awe of a person's many talents, charmed life, successful career, and amazing children, but too often we find ourselves envious, jealous, and even a bit resentful.

Any sense we have of being not-as-good-as can fuel a "poor me" session and snowball into a "why not me, God?" funk. Scripture says that we can combat this green-eyed monster of jealousy by living in reliance on the Spirit and having the eyes of our heart focused on our Savior. A "poor me" session crowds out selfless Christlike thoughts as well as the fruit of His Spirit (love, joy, peace, patience, kindness, and gentleness, to name a few).

So the next time you hear good news about someone, ask God, first, to help you genuinely rejoice for that person and, second, to know His peace regarding your own life.

Holy Spirit, help me to replace any "poor me" thoughts with more Christlike ones that keep me focused on my faithful, glorious, wise, gracious God. Amen.

Be Made Complete

Finally, brethren, rejoice, be made complete, be comforted, be like-minded, live in peace; and the God of love and peace will be with you.

—2 Corinthians 13:11 NASB

Name the ten people you most admire and why each person is on your list. You may have chosen a good parent, devoted friend, or wonderful spouse; a person of remarkable compassion, wisdom, or integrity; a person who makes you feel loved, understood, and complete.

That idea of people completing us reflects the basic fact that God made us in His image to be blessed and completed in community. Do you know people who fill your world with peace and love, who hang with you in tough times? When we consider life without these people, we realize what a hole their absence would leave.

Interestingly, "be made complete" has also been translated "aim for restoration" (ESV) and "repair whatever is broken" (VOICE). God calls us to restore hurting people, repair broken relationships, and offer our strengths where they are weak. We are to seek to live in peace with all people. Do some of your Top 10 do these things?

Whose Top 10 list are you on?

Use me, Lord, to bring restoration, repair, and a sense of completeness to my brothers and sisters in Christ. Give me eyes to see those needs You would have me meet. Amen.

Building a House

Let us therefore make every effort to do what leads to peace and to mutual edification.

—Romans 14:19 NIV

According to *Merriam-Webster,* peace is "harmony in personal relations," and *edify* means "to teach (someone) in a way that improves the mind or character." For Christians, that improvement would be Christlikeness.

Consider that the Latin for *edify* means "to build a house," as opposed to pitch a tent. Our edification of one another is to lead to a solid and lasting faith as opposed to temporary passion and a growth spurt. Learning to become more like Christ means growing in our ability to trust God and submit to His will. Such growth tends to happen during the difficult stretches of our journey of faith. During those stretches we need help from our brothers and sisters in Christ to stay the course—to keep walking with Jesus, to submit to God's plan, to take steps of faith.

Ideally that help is prayer and modeling rather than pep talks and platitudes. We can learn much—we can be greatly edified—by watching how fellow believers not only survive the dark days of their faith journey, but also live out their trust in Jesus and honor Him in all they do.

God, as I walk through the day, please keep my heart open to learning from the believers You have placed in my life how to develop the mind of Christ. Amen.

Living in Peace

If someone does wrong to you, do not pay him back by doing wrong to him. . . . Do your best to live in peace with everyone.

—Romans 12:17–18 NCV

Humility contributes to our living peacefully with one another. In his classic *Mere Christianity*, C. S. Lewis wrote, "True humility is not thinking less of yourself; it is thinking of yourself less."

If I'm not constantly thinking about myself, I'll have an easier time getting along with people, cooperating with them, and living at peace with them. But there is nothing like a jab to my pride to get me thinking about myself—and about both retaliating and proudly rebuilding my wounded reputation. That is certainly the world's approach: society respects individuals who protect their name, their reputation, their pride.

God's kingdom, however, operates on a do-unto-others system. We are to resist repaying a wrong done to us, especially if our primary reason is wounded pride. Christ humbled Himself on the cross, showing no concern about His reputation and yielding to God's will for Him. Following Jesus' model and Paul's exhortation, may we not pay back wrong with wrong, and may we live in peace with everyone.

Lord, help me to be less preoccupied with myself, more attuned to You, and more ready to be used by You, and to live with others in peace. Amen.

On Your Side

In Christ's family there can be no division into Jew and non-Jew, slave and free, male and female. Among us you are all equal.

—Galatians 3:28 MSG

A wise and godly person once commented that the ground is level at the foot of the cross. And the apostle Paul wrote that all of us have sinned and fallen short of God's glory (Romans 3:23). The two statements mean the same thing: we're all sinners—and there is no hierarchy of sin or sinners. Sin is the great equalizer of human beings.

Yet rather than letting that truth contribute to a sense of unity among believers, we still find reason for division. Believers in the church at Galatia found Jew/non-Jew, slave/free, and male/female as reasons for division. Paul reminded them that in Christ's family, all are equal. Today God's people can be divided because of denominational lines and, even more so, theological topics like homosexuality, marriage, and, sadly, the authority of Scripture. These are not unimportant issues, and they should be addressed, but not at the price of unity.

Where there is unity, peace thrives.

Thank You, gracious Lord, for the forgiveness You offer all mankind as a solution for our sin. Use our gratitude and love for You to foster unity in the body. Amen.

There's No "I"

"If your brother or sister sins, go and point out their fault, just between the two of you. If they listen to you, you have won them over."

—Matthew 18:15 NIV

Maybe you've heard it said, "There's no *i* in *team*." Team sports teach players to think in terms of the team, not just self. Evidence of that happening is when a team member confronts a fellow player who isn't working as hard the rest of the group. Teammates hold one another accountable regarding—among other things—focus, effort, attitude, and physical conditioning. The team can only be as strong as its weakest member!

There's also no *i* in *church*. The body of Christ teaches us to think about others and gives us opportunities to serve our brothers and sisters. Being part of the body of believers also means having the responsibility of holding one another accountable to living according to God's Word and in a way that honors Him. In other words, we are to hold one another accountable for our sin. This can be uncomfortable and difficult to do, but such conversations benefit the person being addressed, and your obedience to Jesus' command in Matthew 18:15 glorifies God.

Teach me, Lord, to speak truth in love when You call me to hold someone accountable for sin. And teach me, Lord, to receive truth with love when I'm the one being held accountable. Amen.

Preserving Peace

"While you are going with your opponent to appear before the magistrate, on your way there make an effort to settle with him, so that he may not drag you before the judge, and the judge turn you over to the officer, and the officer throw you into prison."

—Luke 12:58 NASB

Small-claims court was designed to settle disputes between citizens without requiring them to get legal counsel. The disputes must be for small amounts of money and involve matters for which a fair judgment can be made. Disputes taken to small-claims court tend to be resolved quickly and inexpensively. But Jesus encouraged His followers to not even get to the point of going to small claims court.

Jesus did not advise ignoring a disagreement and pretending it never happened. Unsettled disagreements are seeds for bitterness, hatred, and division. That is one reason why Jesus called us to "make an effort to settle" any issues we have with a brother or sister in Christ, especially those involving fellow believers. Doing so brings peace to the two people involved and preserves peace in the body.

Lord, You know the person and situation I'm thinking about right now. Please work in our hearts that we might find a resolution and restore peace. Amen.

Shock Absorbers

"Love your enemies, do good to those who hate you."

—Luke 6:27 NKJV

They have a Volkswagen chassis, a Jeep body, and roll bars. Made for riding over the sand dunes fast, these vehicles are aptly named dune buggies. When a young man speaks of his "girl" or dune buggy, he never fails to brag about her most important feature: shock absorbers. These "babies" are huge tubes connected to the wheels, and without them riding in the dune buggy would be more jarring and teeth-loosening than fun.

Jesus' command to love our enemies is, in a sense, a command to be a shock absorber in the world. We usually want to avoid people who hate us, but Jesus calls us to love them—and to love them with our actions. Choosing to do good to those who have been hurtful or unfair is to receive the blow and absorb it. That takes great strength, and God gives us access to His great strength. Because of our relationship with Jesus, we can be held by Him as we take the blows. Relying on God like that—taking Him up on His offer to absorb an enemy's blows—is one way we followers of Jesus sow peace in this world.

I praise You, God, for absorbing the impact of my sins when I was still Your enemy. Amen.

The Cure

[God's mercy] will shine on those who live in darkness, in the shadow of death. It will guide us into the path of peace.

—Luke 1:79 NCV

We can put a man on the moon, but we can't find a cost-effective alternative to gasoline engines or a cure for the common cold. Or a cure for cancer, Alzheimer's, diabetes, Crohn's, asthma, lupus, or AIDS. Some people with these diseases may easily fall prey to schemes that promise a cure. Desperation may lead them to a reputed miracle cure . . . and potentially crushing disappointment.

Mankind's greatest disease is not listed above. Our most serious disease—one with eternal consequences—is sin. But God offers us the miracle cure of His mercy, and His supply will never run out. Among the benefits of God's mercy is the bright light it shines into the dark places of sin. God's mercy also offers spiritual life to those who sit at the door of eternal spiritual death. And God's mercy guides our wandering souls to peace with Him, and when we accept His grace and His mercy, we have peace in our souls, a peace that comes only from God.

God's mercy is the cure for all what ails us most.

Your mercy is the cure for sin and its symptoms of darkness, death, and lack of direction. Thank You for freely shining Your mercy on me and giving me peace. Amen.

The Salt of the World

"Salt is good, but if the salt loses its flavor, how will you season it? Have salt in yourselves, and have peace with one another."

—Mark 9:50 NKJV

Salt preserves meat by preventing the spread of bacteria. It brightens the taste of food. But salt makes us thirsty, and salt that has lost its flavor prevents growth: scattered throughout fields, it makes them barren.

Jesus likens His followers to salt (Matthew 5:13). God can use us to preserve a world that has turned away from God. God can use us to enhance the flavor of life. Our winsome joy in the Lord, our choice to love, and our willingness to serve make life richer. And God can use us to make people thirsty for Jesus. But if we lose our flavor, our witness for Jesus will no longer encourage growth in other people. It might actually prevent new spiritual life.

We are salt in this world—a preservative, a flavoring, and a contributor to spiritual thirst—when we choose to honor God by how we live. We aren't to hide in the safety of our churches and among our Christian friends. We are to be in the world where Christ can use us to preserve His truth, flavor a godless and therefore bland world, and make people thirsty for Him.

Lord, here I am! Use me to preserve Your truth, flavor a godless and therefore bland world, and make people thirsty for You. Amen.

Sword of the Spirit

Take the . . . sword of the Spirit, which is the word of God.

—Ephesians 6:17 NIV

Located in Sevierville, Tennessee, is Smoky Mountain Knife Works, Home of the World's Largest Knife Showcase. This three-story football-field–sized store has knives, swords, spears, guns, and rifles of all kinds on display and for sale. Most visitors say they didn't know that so many kinds of tools for cutting, slicing, or protecting even existed. The place is packed with people from every walk of life, all looking for the right tool for the job they want done.

Jesus provides us, His followers, with the right tools for the job He has called us to do on this earth. One of those tools is "the sword of the Spirit, which is the word of God." God's Word is an offensive weapon, not a defensive one. When Jesus' truth is met with the world's hostility, battles follow, and we need to be ready. We need to be able to stand with Jesus and do battle for truth.

The Word of God causes people to choose sides. Will you fight for Jesus?

Lord God, make me a bold and effective soldier for Your truth. Genuine peace cannot reign on this earth until darkness and evil are vanquished. Amen.

Glass Slippers

How lovely on the mountains are the feet of him who brings good news, who announces peace and brings good news of happiness.

—Isaiah 52:7 NASB

What do you think of your feet? Few of us would consider them our best physical trait. Some of us have toes that are oddly bent or a second toe that's longer than the big toe. Perhaps the reality of our wide feet makes us self-conscious. We hate the foot-baring summer season. We concluded long ago that feet really aren't pretty.

Feet are primarily for function, not beauty. But, as the verse from Isaiah proclaims, their function can indeed make them lovely. The function God has given us, His people, is to share His good news about the peace with Him that is available because of Jesus' death and resurrection. We can't do much sharing or announcing from where we sit right now. We need to use our feet—regardless of how funny or downright ugly they are—to walk out the door or even to travel the world and spread the good news about Jesus and the peace with God that is now possible for us sinners. There is no better function for our feet. No wonder the prophet calls them "lovely."

Thank You, Lord, for the privilege of sharing the gospel. Help me to be bold and articulate. Amen.

Instrument of Peace

Join us, and pursue a life that creates peace and builds up our brothers and sisters.

—Romans 14:19 VOICE

It is a beautiful prayer, and it is commonly known as the Prayer of Saint Francis. Around 1920, a Franciscan priest in France had the prayer printed on a small card that had a picture of Saint Francis on the other side. Although the card did not make any claim that the prayer was written by Saint Francis, the implication led many people to that conclusion. Whatever its earthly origins, its principles indicate its ultimately divine origin:

Lord, make me an instrument of Your peace. Where there is hatred, let me sow love; where there is injury, pardon; where there is doubt, faith; where there is despair, hope; where there is darkness, light; where there is sadness, joy. O Divine Master, grant that I may not so much seek to be consoled as to console; to be understood as to understand; to be loved as to love; for it is in giving that we receive; it is in pardoning that we are pardoned; and it is in dying that we are born to eternal life.

Make this prayer your prayer today by living it.

Lord, "make me an instrument of Your peace" in this world—in the world of my family, church, and neighborhood as well as in the world at large. Amen.

Just a Crack

The beginning of strife is like letting out water, so abandon the quarrel before it breaks out.

—Proverbs 17:14 NASB

Some very big things start small. An international corporation was once an individual's idea. A human being was once a pair of cells. A tsunami was once a gentle wave. And an argument was once a single word sharply spoken.

That single sharp word can, however, be a crack in a dam if we choose to either disagree or respond with an equally sharp retort. Even that little crack can be enough to allow emotions to come rushing out, hurting people and damaging relationships.

So what counsel did the wise King Solomon offer? Abandon before it even starts the quarrel that a sharp word might prompt. Don't let that crack get bigger. Instead, in the moment, ask for the Holy Spirit to help you control your tongue. You'll be glad you did. Your day will be more peaceful.

Lord, help me control both my tongue and the tone of my voice. I don't want to cause a crack in the dam, and I don't want to cause a crack to get bigger. Amen.

J-O-Y

Those who promote peace have joy.

—Proverbs 12:20 NIV

Joy is one of those things that is difficult to describe, but you definitely know it when you see it. Think of a child's eyes on Christmas morning, the reunion of two friends, the long-awaited answer to prayers for healing, and the woman who accepts a proposal of marriage. You can probably think of other times.

Joy—with and without tears—is to be an identifying characteristic of Christians. Today's verse clearly states that those who promote peace display joy. So how does one go about promoting peace? A hint lies in the word *joy* itself. Think of it as an acronym: the *J* stands for *Jesus* first; the *O*, *others* second; and *Y*, *yourself* last. That is a great way to think about promoting peace. When we have our priorities straight and a willingness to serve others, peace and joy will be ours.

Teach me to live, Lord, with You as my number one priority and with the willingness to serve others. Thank You that You will bless me with joy when I attempt to promote peace. Amen.

Friends, Not Enemies!

When a man's ways please the LORD, He makes even his enemies to be at peace with him.

—Proverbs 16:7 NKJV

The oldest member of the church was talking to the new minister. "I am ninety years old, sir, and I haven't an enemy in the world." The minister responded with great interest: "That is an amazing feat." Proudly, the woman added, "Yes, sir. I'm thankful to say that I've outlived 'em all."

If you've lived any length of time, you've made some enemies. Sadly, even friends can become enemies. Sometimes they turn on us because of something we've done or something we shouldn't have done. At other times, though, a friend becomes an enemy for no reason we can figure out.

We can work hard to make peace with all people, but this becomes difficult when we don't know the underlying issue. In that case, we can trust that God knows and focus on keeping our ways aligned with His. We aren't to worry about the situation; instead, we are to leave it in God's hands. In the end, perhaps when we don't expect it, our grace-filled God will bless our right living with the peace between friends we had hoped would come.

God, You know the friend who is now an enemy. Help me trust the situation to You while I focus on living in a way that pleases You. Amen.

The Sun and the Rain

"He causes the sun to rise on good people and on evil people, and he sends rain to those who do right and to those who do wrong."

—Matthew 5:45 NCV

It is a dirty little secret. It's a dirty little—or maybe not so little—sin! We don't do it intentionally. It just happens (our sin nature is alive and well) when we learn of a "bad" person's misfortune. What do we do? We celebrate. No, we don't jump up and down and throw a party, but secretly, deep inside, we are happy the bad person finally got his due.

Yet, if we take this line of reasoning further, we realize we have to believe that bad things are retribution for living a bad life. Logically, however, we know this is not true. Too often we've seen the innocent suffer tremendously.

When we hold in our hearts the truth of what Jesus said here, we are more able to accept the good that is enjoyed by people who are not good. When bad things happen to anyone, whether—in our estimation—the people deserve it or not, we can have compassion because bad things happen to everyone, good and bad.

The sun rises and sets on the good as well as the evil.

Forgive me for the silent but real celebration I have in my heart when bad things happen to those who "deserve" it. Forgive me, Lord, for judging them rather than praying for them. Amen.

How's Your Alignment?

Do not drag me away with the wicked and with those who work iniquity, who speak peace with their neighbors, while evil is in their hearts.

—Psalm 28:3 NASB

Some people can't be trusted. They'll tell you what you want to hear, but is it true? They'll make promises to please you, but they have no intention of fulfilling those promises. Or, as the psalmist observed, some people speak of peace while they are sowing seeds of disharmony. And some can sound like the good guy but be planning bad things.

The sad truth is that any of us can find ourselves doing these same things. Maybe the untruths are not premeditated. Or maybe we've thought it through and tell ourselves that everyone is doing it.

Granted, it can be difficult to align what we say and what we do, especially when what we say and do sets us apart from people we long to associate with and against society's accepted yet immoral practices. God's Spirit will give us the self-discipline we need so that we do align our words and our actions. By the way, inner peace is a nice side effect.

God, help me to live with my words and actions aligned with each other and, more importantly, aligned with Your ways. Amen.

A Crooked Path

They do not know the way of peace, and there is no justice in their tracks; they have made their paths crooked, whoever treads on them does not know peace.

—Isaiah 59:8 NASB

Anytime we hear about a new corporate scandal, it's easy to join in the condemnation of those responsible. Many of us have said, "They deserve whatever they get," but if we are honest, we know we may have done the same thing on a much smaller scale and out of the public eye.

Granted, we haven't embezzled millions of dollars or misrepresented financials to our shareholders, but we have done things in secret. We have lied (white lies are lies), cheated (that extra meal we put on our expense report), stolen (paper clips and sticky notes from the office), manipulated evidence (to put ourselves in a better light), and stepped on others (to protect or to advance ourselves).

Isaiah warned of the danger in following crooked paths like these. If we choose to walk a crooked path, we will be dodging, hiding, and sneaking around, fearing that we will be discovered.

Choosing to live with integrity is choosing to know peace.

Lord, forgive me for the little things I try to hide—and thank You for this reminder that they're not so little. Help me live a life with nothing to hide. Amen.

Priority Mail

Quiet down before God, be prayerful before him.

—Psalm 37:7 MSG

Priority Mail is a great invention: the post office charges a flat fee to ship an envelope or a box. No matter how much we stuff into it and how much it weighs, we give them the parcel and the fee, and they take it from there.

In a sense, God has always been acting on this principle. He will take as much as we want to send His way. No matter how much sin we stuff in the envelope, no matter how weighty the issues we lay before Him, and no matter how much disappointment in Him or even anger at Him we express and confess, He will accept the package and take care of all we sent. God will always receive all of our prayers; He will always listen and act.

As the psalmist encouraged above, whatever the circumstances of your life or emotions in your heart, quiet down. Go before your heavenly Father, the almighty God, and pray. God will always receive whatever we send His way.

Thank You, Lord, that You will receive anything and everything I send Your way. Amen.

Be Reconciled

"Leave your gift there before the altar, and go your way. First be reconciled to your brother, and then come and offer your gift."

—Matthew 5:24 NKJV

When we use the word *reconcile* in the context of a relationship, we are talking about restoring friendly relations between those who have been estranged. In the banking world, *reconcile* means making our checkbook register consistent with our bank statement. In both contexts, we are looking to restore people or things to harmony.

In Matthew 5, Jesus was speaking about reconciliation between people: the goal was to restore peace and harmony to a broken relationship. Reconciliation of relationships is so important to Jesus that He instructed us to not even give our offering if we have an unresolved issue with a brother or sister in the faith. Jesus was clear that we are to leave our offering at the altar and go make peace. Only after the relationship has been restored can we return to complete our offering. God will receive that offering with an open heart because we gave it with a cleansed heart. We were reconciled to our brothers and sisters in the faith as well as with God. With such reconciliation comes great peace.

Lord, I know with whom I need to be reconciled. Give me the courage to make peace with this person. Amen.

Rolled Together

Commit your way to the LORD, trust also in Him, and He will do it. He will bring forth your righteousness as the light and your judgment as the noonday.

—Psalm 37:5–6 NASB

With the advent of slice-and-bake cookies or good-as-homemade grocery-store bakeries, rolling out cookie dough is one skill disappearing from the art of baking. But baking can be fun, especially with new time-saving tips. One is to roll the dough between two pieces of waxed paper or parchment paper. Another suggestion is to freeze the dough in smaller, flatter portions to make rolling easier. One of the best tips I've found is to use powdered sugar to coat the rolling pin. Sugar won't toughen the cookies as flour does.

And what do cookies have to do with today's passage? In verse 5, *commit* means, in Hebrew, "roll into." When we roll the ingredients to make dough, they blend together and can't be separated again. Imagine our will being so blended with God's that it can never again be separated from His. Furthermore, when we confess our sin and accept Jesus as our Savior, His righteousness becomes ours. And so will His peace.

Lord, I want my will rolled into Yours so the two can never be separated, so that Your will is my will and the way I walk is the way You want me to walk. Amen.

Peace and Thankfulness

Let the peace of God rule in your hearts . . . and be thankful.

—Colossians 3:15 NKJV

Take a long, slooooow, deep breath . . . And another. What benefits came with doing so? Maybe your heart slowed down a bit, some weight lifted off your shoulders, and a spark of hope came from somewhere.

Moments of peace like this don't come naturally or automatically. That may be one reason the apostle Paul charged us to "let the peace of God rule." God longs to bless us with His peace—but will we let Him? Will we receive it from Him?

Another action that doesn't come naturally or automatically is saying "thank you." Interestingly, in the same verse that he invited us receive God's peace, Paul called us to be thankful. Consider the connection.

When we are at peace, we slow down and find ourselves more aware of the many blessings we can thank God for. When we choose to be thankful for all that God has given us, we can find ourselves more at peace in the world, more at peace with Him, more at peace within. The two can fuel each other, blessing us with a joy-filled life rooted in peace and gratitude.

Lord, please start in my life the cycle of peace fueling thanksgiving and thanksgiving fueling peace. Amen.

Plowshares of Peace

He will judge between the nations and will settle disputes for many peoples. They will beat their swords into plowshares and their spears into pruning hooks.

—Isaiah 2:4 NIV

"Swords to plowshares" refers to the practice of using military weapons and technologies for civilian purposes. Nuclear-weapons fuel is now used in electric power stations, and nuclear fission is now used in radiopharmaceutical production. Relief organizations promote this "swords to plowshares" concept for reconstruction after a war ends.

That phrase is much older than this modern-day practice. Seven hundred years before the birth of Jesus, the prophet Isaiah spoke of the Messiah's coming that would prompt the conversion of weapons into farm tools. As followers of Jesus, we can be involved in this kind of transformation, helping to make the peace Isaiah spoke of a reality.

Instruments of war that we have access to—our words, our money, our belongings—need to be used for peaceful purposes. Kind words can sow peace in our family and our church. A check can help bring peace to drug addicts and the homeless. And we can use our home to host informational meetings and times for prayer. What might you do?

God, I want to be an instrument of Your peace. Show me which swords You want me to turn into plowshares for Your good purposes. Amen.

PEACE THROUGH THANKSGIVING

Special Gifts

The special gift of ministry you received when I laid hands on you and prayed—keep that ablaze! God doesn't want us to be shy with his gifts, but bold and loving and sensible.

—2 Timothy 1:6–7 MSG

The child had stood in line for hours. The missionaries had told the villagers a truck was coming from America with gifts. This young girl had never received a gift. In her world, every day was a struggle just to find enough food to eat.

Finally the truck arrived. The children watched with even greater anticipation as the boxes were unloaded.

The magical moment arrived: a box was placed in the little girl's hands. She opened the lid, and nestled alongside the hairbrush and soap was the most beautiful doll she'd ever seen. Her eyes filled with tears as over and over again she repeated the only words she knew in English: "Thank you."

Each of us is given many tangible gifts, but we also receive the special gift of ministry. Have we ever thanked God for our gift of teaching, encouragement, or hospitality? Of course we can pray our thank You, but may we also live our thank You by using these gifts to boldly serve others—in the name of Jesus—with joy, peace, and love.

Thank You, Lord, for gifts of ministry and for opportunities to use those gifts. Enable me to serve boldly and with joy. Amen.

The Importance of Stories

Say, "Save us, Savior God, round us up and get us out of these godless places, so we can give thanks to your holy Name, and bask in your life of praise."

—1 Chronicles 16:35 MSG

The holiday season is here! It's a time of being together as a family and thanking God for blessings. Inevitably stories are shared that bring laughter and tears. Stories connect us to our past, knit our hearts together in the present, and remind us of God's faithfulness as we consider the future.

Throughout Scripture we see God's people telling and retelling stories to stay connected to their holy roots and to remind themselves of God's faithfulness to them. First and 2 Chronicles features the prophet Ezra as the storyteller. When the people of God gathered in Jerusalem after the exile, Ezra told them about God's faithfulness. That story cannot be told or God's goodness fully appreciated without discussing Israel's faithlessness and evil behavior. Ezra didn't gloss over the tough times but told how God saved them again and again from godless places and their own godless behavior.

When you gather this holiday season, listen to the stories and give thanks to the faithful One.

God, as I listen to family stories, Your faithfulness is unmistakable. How You are glorified and praised for being faithful from generation to generation. Amen.

Like a Tween?

I will praise you in the great meeting. I will praise you among crowds of people.

—Psalm 35:18 NCV

For years you drove your child to school. Those few minutes together became a favorite time of your day. But then came that fateful morning when your child asked if you wouldn't mind dropping her off a little sooner—down the street. You were crushed by this rite of passage, and you hold on to the hope that someday your child will once again not mind being seen in public with you.

Are there times when we're like a tween, times when we don't want others to know about our connection to God, times when we park down the block so our friends won't see who's driving? What a contrast to the psalmist's attitude above.

God wants us to sing His praises "among crowds of people." Perhaps you are a private person by nature, but the real issue is why some of us choose to praise God only in private. Is it really a personality thing, or are we somewhat embarrassed by God and worried about what others might think? Be honest with yourself and the Lord. Ask Him to help you. One of the blessings will be peace in your heart.

Lord, I wish I were more comfortable talking about You in public and sharing my faith with others. Help me to become bolder in talking about You. Amen.

Herding Sheep

We Your people and the sheep of Your pasture will give thanks to You forever; to all generations we will tell of Your praise.

—Psalm 79:13 NASB

A flock of sheep can number near one thousand, and shepherds depend on sheepdogs to herd and help protect the sheep. A herding dog must be able to help move the flock several miles, keep the sheep on the road, and, if needed, move the flock to the side of the road to allow cars to pass. Once the sheep are safely in the pasture, sheepdogs become living fences, keeping the sheep out of the crops that often border their grazing land.

God compares us to sheep (that's not a compliment!) that He must herd like a sheepdog with its herd. He must be able to move us along the road for good distances and get us out of harm's way when danger arises. He must keep us out of nearby crops that aren't ours and safely in our pasture.

Take time today to praise God for the lush and peaceful pastures where you eat, work, and play. You are blessed to be in His flock and in His pasture, safe and at peace.

Lord, thank You for protecting me from danger I am unaware of. Thank You for the peace and safety I find in Your pasture. Amen.

God Is Good

Praise the LORD! Oh, give thanks to the LORD, for He is good! For His mercy endures forever.

—Psalm 106:1 NKJV

Perhaps during a worship service you've heard this call and response. Half of the worshippers proclaim, "God is good!" The other half respond with, "All the time!" Then the congregation declares together, "All the time God is good."

God's blessings are evidence of His goodness, but this proclamation does the important job of reminding us that God is good even when life is hard, the pain is unrelenting, and He seems unaware and uncaring. Difficulties and pain don't mean that God is no longer good.

The truth is that our circumstances are no indication of God's goodness. In the most horrific situations, God is still good. A faith that acknowledges the goodness of God only when things are going well isn't faith at all.

Not everything was good when the psalmist wrote Psalm 106, yet he named God's goodness and mercy as a reason to praise Him. We find peace in dark days when we remind ourselves that God is good *all the time*, even when we don't understand the bad in our lives, in the world.

God, whatever my circumstances, I find peace in choosing to believe what Your Word teaches: You are always good. Amen.

Night and Day

At midnight I rise to give you thanks for your righteous laws.

—Psalm 119:62 NIV

Are you a morning person who wakes up singing with the birds, or do you prefer to burn the midnight oil? Night owls have a difficult time with morning songbirds who want to carry on meaningful conversations before the rooster crows. Likewise, songbirds have a tough time staying awake when night owls are ready to talk.

King David, however, was neither songbird nor night owl; his heart was so filled with thanksgiving that he found himself waking at all hours of the night with God's praise on his lips. When some people were rising to start their day and others were crawling into bed after a long night's work, David was on his knees with hands lifted high to thank God for His goodness, His grace, and His blessings. David's life was hardly easy, but he knew joy and hope because he knew God.

Whether you are a morning songbird or a night owl, peace will be in your heart when praise for God is on your lips. And God is worthy of that praise every hour of the day and every hour of the night.

Lord, when I lie down and when I awaken, may Your praise be ever on my lips and, as a gracious result, Your peace in my heart. Amen.

Thank You, God

[Jesus] took a cup of wine; and when He had given thanks for it, He passed it to [the disciples], and they all drank from it.

—Mark 14:23 VOICE

The elderly woman stood before the pile of rubble that, before the tornado, had been her home. She told the media gathered around her that although she'd lost everything, she was genuinely thankful to be alive.

At another gathering two thousand years earlier, Jesus also gave thanks at a surprising moment. He was sharing His last meal with His followers, and He knew all too well that He was about to face death—physical death on the cross as well as the spiritual death of never-before-experienced separation from His father. Once again communicating His imminent death to His disciples, He took the cup of wine and said it was His blood that would be spilled. Then Jesus did an amazing thing: He gave thanks to God. Thanking God in the midst of suffering and loss may not make sense, but by thanking God even during the most difficult or horrific things, we allow Him to transform that loss into new life.

Help me, even in the hardest circumstances, to find much to praise You for and reasons to give You thanks. I find peace knowing that You transform suffering and loss into new life. Amen.

The Greatest Victory

In a single victorious stroke of Life, all three—sin, guilt, death—are gone, the gift of our Master, Jesus Christ. Thank God!

—1 Corinthians 15:57 MSG

In 1913, Francis Ouimet, a twenty-year-old amateur golfer, beat the world's two best professionals in an eighteen-hole playoff to win the U.S. Open. He was ahead by one stroke going to the seventeenth.

Ouimet drove onto the fairway, sent his second shot onto the green, and knocked in his putt for a three. His lead now stood at three shots. At the eighteenth, he drove onto the fairway, the second shot put him on the green, and, with two breath-holding putts, he won the championship. It remains one of golf's greatest upsets.

But Ouimet's victory can't compare to the greatest victory of all. Surely, all of heaven must have held its breath when Jesus stepped onto the cross. And imagine the celebration when, with a single stroke, Jesus defeated our greatest adversaries—sin, guilt, and death—in the greatest victory of all time. And because of Jesus' victory, you and I have victory over sin, guilt, and death—and a reason to give thanks and praise God forever and ever.

Lord Jesus, Your victory on the cross will always be the greatest victory in history—and the greatest reason to give You thanks and praise for eternity. Amen.

God's Will

Pray without ceasing; in everything give thanks; for this is God's will for you in Christ Jesus.

—1 Thessalonians 5:17–18 NASB

What were your answers to the childhood question, "What do you want to be when you grow up?" A teacher? A firefighter? A mommy? A doctor? Perhaps you wanted to be president of the United States. As you got older and your faith grew, the question changed to, "What is God's will for my life?"

But Scripture never answers that question with a career path or job title. God's will isn't a hidden plan for your life that, once discovered, will lead to peace and happiness. Where God's will is mentioned in the Bible, it is always spelled out clearly: it is God's will that you believe in Him, trust Him, pray without ceasing, and give Him thanks in all things. When you do these things, you can be assured you're living in God's will for your life. What a source of peace that is!

Lord, thank You for making known the purpose You have for my life, which is to believe, trust, pray, and give thanks to You in all circumstances. Amen.

NOVEMBER 12

Celebrating God's Presence

The trumpeters and musicians joined in unison to give praise and thanks to the Lord. Accompanied by trumpets, cymbals and other instruments, the singers raised their voices in praise to the Lord.

—2 Chronicles 5:13 NIV

Did you play a musical instrument in school? Maybe you played the guitar or harmonica or you joined the school band and mastered the clarinet or tuba. You may still play in a community orchestra or the church praise band. Imagine one glorious day being invited to play in heaven's orchestra (Revelation 18:21).

Harps, lyres, trumpets, cymbals, tambourines, flutes, and that catch-all "instruments of music" or "other instruments" are mentioned throughout the Bible in scenes of praise, worship, thanksgiving, and celebration. In 2 Chronicles 5, for instance, music was playing as the priests took the Ark of the Covenant into Solomon's Temple. To the people of Israel, the ark represented God's presence, and His presence with them prompted great joy. As New Testament believers, we know that God's presence is both within us and always with us. So we have a 24/7 reason for joy and celebration: God *is* with us!

What difference will this reminder make in your life?

God, may the truth that You are always with me prompt me to live a life of worship! Amen.

Thanksgiving and Praise

Enter into His gates with thanksgiving, and into His courts with praise. Be thankful to Him, and bless His name.

—Psalm 100:4 NKJV

It's cause and effect: children who are praised only for the tasks that they do, but rarely for who they are, too easily conclude that they are loved for what they do. That sense often compels them to try to do bigger and more impressive things in hopes of receiving affirmation that will fill their souls. Children who receive praise for what they do *and* especially for who they are will be blessed with a soul that is healthier and more at peace.

We also go before God with both praise for His actions and praise for who He is. This psalm—written for the ceremony of offerings—reflects that balance. The gates were the entryway to the courtyard where the unclean washed and prepared to meet God by yielding their hearts to Him. "Enter into His courts with praise" refers to the inner courtyard where we praise God for the marvelous things He has done. After that we enter the inner courtyard and God's very presence. When we are in God's glorious presence, what better response than blessing His holy name, praising Him for who He is!

Lord, it's a privilege to enter the gates of prayer. I come with a yielded heart, gratitude for all You do, and praise for who You are. I love You, Lord. Amen.

NOVEMBER 14

Sweet Hour of Prayer

Three times each day Daniel would kneel down to pray and thank God, just as he always had done.

—Daniel 6:10 NCV

Did you know that God has ordained certain specific times—also called "hours"—for prayer? Three memorial hours of prayer are practiced today: the third hour (9 a.m.) when Christ was crucified; the sixth hour (12 p.m.) when darkness covered the earth; and the ninth hour (3 p.m.) when Christ uttered the words, "It is finished" and gave up His life. Those who practice this discipline can do so by simply praying the Lord's Prayer, or the hours can be more structured with preselected hymns and readings.

Although we can go to God anytime in prayer, setting aside a specific time slot is a discipline that brings great reward. Daniel, for instance, was known as a man of prayer: he regularly went before God to pray. Daniel began his prayers with praise, not requests. Likewise, when we pray to God for mercies, let's begin by praising Him for all He has given us. Being in prayer brings the blessing of God's peace.

Holy Spirit, grow in me the fruit of Your presence in my life, the fruit of self-control, so I may be more disciplined in my prayer life and come to know Jesus better. Amen.

A Change Agent

Work out your salvation with fear and trembling; for it is God who is at work in you, both to will and to work for His good pleasure.

—Philippians 2:12–13 NASB

If you've ever tried to make a big change in your life, you know it can be a one-step-forward, two-steps-back process. Most of us would benefit from having a change agent—or champion—in our life when it's time for some significant modifications. Ideally, this change agent would have a vision of what could be. Of course that vision would be aligned with yours, but it might be bigger, more worthwhile, yet still achievable. With this vision as the specific goal, the change agent would encourage and support you during the difficult but often necessary growth.

Does that description of a change agent remind you of anyone? Yes: Jesus. He knows you and knows what is best for you. He understands you and loves you, and He longs for you to be as God-honoring, joyful, and peaceful you as you can be. Jesus not only supports and encourages you in your growth, but He also provides His power to make it happen.

Jesus can change our pattern initially to two steps forward for every one step backward.

I am tired of this two-step pattern in my effort to change, but I'm encouraged, Jesus, that You will empower me to move forward, for my growth and Your good pleasure. Amen.

Our God Reigns!

We give thanks to you, Lord God Almighty, the One who is and who was, because you have taken your great power and have begun to reign.

—Revelation 11:17 NIV

The longest reigning monarch in history was King Sobhuza II of Swaziland: he governed for eighty-two years from 1899 to 1982. Queen Victoria had the longest reign—sixty-three years—of any king or queen in the English monarchy. Yet, when speaking of kings, no one in the course of history has ever or will ever match King Jesus in power and reign.

Our eternal Lord has reigned in heaven for eternity past and will reign for eternity future. He became flesh before dying on a cross, rising victorious over the power of death and the sin that caused it. King Jesus will one day return to finally put an end to Satan, to gather the faithful, and to begin to reign over a new heaven and a new earth.

Even more amazing is the fact that King Jesus is the same today as He was in the beginning: pure, holy, wise, powerful, just, true, compassionate, faithful, sovereign—and so much more. To this unchanging and indescribably wonderful King belong all honor and glory forever and ever.

I find much comfort and peace in knowing You are the One who is and who was. I know that I can trust in Your stable, reliable, unchanging character. Amen.

Our Sacrifice of Praise

By [Jesus] let us continually offer the sacrifice of praise to God, that is, the fruit of our lips, giving thanks to His name.

—Hebrews 13:15 NKJV

A sacrifice, according to *Merriam-Webster,* is "an act of offering . . . something precious; *especially:* the killing of a victim on an altar." Parents, for example, sacrifice time and sleep to take care of their babies, while young people might sacrifice time with their friends to spend some time with Mom and Dad.

Why, then, does the Bible sometimes refer to praising God as a sacrifice? Because praise requires that we "kill" our pride, confess our sin, relinquish our independence, and recognize His lordship. This act—this sacrifice—requires us to approach God with a heartfelt and appropriate yet unnatural humility. And this privilege of coming before God with a sacrifice of praise, for who He is and for the forgiveness we'll receive, is possible because of the ultimate sacrifice offered by Jesus, the One whom we are praising. It is *by* Him, *in* Him, *with* Him, *to* Him, and *for* Him that we offer our sacrifice of praise to God.

Father, please help me to put to death my pride, to fully surrender my will to Yours, to live my life for Your glory. Amen.

Sing to the Lord!

Sing to the Lord *with thanksgiving; sing praises to our God on the lyre.*

—Psalm 147:7 NASB

Singing is something virtually everyone can do, but some of us do it better than others. Some people are born with an ear for music, a natural vibrato, or a remarkably clear voice. Others are less skilled, but confident doing exactly what the psalmist called us to do: "Make a joyful noise unto the Lord" (Psalm 100:1 KJV). Wherever you fall on the spectrum of vocal ability, know that singing with a joyful heart makes all of us sound better.

Since Psalms is the Bible's hymnbook, we shouldn't be surprised that—like Psalm 100—many psalms mention singing. Research has shown that our bodies were designed to sing. God created us with a diaphragm and thirty-six muscles that support its work of pushing air upward to vibrate the vocal cords so we can sing.

Yes, your body was physically made to sing and praise God. And I'm guessing at least once in your life you've been blessed with the sense in your heart of hearts that, yes, you as a spiritual being were created to sing and praise your God.

What a miracle the human body is! Help me use it to wholeheartedly sing Your praises, to make a joyful noise, because of Your goodness and grace. Amen.

A Parent's Heart

These things did not really come from me and my people. Everything comes from you; we have given you back what you gave us.

—1 Chronicles 29:14 NCV

Gifts to Mom and Dad from their children are some of the most precious. It doesn't matter in the least that the ingredients for Mom's cake were bought by Mom or the craft supplies for Dad's card were financed by Dad. That thought never crosses the parents' minds. It is the gift—and the thought, the effort, and especially the love behind the gift—that melts their hearts.

That is a good truth to keep in mind when we find ourselves wondering what we can give God. After all, every single thing we have came from God. But that thought never crosses our heavenly Father's mind. It is the thought, the effort, and especially the love behind our gift that melts God's heart.

Keep that in mind when you wish you could place more in the offering plate or sponsor another orphaned child. In the meantime rejoice with King David that everything you have comes from God and you have the joy of giving some back to your heavenly Father. His heart melts.

Thank You for knowing my heart, my circumstances, and my responsibilities. Thank You for receiving my gifts—which were first Your gifts to me—with Your heart of love. Amen.

A Simple "Thank You"

I will give you thanks, for you answered me; you have become my salvation.

—Psalm 118:21 NIV

What could you possibly say to the person who saved your life? What could you possibly do for that person to show your gratitude? In a classic episode of *The Andy Griffith Show*, Andy saves Goober's life, and for days afterward Goober tries to repay Andy. He washes Andy's car, takes out his garbage, and even cuts his meat on his dinner plate. After several days Andy can't take any more gratitude! So he devises a way for Goober to save his life, thereby erasing the need for repayment.

Jesus Christ saved our lives for eternity. What can we possibly say or do to show our gratitude? We are well aware of how desperately we need a Savior. We understand that absolutely nothing about us makes us worthy of saving. We are overwhelmed by the humbling Ephesians 2:8 truth that only by God's grace are we saved. We, like Goober, long to repay God, yet there is nothing God wants more than our thanks. A simple "thank You" whispered from a genuinely grateful heart is all God desires.

Lord, I thank You from a genuinely grateful heart for the gift of my salvation. Enable me to live my thanks as well. Amen.

A Masterpiece

I will offer You my grateful heart, for I am Your unique creation, filled with wonder and awe. You have approached even the smallest details with excellence; Your works are wonderful; I carry this knowledge deep within my soul.

—Psalm 139:14 VOICE

Most women would reshape at least one part of their body if they could. Compounding this unsettledness about our appearance are the worlds of advertising and entertainment that in many ways make it clear that we don't measure up to their standards.

We so need to hear truth! And Scripture is straightforward in its presentation of the truth: you are wonderfully made. When God looks at you, He sees a masterpiece—a one-of-a-kind creation that He lovingly crafted. God fashioned every detail—even that part we and/or society deems inferior. God is especially pleased with the part of us that makes us who we are—our souls.

So the next time you look in the mirror, tell that image looking back at you, "You are a masterpiece, crafted and cherished by the God of all creation." Then spend a few minutes in His loving, peaceful presence. Let Him give you peace about the body He so lovingly knit together.

Lord, thank You for today's mirror of Your love. May I be at peace knowing that You, Creator God, made me, love me, and cherish me. Amen.

A Prayer Away

The LORD is my strength and my shield; my heart trusts in Him, and I am helped; therefore my heart exults, and with my song I shall thank Him.

—Psalm 28:7 NASB

Did you know that falling is the leading cause of death among the elderly? Death comes due to trauma to the brain sustained in the fall, a risky surgical procedure to repair a bone broken in the fall, or a longer recovery time in the hospital that increases the person's vulnerability to disease. It is therefore a sobering statistic that one out of three older adults, aged sixty-five or older, falls each year. Medical alert devices, however, enable many seniors to call immediately for help they need.

You and I can also call immediately for any help we need: Jesus is just a prayer away. When you call on Him, you can know God's peace that passes understanding. You'll find yourself waiting with confidence for the Helper to deliver exactly what you need. You can trust Him to know your need, and then meet it.

You never need to fear falling: Jesus is only a prayer away.

God, I find great comfort and peace in knowing that You are only a prayer away and that when I need help, You will send exactly what I need exactly when I need it. Amen.

A Ticker-Tape Parade

In the Messiah, in Christ, God leads us from place to place in one perpetual victory parade. Through us, he brings knowledge of Christ. Everywhere we go, people breathe in the exquisite fragrance.

—2 Corinthians 2:14 MSG

On August 14 and 15, 1945, New York City marked the end of World War II with a ticker-tape parade. The term *ticker tape* referred to the paper generated by machines that provided updated stock market quotes. Ticker-tape parades continue, but the pieces of tape have been replaced by confetti.

Of course parades are not modern, western-hemisphere events. In his first-century letter to the Corinthian church, the apostle Paul envisioned God leading a victory parade of believers into a world looking for a hero. As believers, we are part of that "triumphal procession" (NIV), proclaiming and celebrating the life, death, and resurrection of Jesus, the Messiah. He is the Hero people are looking for. As we pass by, may these searching people notice, marvel, and wonder at "the aroma of the knowledge of [Christ]" (NIV). As we travel the parade route of life, may the "exquisite fragrance" of salvation, purpose, and hope fill the air, inviting friends to investigate and experience the peace that we have found in Jesus.

Lord, it's an honor to part of a "perpetual victory parade" that glorifies You and attracts people to want to know You and join the parade themselves. Amen.

PEACEMAKERS

Peace Activists

"They are blessed who work for peace, for they will be called God's children."

—Matthew 5:9 NCV

What do you think of when you hear the word *peacemaker*? Someone negotiating a peace agreement in an effort to end a war? A person who chose peaceful acts of civil disobedience to make a point?

Mahatma Gandhi, perhaps the most famous peacemaker in modern history, practiced civil disobedience, nonviolence, and passive resistance as he worked for peace. Inspired by Gandhi, Dr. Martin Luther King Jr. encouraged African-Americans to maintain the moral high ground by practicing nonviolence in their fight for civil rights.

Peacemaking is hard work; perhaps it is even divine work. It is hardly surprising that the particular blessing for peacemakers is that "they will be called God's children": peacemakers surely are doing both God's will and His work on this planet.

So, as children of the heavenly Father, let us seek to do what He has done and continues to do: love people and find common ground so bridges can be built where war and hostility have taken hold.

Lord, please love others through me that they may better know Your love for them—and please use me as a peacemaker in this world. Amen.

What Will They Say?

Consider the blameless, observe the upright; a future awaits those who seek peace.

—Psalm 37:37 NIV

What do you think people will say about you after you're gone? What might be inscribed on your tombstone or said at your funeral? Think about it.

What would your neighbors say or your coworkers, your boss, your family, and your friends? Would all of them know you were a Christian? Would they talk only of your accomplishments, or would they also speak of your character? If so, would *peacemaker* be one of the words they use?

Peacemakers are among our world's unsung heroes. They do their work behind the scenes. They lead blameless lives, walking upright in their families, workplaces, and communities. They aren't famous or flashy. Instead they humbly and persistently work for peace, model peace, fight for peace, and nudge others toward peace. They serve the cause of peace in humble and selfless ways.

Would *peacemaker* be one of the words they use? Even more important, however, would they know you followed Jesus?

Lord, please help me live in such a way that people have no doubt that I am living for You. May You and Your gospel be the take-away from my funeral. Amen.

War and Peace

Nation shall not lift up sword against nation, neither shall they learn war anymore.

—Isaiah 2:4 NKJV

The epic novel *War and Peace* is set against the background of Napoleon's invasion of Russia in 1812. Author Leo Tolstoy focused on five aristocratic families and the impact the French invasion had on them, but he also revealed the struggles of peasants, civilians, and soldiers during the Napoleonic era. In addition, Tolstoy juxtaposed the peace that followed war with the more fragile and profound peace found in the human soul.

Many of us long for the day when peace is not so fragile and war will be no more, the day when swords, guns, and bombs will be set aside forever. Christians have long looked to Isaiah's promises that war will cease when the Messiah begins His forever reign. What a glorious day that will be! However, it is easy to look ahead to that day and overlook what Tolstoy knew: securing peace within the soul is the beginning of securing world peace.

God, I long for the day when war is only in the history books, and peace fills the earth, our nation, our homes, and our own hearts. Amen.

Getting Centered

Is God the God of Jews only? Is he not the God of Gentiles too? Yes, of Gentiles too, since there is only one God, who will justify the circumcised by faith and the uncircumcised through that same faith.

—Romans 3:29–30 NIV

It was a radical proposal, one that directly contradicted the theory that had been accepted as truth for more than ten centuries. The proposal required a significant paradigm shift, one that might get the scientist in trouble with the Catholic Church. Yet Nicolaus Copernicus stood by his conclusion that the sun is the center of the universe, not the earth. Scholars criticized his so-called theory, and the Roman Catholic Church banned his writings.

Proposing a different center of the universe is a bold act, and that is basically what Jesus of Nazareth did as well—and neither the claim nor Jesus Himself was readily accepted. Jesus said that grace—the holy God's sacrificial and redeeming love for sinful people—was at the center of salvation, not one's family tree, not membership in a particular group, and not the ability to follow rules.

It's a paradigm shift: our gracious Jesus is at the center of salvation, not anything you or I do. May that truth make you grateful and give you peace.

Jesus, You are at the center of my salvation. Thank You for Your amazing grace. Amen.

Love and Patience

Love patiently accepts all things. It always trusts, always hopes, and always endures.

—1 Corinthians 13:7 NCV

When the Lord was handing out virtues in the heavenly birthing room, did you get in the line labeled *patience* or did you miss it? Looking at many of the drivers on our roadways, it appears many, if not most, of us missed that line!

But patience can be improved or even learned. Yet common wisdom warns not to pray for patience—if you do, you might get children! Parenthood will test your patience well into grandparenthood.

The Bible tells us that Christian love is patient, and *patience* is defined as "the capacity to accept or tolerate delay, trouble, or suffering without getting angry or upset." Each one of us has struggled to love someone who tests our patience, yet, by God's grace, we persist. To trust, hope, and endure in our efforts is to love as Jesus loves. To persist without getting angry, without growing weary, is to love as Jesus loves. Loving a difficult person is an act of Christlike peacemaking at its best.

God, I am not naturally patient! Add tiredness or stress, and I'm a total failure. Please continue to make me more like Jesus. Amen.

Slap! Whack! Wham!

"You have heard that it was said, 'An eye for an eye, and a tooth for a tooth.' But I say to you, do not resist an evil person; but whoever slaps you on your right cheek, turn the other to him also."

—Matthew 5:38–39 NASB

Onomatopoeia refers to words that imitate or resemble the sounds they refer to. Animal sounds offer great examples: *hee-haw, meow, neigh, ribbit,* and *woof.* And from the comic books we have *pow, whack, wham, boink,* and *swish!*

That last set of words comes to mind when I read Jesus' words above. When we are slapped, He instructed us to turn the other cheek for a second slap rather than returning the initial slap. As we turn our cheek, we can almost see the speech bubbles pop up above our heads: *POW! WHACK! WHAM!* And, as we turn the other cheek, we feel almost like we're living a cartoon. After all, real people live "an eye for an eye," not "turn the other cheek."

But Jesus was clear: if we are to be real peacemakers, we are not to retaliate but instead allow that second *WHACK!* to come. Though it may be counterintuitive, it's exactly what Jesus did when He stood silent before accusers and let Himself be nailed to a cross.

This is the most difficult part of peacemaking. Lord, it seems so unfair. Change my heart into that of a real peacemaker so that, when I am attacked, I choose to turn the other cheek. Amen.

A Million Tiny Pieces

Not only that, but all the broken and dislocated pieces of the universe—people and things, animals and atoms—get properly fixed and fit together in vibrant harmonies, all because of his death, his blood that poured down from the cross.

—Colossians 1:20 MSG

The fifty-year-old woman proudly showed her friend a set of sixteen china dolls. And she had quite a story to tell about them.

"Shortly after I turned sixteen, I let my mother use them at a banquet. The dolls were carefully wrapped and placed in a cardboard box. The cat, however, thought the box looked inviting, and I watched as the box, with all its precious treasures, crashed to the floor. What makes these dolls so precious to me is that my mother spent weeks lovingly gluing together all those pieces of porcelain, making whole each doll—and her daughter's heart."

Jesus came to repair all of the broken and dislocated pieces of the universe—and of His children's hearts. The glue He used was His own blood, and that precious glue brings peace. So if circumstances have left you feeling shattered, allow your heavenly Father to pick up all those pieces and make you whole.

I realize I need to be made whole. So I thank You, Jesus, for providing the precious glue necessary to repair my brokenness. Amen.

A Bond for Battle

Make every effort to keep the unity of the Spirit through the bond of peace.

—Ephesians 4:3 NIV

He went back toward enemy lines when he realized his buddy had not retreated with the rest of the platoon . . . Without thinking, the Medal of Honor winner fell on the grenade, saving dozens of lives at the cost of his own . . . Incidents like these happen when soldiers' hearts are bonded together by a common passion and profound friendship. The battlefield offers amazing examples of the loyalty and love that exist between brothers and sisters in arms.

We believers are also in battle, fighting an enemy who wants people stuck in living for themselves, distant from God, and burdened by unforgiven sins. We aren't much of a force against the enemy if we are not unified, if philosophical differences, the world's distractions, or even personalities keep us from working together as one.

May we focus on Jesus even as we come together to serve Him in our battle against darkness. He who brought peace between the holy God and us will enable us to be at peace with other believers and forge bonds in us, so that we can bring peace to those still far away from the Savior.

Holy God, thank You for making possible both forgiveness of my sins and peace with You. Please use me in this world to bring peace with You to others. Amen.

Harmony

The Jewish law had many commands and rules, but Christ ended that law. His purpose was to make the two groups of people become one new people in him and in this way make peace.

—Ephesians 2:15 NCV

As a fourth-grader, he could choose to do vocal music or instrumental. He opted for instrumental, and that meant taking up the violin. Soon the Christmas concert arrived. Parents were amazed at how good their rookie musicians sounded when they played together!

Bringing people together may also result in unexpected harmony, but such was not the case in the early church. The Jews were not about to relinquish their rule following; the new followers of Jesus were blessed by grace, and they were not going to be enslaved by laws He had fulfilled. Jesus wanted "the two groups of people [to] become one new people in him."

We help that happen when we bring our unique gifts to God; He combines them with the gifts of others and transforms that combination into something beautiful. When we place them in God's hands, He harmonizes what we thought were incongruent gifts so that He can use us mightily as His tools for the cause of peace.

Lord, I lay before You the gifts You have given me. Use them—use me—in harmony with Your people to make peace in this world. Amen.

DECEMBER 3

A Perspective for Peace

If it is possible, as much as depends on you, live peaceably with all men.

—Romans 12:18 NKJV

At the end of the battle, two warriors from opposing sides stood among the lifeless bodies of their comrades. "Shall we end this now?" one of the soldiers asked.

Weary and tired, the other suggested, "Let us rest until dawn and then finish this fight." Struggling to find sleep, the warriors started talking. "I have a son back home who dreams of being a soldier like me." The other responded, "I have a son who dreams the same dreams."

Through the night the two exchanged stories about their families. When day broke, they drew their swords, but neither could make the first move. We are less likely to hate each other when we know each other's stories.

Being a peacemaker is facilitated by remembering that an enemy is someone's son or daughter, brother or sister, husband or wife, friend. We can choose to remember that he or she has experiences that invite our compassion rather than our opposition. Peacemakers make peace possible by choosing to see the enemy as a person.

Lord, give me compassion for my enemies by keeping me mindful that they are people with stories, people who love and are loved by other people and especially by You. Amen.

The Rule of Reciprocity

"Treat others the same way you want them to treat you."

—Luke 6:31 NASB

Marketers use a wide range of strategies to convince consumers to make certain purchases. Some tactics are straightforward: sales, coupons, and special promotions, for example. Other approaches are more subtle, often based on the psychological principle known as the rule of reciprocity: we tend to feel obligated to return favors after people do favors for us.

Reciprocating like this is not hard when we consider other people deserving of fair or even generous treatment. When someone treats us well, we readily want to return the favor. But reciprocity is difficult when we regard someone as less than deserving. In these instances, the Bible tells us, we are to practice reciprocity anyway. We are to follow the foundational rule for peacekeeping, referred to as the Golden Rule. As Jesus stated above, we are to treat others the way we want them to treat us—regardless of how we have been treated. That divine guideline is a principle for peacekeeping.

Lord, forgive me for judging that certain individuals don't deserve fair treatment. Enable me to live according to Your rule of reciprocity. Amen.

DECEMBER 5

The Beginning of Thanks

When you think about [the leaders in your church], let it be with great love in your heart because of all the work they have done. Let peace live and reign among you.

—1 Thessalonians 5:13 VOICE

We often complain more than we say "thank you." We might choose to blame our busyness, or we might judge the less thankful among us as having a sense of entitlement ("I should get what I want.") or being narcissistic ("Yes, the world revolves around me! I'm wonderful!").

Maybe we need to ask God to show us why we aren't saying "thank you." Nineteenth-century clergyman Henry Ward Beecher observed, "A proud man is seldom a grateful man, for he never thinks he gets as much as he deserves." Pride and gratitude are incompatible: we don't thank someone—or Someone—when we believe we are simply getting what we deserve. So what is the antidote? God's Word and its teaching that all we have is from Him—this is where the thanks can begin.

So spend time thanking God. Mentally walk through your day and thank God for everything and everyone. Thank God for the leaders at your church—and then thank *them*!

Lord, thank You for this exercise in gratitude. Use it to change me and grow me. Amen.

Covenant Keepers

"Tell [Phinehas] that I am making a Covenant-of-Peace with him. He and his descendants are joined in a covenant of eternal priesthood, because he was zealous for his God and made atonement for the People of Israel."

—Numbers 25:12–13 MSG

We see it in children, young people, and adults: the unwillingness to make a commitment and stick to it. We like to keep all of our options open. Children sign up for lessons only to attend the first and never return. Young people on a soccer team miss practice because they went to the midnight release of the new movie. Adults won't RSVP to an invitation because something better might come up.

Our God, however, is the absolute and ultimate Covenant Keeper who makes commitments to His people and honors those commitments. Even when we don't hold up our end of the bargain, God keeps His covenant of peace with His people. He expects no less from those who claim His name. This means that we, too, should honor our commitments. This impacts all of life, including the hard work of peacekeeping, the hard work of following after Christ.

Lord God, even when it costs more than I anticipated or want it to, help me to be a covenant keeper just like You. Amen.

DECEMBER 7

Unbridled Love

Jesus replied: "'Love the Lord your God with all your heart and with all your soul and with all your mind.' This is the first and greatest commandment. And the second is like it: 'Love your neighbor as yourself.'"

—Matthew 22:37–39 NIV

Oh, to be able to love God with all that we are! To carry on a day-long conversation with our heavenly Father! To be mindful of His presence with us every minute of every day! We so long to love God with lavish, unbridled love. As with every command He gives us, we need His help to do so.

Even the next words out of Jesus' mouth remind us how much we need His help to obey. Loving our neighbor as ourselves means loving ourselves, and that's where some of us get hung up. We may find it easier to love ourselves if we ask Jesus, our Beloved, to help us see ourselves the way He sees us. Being so wholeheartedly accepted, celebrated, and loved, we just might find our hearts overflowing with so much love that loving others comes more easily.

Love God, love ourselves, love others: obedience to these commands can indeed make for peace in a world desperate for love.

By Your grace and Your Spirit's power, help me receive Your love, not only in my mind, but in my heart, so that I am better able to love others as You have loved me. Amen.

No Small Wounds

"They tried to heal my people's serious injuries as if they were small wounds. They said, 'It's all right, it's all right.' But really, it is not all right."

—Jeremiah 8:11 NCV

Maybe it was a rock, a moment of distraction, or the uneven sidewalk, but suddenly the little boy was flying over the bicycle handlebars. When he hit the concrete, the bike landed on top of him, driving the broken pedal into his ankle. His mother took a look at the wound and grabbed her purse and a towel. "Hold this on your ankle until we get to the ER," she said. The boy protested, "Can't we just put a Band-Aid on it?"

Perhaps you've walked around with a gaping wound in your heart only to hear people say, "It's not that bad. Just put a Band-Aid on it." You want to shout, "Don't you see this huge hole?" Their words add to your pain.

A basic principle of peacemaking is to never minimize someone's pain or suffering. Suggesting the pain just needs a bandage or that the time for grieving has expired shuts down the peacemaking process. Sometimes peacemaking requires us to go with others to God's ER.

Enable me to love with Your compassion, never minimizing someone's suffering and always willing to go with someone to God's ER, where true healing takes place. Amen.

DECEMBER 9

Healing, Freedom, and Joy

Counselors of peace have joy.

—Proverbs 12:20 NKJV

Thankfully, Christian counseling is becoming more accepted among believers. Churches now host counseling centers, and Christian schools offer accredited programs to train these compassionate people. For too long, Satan enjoyed free range in the Christian community because, ashamed and feeling lesser-than, we hid our hurts and struggles. Christian counselors allow us to bring that pain into the open where healing can take place.

If you want to see the joy that comes with such healing, attend a meeting of people who have been set free from the bonds of secrecy, the bonds of darkness and sin. They are freer now to love themselves and to love others because they better understand God's love and have experienced His healing power. The godly professionals who help individuals make peace with themselves are answering Jesus' commands to love others and to be a peacemaker.

Don't hesitate to let one of these fellow brothers or sisters in Christ come alongside you and enable you to receive from the great Physician, your heavenly Father, the healing and peace He wants you to know.

Lord, I pray for those who counsel others. Give them wisdom. Enable them to help people find freedom and know peace in their souls. Amen.

PEACE FOR THE FUTURE

One Fine Day

In my vision at night I looked, and there before me was one like a son of man, coming with the clouds of heaven. He approached the Ancient of Days and was led into his presence. He was given authority, glory and sovereign power; all nations and peoples of every language worshiped him.

—Daniel 7:13–14 NIV

We open the newspaper or turn on the news. Our hearts sink, and we try to pray. How evil can humanity get? How far away from God's standards for moral behavior can we run? It's hard not to ask one more question: where is God?

First, we remind ourselves of truths from Scripture. God is sovereign throughout time, God is with us always, and God's ways aren't our ways. Daniel's vision shows us the hope of Christ's return. The risen and glorious Jesus will come from the heavens, and we will watch as He approaches God. The Almighty will then give Jesus authority over heaven and earth. All wars, hatred, and evil will cease to exist. All nations and people of every language will bow before our Lord, and peace will rule. Cling today to the promise of a world that will one day be at peace.

I wait expectantly for the day when You, Lord, rule the heavens and the earth, when evil has been vanquished and replaced by Your unshakable and eternal peace. Amen.

DECEMBER 11

Swords into Shovels

They'll turn their swords into shovels, their spears into hoes. No more will nation fight nation; they won't play war anymore.

—Isaiah 2:4 MSG

Any study of human history will reveal that the human race has always been at war. Some people naively thought that World War I was the "war to end all wars." That was hardly the case. Not too many years later, other people imagined that dropping the bomb at Hiroshima would end the need for war. Others are still convinced that we can talk our way out of war, but that hasn't happened either. History as well as today's news stories suggest that there will be war somewhere in the world until Christ returns.

But when He returns, implements of war will be turned into tools for peace: swords will become shovels and spears, hoes. No longer will weapons be needed, for nations will not fight against one another but instead live together in harmony and peace, ruled by our King who reigns in peace and love. War will be no more; and peace will reign into eternity.

What a glorious day! Until this scene of ultimate peace arrives, Jesus, use me as a peacemaker as well as Your gospel messenger. Amen.

No Term Limit

Of the increase of His government and peace there will be no end, upon the throne of David and over His kingdom, to order it and establish it with judgment and justice from that time forward, even forever.

—Isaiah 9:7 NKJV

Have you ever imagined being president of the United States? If you were president for just a week or a month, what would be your top two or three priorities? Would it be Middle East peace? Would you address health care, the nation's deficit, or nuclear weapons?

Jesus has already told us what His priorities will be when He returns to this earth as King of kings. First, He will be a one-term president, but that term will last for eternity: "Of . . . His government . . . there will be no end." Second, His throne will be the highest, the final, the absolute authority: that is only appropriate considering He is the Redeemer; He is love; and He is perfectly just, wise, and merciful. Finally, Jesus' governing priority will be justice and peace: His justice will be pure and holy; His peace will be perfect.

And—thank you, Mr. Handel—"He shall reign forever and ever"!

Lord, thank You that our perfect King of kings will lead a perfect and eternal government as every knee, in heaven and on earth and under the earth, bows before Him. Amen.

DECEMBER 13

The Lord's Compassion

"So you will go out with joy and be led out in peace. The mountains and hills will burst into song before you, and all the trees in the fields will clap their hands."

—Isaiah 55:12 NCV

We can grin and bear some tough situations when we know how long we will have to endure. We run the five laps. We read the ten chapters. We diet for six weeks. We dog sit for ten days. We are pregnant for forty weeks. Just don't move the finish line!

Interestingly, we don't know how long this world—how long God's people—need to wait before Jesus returns. But the Holy Spirit sustains us, as does God's Word.

Take some time to read Isaiah 55. Hear the love in God's invitation to "Come!" Read His promises. And note the unmistakable joy, such joy that creation itself joins in. Mountains will sing, and trees will clap their hands. By the end of Isaiah 55, you may be singing and clapping! What an amazing God we serve—and He will not only sustain us, but He will richly bless us with His presence as we await Jesus' return.

What a glorious and joyful day when Jesus returns, King of kings and Lord of lords! What a glorious and joyful day when the mountains sing Your praises and the trees clap their hands! Amen.

To the End

"I will be with you, day after day, to the end of the age."

—Matthew 28:20 VOICE

Have you been with someone as he or she has passed from this life into the next? Depending on the person's physical condition and especially his or her spiritual health, that passing can be difficult to witness or a sacred time with your heavenly Father. Even when those moments or days or weeks are difficult, many people consider it a privilege to walk alongside their loved one as this life ends. Sometimes these people are rewarded by the loved one's parting words; they can be the most precious words ever heard.

Jesus had some significant parting words for His friends before He, risen from the dead, ascended into heaven. First, He instructed His disciples to tell everyone what they'd seen and heard during His ministry. Jesus also told these faithful followers to wait for the gift of the Holy Spirit, and then He spoke these words of promise and encouragement: "I will be with you, day after day," all the way to the end of time.

Jesus is with us—is within us—through His Holy Spirit. What peace and comfort come with knowing He will never leave us.

Lord, You are Victor over sin and death. And You will be with me "to the end of the age." All glory and praise to You! Amen.

DECEMBER 15

Knowing What's Best

"Nevertheless I tell you the truth. It is to your advantage that I go away; for if I do not go away, the Helper will not come to you; but if I depart, I will send Him to you."

—John 16:7 NKJV

Parents usually know best, but kids usually don't appreciate that fact. When Dad says, "Eat your veggies so you can grow up strong," a child looks at that pile of peas and finds it hard to see how they can do anything good! When tragedy strikes, we look at the circumstances and find it hard to see how anything good could come out of them. Why did our heavenly Father allow it?

Similarly, when Jesus told His friends He had to leave in order to be with them, it didn't make sense to them. Jesus essentially said that the very thing they wanted—for Him to stay with them—was not what was best. The disciples didn't understand that the risen Jesus had to leave this earth so His Spirit could come.

Jesus knew that God's Spirit would be the best for us. And today, two thousand years later, we who follow Jesus agree. We are blessed, sustained, comforted, and guided by the Holy Spirit Jesus sent.

Jesus, You knew best. Of course I long for the day when You return, and I am grateful beyond words for the gift of Your Spirit, truly the best gift You could have given. Amen.

Downtime

The church throughout Judea, Galilee and Samaria enjoyed a time of peace and was strengthened. Living in the fear of the Lord and encouraged by the Holy Spirit, it increased in numbers.

—Acts 9:31 NIV

Downtime is in short supply in our hectic and busy world. It can be planned, it can occur because work has slowed, or it can come for no explainable reason. Regardless of the reason, we must be prepared to take advantage of this opportunity to renew, refocus, and refuel.

Downtime is an opportunity to experience peace. Sometimes we get so busy that peace could knock at our door, and we wouldn't hear it. So in God's goodness, He puts on the brakes for us. The trick is being aware when the opportunity comes so we don't miss the chance to soak in the peace He's offering.

The newly formed church experienced this time of peace, even though things never slowed down. They were in tune with the Spirit and took full advantage of this time to renew their spirits, refocus on Christ's teachings, and refuel for the growth ahead.

Are you enough in tune with the Spirit so that you won't miss your downtime?

Lord, help me to never miss the opportunity to soak in the peace You graciously offer. Amen.

The Important Things

In the kingdom of God, eating and drinking are not important. The important things are living right with God, peace, and joy in the Holy Spirit.

—Romans 14:17 NCV

What tends to be your response to rules? Are you a rule follower, content to stay within the lines that are drawn? Or do you automatically go left when the rules say to go right? Maybe you're in the middle: you're fine with following rules—and you're fine with bending them when necessary.

The Jewish religion in Jesus' day had a lot of rules. Some of them were God's rules, but others were man's attempt to clarify God's rules. Still other rules were simply manmade.

Our loving God established rules for our good and for the good of our relationship with Him. To keep us from getting entangled in rules for rules' sake, God made His priorities clear: "The important things are living right with God, peace, and joy in the Holy Spirit." The rules are important, but they aren't as important as their purpose, which is to help us live God-honoring lives according to His will, to know His peace, and to share in His joy.

Lord, help me never to lose You in a tangle of rules. Help me never lose focus on You because I'm evaluating how well I'm keeping rules! Amen.

Hidden Healing

So we're not giving up. How could we! Even though on the outside it often looks like things are falling apart on us, on the inside, where God is making new life, not a day goes by without his unfolding grace.

—2 Corinthians 4:16 MSG

We live in a time when miracle drugs offer amazing cures and when diagnoses that once were death sentences no longer are. We are living longer, healthier lives because of medical advancements. But no medical advancement can improve our spiritual health.

Sin has been likened to a disease, with God's grace and forgiveness being the life-saving, life-giving cure. And just as we can't watch today's drugs do their internal work, neither can we see the healing that is happening in our hearts and souls. Though on the outside we might not look like we are changing, on the inside God is at work to heal us and make us whole.

So if you're feeling discouraged about your spiritual growth, remind yourself of this simple yet profound truth: "on the inside . . . God is making new life." Stand strong in that truth and its companion promise: "not a day goes by without his unfolding grace." God *is* at work for your good and His glory!

Thank You, Lord, for Your grace and forgiveness, which is a reminder that You are making me new from the inside out. Amen.

The Secret

The word which God sent to the children of Israel, preaching peace through Jesus Christ—He is Lord of all—that word you know.

—Acts 10:36–37 NKJV

We all want to know the secret. Maybe we want to know the secret to beautiful skin, to wealth, or to safety and security. Or perhaps we're searching for the secret to happiness, to long life, and to a fulfilling retirement. Many secrets are elusive at best. Such is not the case when it comes to the secret for finding peace.

Here it is: peace is found in the Word of God. The more you read God's Word and the better you know God's Word, the more peace you will experience. The more you allow God's Word to fill your heart and mind, the more peace will flood your soul. And the more you align your life with guidance and instructions from God's Word, the more peace will fill your life.

The secret of knowing peace is out: it is knowing God's Word.

God, the secret to having peace seems so simple: know Your Word and then do what I know You want me to do. Thank You for sharing Your secret to peace. Amen.

The King of Kings

The demons begged Jesus, "If you drive us out, send us into the herd of pigs." He said to them, "Go!" So they came out and went into the pigs, and the whole herd rushed down the steep bank into the lake and died in the water.

—Matthew 8:31–32 NIV

The Grand Canyon is one of the most amazing and breathtakingly beautiful places on earth. Standing on the edge, it's difficult to take in the magnitude of its colors and size. The water that wore away this rock could have been its destruction. Yet God took the potentially disastrous and made it into something spectacularly gorgeous. God *is* God over all creation. He commands the seas, the winds, and the spirits of this world. And, yes, He even commands Satan.

Although Satan is the prince of this world and we are living on his terrain, our God is still the ruler over him. When Jesus died, He conquered the power of death. As the life, death, and resurrection of Jesus reveal, there is nothing He does not command. Does that rock-solid biblical truth bring peace to your soul? Jesus truly is the King of kings and Lord of lords. There is nothing on this earth, including death, over which He is not Lord.

What a glorious God You are! You command the seas, the winds, and the spirits of this world! You have defeated death itself! Amen.

DECEMBER 21

The Promise Keeper

You need to persevere so that when you have done the will of God, you will receive what he has promised. For, "In just a little while, he who is coming will come and will not delay."

—Hebrews 10:36–37 NIV

"Pinky promise?" your childhood friend would ask, extending a curved pinky finger in your direction. This practice can be traced to the 1860s when a rhyme accompanied the promising: "Pinky, pinky bow-bell / Whoever tells a lie / Will sink down to the bad place / And never rise up again." Most little girls would not have made the promise if they had known that rhyme!

God knows the ins and outs of what He is promising, and He is always straightforward. You can depend on God to fulfill every single promise He makes. What does God want in return for His promise making and promise keeping? He expects us to keep trying to obey and live a life that honors Him. He expects us to persevere in our faith and never give up, whatever the trials, afflictions, or discrimination. And when we persevere, we can count on the Promise Keeper to keep His promises, including this big one: our sovereign God will return for us.

You know I get weary and struggle to persevere in my faith, Father God. Thank You for providing Your Word, Your Spirit, and Your promises to strengthen and sustain me. Amen.

PEACE FOR THE WORLD

Hold On!

Be patient, brethren, until the coming of the Lord. The farmer waits for the precious produce of the soil, being patient about it, until it gets the early and late rains. You too be patient; strengthen your hearts, for the coming of the Lord is near.

—James 5:7–8 NASB

As Christmas Day approaches, you can feel the excitement building. The children are out of school, family begins to arrive, last-minute packages are wrapped. But what if, by declaration of Congress, Christmas Day were delayed? How long would the anticipation hold?

The disciples were certain Jesus would return shortly. Yet as the years passed, these faithful found it harder to hold on to that belief. James wrote to encourage them. He likened their wait for Jesus' return to a farmer who patiently waits for his crops to grow. If you, like those first disciples, grow weary in waiting for the Lord's Second Coming, take a cue from the farmer. He doesn't stand in the field and stare at the ground, watching for the first sprout to push through the soil. Instead, the farmer keeps busy every day with the tasks at hand. So stay busy doing the good things God has called you to do while you wait for Jesus' return.

Help me to wait for Your Second Coming with the same anticipation we wait for Christmas Day. When You return, may You find me busy doing what You called me to do. Amen.

No Room for Them

[Mary] brought forth her firstborn Son, and wrapped Him in swaddling cloths, and laid Him in a manger, because there was no room for them in the inn.

—Luke 2:7 NKJV

The drive was long, and you are bone-tired. Finally, you've arrived, only to discover there is not a hotel room to be found. Unbeknownst to you, a convention, a race, or some festival means all the rooms at every hotel are taken. Reluctantly, you decide to grab a few winks in the car before driving on.

Mary and Joseph had a similar experience when they arrived in Bethlehem. No vacancy. No space available. No room for one more person—not even the Son of God.

How many of us have filled our lives with so much that if God wanted to visit for just an hour, there wouldn't be any room? Our hearts are filled with so many things that call for our attention that when He desires to fill us with His love and peace, there is no room.

Before Christmas morning, make room in your heart so you can celebrate with joy and receive His Christmas peace with gratitude.

Thank You for these important words in this busy season. Forgive me for not making room for You. Help me get and keep the clutter out of the way, Jesus. Amen.

Expectant

For unto us a Child is born, unto us a Son is given; and the government will be upon His shoulder. And His name will be called Wonderful, Counselor, Mighty God, Everlasting Father, Prince of Peace.

—Isaiah 9:6 NKJV

Experts say that babies in utero are impacted by the atmosphere of their parents' home and the attitude of their parents. If God had chosen you to carry the infant Jesus into the world, would your home life and the attitude of your heart have nurtured in the holy child such traits as kindness, gentleness, patience, and trust in God? Would God have chosen you for such an important assignment? The answer is, He has. . . .

Isaiah wrote the well-known words above more than seven hundred years before Christ was born. God's chosen people had been waiting for the promised Messiah for a lot longer than they had anticipated. Finally the wait was over. God chose a human being named Mary to bring Him into the world. And God has chosen you and me to carry the truth and the love of this Christ child into the rest of the world.

Lord Jesus, may the atmosphere of my life and the attitude of my heart make my life a place where You want to be and a place where people can meet You. Amen.

Behold, the Lamb

Those people will never be hungry again, and they will never be thirsty again. The sun will not hurt them, and no heat will burn them, because the Lamb at the center of the throne will be their shepherd.

—Revelation 7:16–17 NCV

I love decorating the house with nativity scenes at Christmastime. In each one, young Mary tends to her newborn while her faithful husband stands guard. Wise men and shepherds stand in awe. And often near the Christ child is a little lamb. Jesus is known as the Lamb of God, and the symbolism is not lost on us.

Throughout the Old Testament, the people of Israel sacrificed lambs as sin offerings. John the Baptist was direct in drawing the comparison. When he saw Jesus coming toward him, he said, "Behold! The Lamb of God who takes away the sin of the world" (John 1:29 NKJV). Then on the cross Jesus was the perfect sacrifice—the perfect once-and-for-all sin offering—that removed our sins as far as the east is from the west.

This Christmas, when you spend time in front of a nativity, may you be filled with peace and awe as you behold the Lamb of God.

I stand in awe before the manger as my soul whispers, "Behold, the Lamb." Amen.

Comfort and Peace

Shout for joy, O heavens! And rejoice, O earth! Break forth into joyful shouting, O mountains! For the LORD has comforted His people and will have compassion on His afflicted.

—Isaiah 49:13 NASB

When you hear the word *comfort*, what comes to mind? Mashed potatoes or homemade chicken noodle soup? Your favorite chair, your Bible, and a soft blanket just warmed up in the dryer? Or maybe time with a friend?

The trials and tribulations in this life mean we all need comfort at one time or another. For one long period of history, comfort was hard to come by because God was silent. Had He forgotten His people? Not a sound for four hundred years between the Old Testament's account of history and where the New Testament picks up the story.

At the end of this four-hundred-year period, the heavens broke forth in praise. The angel announced the birth of the Messiah, and a multitude of the heavenly host praised and glorified God.

The Lord God *had* heard His people's cries—and He has heard yours. Receive from Him the light, the joy, the comfort, and the peace He has for you.

God, it is a gift to be reminded that You hear my cries, You respond according to Your good timing, and You bring comfort and peace. Amen.

All of Creation

The wolves will live in peace with lambs, and leopards will lie down to rest with goats. Calves, lions, and young bulls will eat together, and a little child will lead them.

—Isaiah 11:6 NCV

A beautiful bond naturally exists between young children and animals. When a child is sick, the family dog will hover around her protectively. And what child doesn't love a trip to the zoo?

It should be no great surprise that, here in Isaiah 11:6, a child is able to lead animals that are natural enemies, even predator and prey. This image beautifully portrays the reign of peace that Jesus Christ would inaugurate at His first coming. During His eternal reign, peace would be evident in the way a wolf would live with a lamb and a lion would lie down with a calf.

The Lord Jesus truly is our Prince of Peace. Because of Him, we know peace with our holy God, peace with one another, internal peace, and a creation that will one day be at peace as well. "Hail the Heaven-born Prince of Peace!"

What a picture of Messiah's reign, of natural enemies no longer at odds, of a child—of *the* Child—leading the way. Come quickly, Lord! Amen.

Goodwill to All!

Glory to God in the highest, and on earth peace, goodwill toward men!

—Luke 2:14 NKJV

When we hear the word *goodwill*, most of us probably think first of Goodwill Industries International. Founded in 1902, the organization has the following as its mission statement: "Goodwill works to enhance the dignity and quality of life of individuals and families by strengthening communities, eliminating barriers to opportunity, and helping people in need reach their full potential through learning and the power of work."

Goodwill Industries is an example of the goodwill the heavenly host proclaimed and celebrated at Christ's birth. Jesus brought peace in more profound ways than humankind had known, and nothing can surpass His supreme act of goodwill: the Holy One died for sinners.

Opportunities abound for you to continue Jesus' work of peace and goodwill. Consider the homeless person asking for food, the neighbor whose health is failing, and your friend who is struggling financially.

May the peace and goodwill sung about at Christmas keep our hearts soft and inform our actions throughout the year.

Lord God, please help me be a person of peace and goodwill, not only at Christmas but all year long. Amen.

Truly Waiting

"The vision is yet for the appointed time; it hastens toward the goal and it will not fail. Though it tarries, wait for it; for it will certainly come, it will not delay."

—Habakkuk 2:3 NASB

Are you good at waiting? Some people seem to possess a wonderful abundance of patience that serves them well while they're waiting—but they may be pacing, making lists, and doing a lot of research as they think through the various possibilities. We also don't necessarily see that, inside, they are actually agitated and impatient.

And when we are not *waiting* patiently, we are *wanting* the event to start, the situation to improve, or the circumstances to change. In contrast, when we're truly waiting patiently, we have a peace that says we know the event, the situation, and the circumstances have already been resolved. We don't need to fret or worry. And this principle applies to waiting for Christ's return.

The Christmas season reminds us to anticipate the Lord's Second Coming just as we anticipated His first, knowing full well that He—the greatest gift of all—will arrive on time.

Lord, it's difficult for me to wait for You and for the unfolding of Your plans. Help me to patiently, expectantly, and peacefully wait for Your answers to prayer. Amen.

Post-Christmas Blues

Remember the miracles he has done; remember his wonders and his decisions.

—Psalm 105:5 NCV

The frantic pace of the Christmas season will be winding down soon. The presents you painstakingly chose are all unwrapped, and some of them have already been returned! Your family's traditional holiday treats have been eaten. The stress of parties, family gatherings, and endless lists has waned. But after all of the weeks of anticipation, planning, preparation, holiday busyness, and fun, it's easy to slip into the post-Christmas blues.

To avoid feeling let down after all of the hustle and bustle, thank God for these moments of peace when they come. Accept this refreshment as a gift from the Prince of Peace. And before you jump ahead to the new year, reflect on the Creator's faithfulness to you throughout this year. As you remember His goodness, notice the peace and thankfulness that come to rule in your heart.

Lord, instead of longing for days gone by or trying to run into the future, I would like to focus on the present and Your goodness. Amen.

DECEMBER 31

Back to the Beginning

Thank the Lord *because he is good. His love continues forever. No one can tell all the mighty things the* Lord *has done; no one can speak all his praise. Happy are those who do right, who do what is fair at all times.*

—Psalm 106:1–3 NCV

As you prepare to begin another year, go into it with peace. Remember that God, your Redeemer and Creator, goes before you wherever you go. He leads you with peace, with patience, and with love. He knows you. In fact, He knows everything about you, and He won't let anything happen to you that won't help shape and mold you into the person you are meant to be.

As you end the year today, prepare to embrace the new one with joy and thanksgiving. After all, you are in the hands of the One who loves you and who has designed you to live in peace with Him and with those around you. Stand firm and be a peacemaker, able to assume that role because you live in God's grace and mercy each day.

Thank You, God, for giving me peace this year. And throughout the new year, Lord, may I be mindful that I will only know genuine peace when I abide in Your presence. Amen.

LOOK FOR OTHER TITLES IN THE SERIES

365 Devotions

AVAILABLE AT BOOKSTORES EVERYWHERE

365 DEVOTIONS
TO EMBRACE WHAT
MATTERS MOST

365 DEVOTIONS
FOR FINDING REST

365 DEVOTIONS
FOR LIVING JOYFULLY

365 DEVOTIONS
TO LOVE GOD AND
LOVE OTHERS WELL

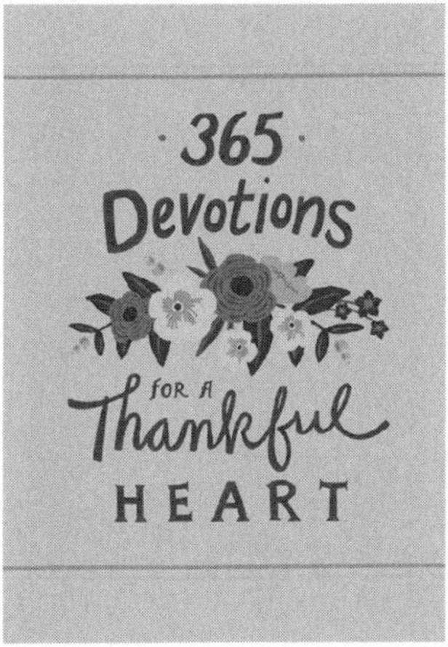

365 DEVOTIONS
FOR A THANKFUL HEART

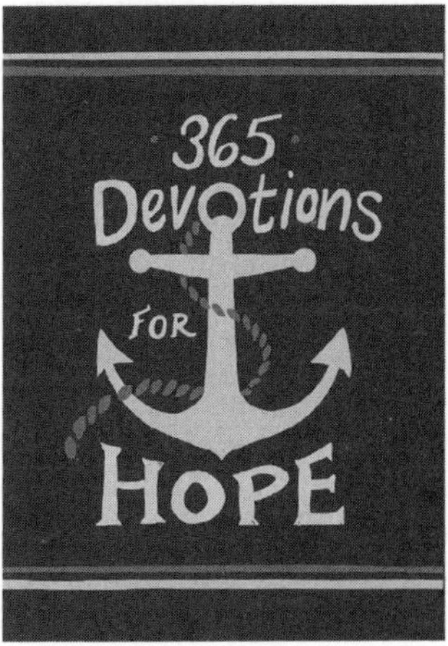

365 DEVOTIONS
FOR HOPE